The
GREAT ADVENTURE
of the
End Time Church

by Jim Sayles

The GREAT ADVENTURE of the End Time Church

By Jim Sayles

Edited by Kim Perrine

Printed in the United States of America

First Edition: 2019

IBSN: 978-0-579-05393-6

Foreword:

We rightly revere the great heroes of God, the prophets, kings, warriors, apostles, and men and women of faith documented in scripture, and in history. Yet, the vast majority of the body of Christ today is unaware that scripture reveals a final heroic body of believers who will be heralded throughout the ages as the Joshua generation of the end time church who will persevere, endure, and overcome Satan's ultimate beast kingdom assaults during the final three and a half years of this present age identified as "*great tribulation.*"

This book is, therefore, dedicated to these persevering, "wise virgins" of the end time Philadelphian identity who will become the ultimate manifestation of the spiritual body of Christ as they bring in the harvest of the multitude from every nation, tribe, and tongue in the face of the worst Satan can do through his beast kingdom.

And, to the fathers of our faith ministering in the spirit of Elijah to prepare this heroic, Joshua generation of "wise virgins" for their amazing adventure.

> *Arise, shine; for your light has come,*
> *And the glory of the LORD has risen upon you.*
>> *For behold, darkness will cover the earth*
>> *And deep darkness the peoples;*
>> *But the LORD will rise upon you*
>>> *And His glory will appear upon you.*
> Isaiah 60:1-2 NASB

My deepest gratitude to Kim Perrine, the original manuscript editor for this book, whose Biblical scholarship and Spirit-revealed insights made invaluable contributions to the finished work.

To Pastor Jerry Roach of Victory Christian Center in San Angelo, Texas in whose home I first received the prophetic assignment given to me by the Lord.

My thanks also to Sue Patterson, associated with Christian Media, whose article "The 144,000 and the Multitude" initiated my meditative research into this profound and intensely encouraging subject.

And to Chris Johnson, director of Jubilee World Missions, for his fellowship and profound prophetic confirmation.

1 – Whispered Warnings for a Sleeping Bride - God's prophetic warnings for this generation

2 – The Tribulation Parables - Prophetic parables concerning the time of the end

3 - The Strong Delusion – The covenant intent of God, and the "strong delusion" that will condemn many

4 – God's Prophetic Calendar of Redemption - The timing of the seven primary events of covenant redemption

5 – Paul's Unknown Prophecy - Paul's prophesy concerning God's prophetic end time intent for the spiritual body of Christ

6 – Daniel's 70 Weeks Prophecy - The interpretive key for the specific timing of the Lord's fulfillment of the seven primary events of redemption

7 – The Awakening - An awakening to come for the entire body of Christ in our immediate future

8 – The Former and Latter Rains - Ours since Pentecost revived to fullness in the final days

9 – The "Naked" Church - The Lord's demand for repentance after our awakening, and the believer's "wise" or "foolish" response

10 –The Doctrine and Practice the Lord HATES The end time Nicolaitans identified

11 –False Prophets and Lying Shepherds - The unknowing "wicked," shepherds of spiritual Israel who will lead the "foolish" into Satan's trap

12 –Apostasy of the "Foolish" Virgins – Specific events and understanding related to the great "falling away"

13 –The 144,000 - The ultimate identity of the "wise virgins"

14 –The Woman Clothed With the Sun - God's glorious intent for spiritual, "born again" Israel during the 7th seal

15 –The Heroic End Time Joshua Generation - The ultimate manifestation of the body of Christ in this age

1 – Whispered Warnings for a Sleeping Bride

As I stood on a lush green hill looking out over the brilliant blue sea I was shocked by the sudden appearance of a tsunami wave on the horizon. Frozen in fear, I realized that the gigantic wave rapidly approaching the shore was no ordinary tsunami. This wave was thousands of feet tall, and I knew with absolute certainty that it was about to destroy me and everything in its path.

As the wave towered above me, I was instantly transported to the crest where instead of destroying me, the wave carried me along like a body surfer as euphoric joy filled my soul.

Then I awakened one minute before my alarm was set to go off.

I quickly rehearsed the details of the dream in my mind so that I could write them down in my journal. Then, as I prayed and meditated on the dream, the Spirit caused me to understand that the sudden appearance of a tsunami wave on the horizon, breaking the peace and tranquility of the moment, is how the coming storm of the Lord will awaken the entire unexpecting and heavily deceived body of Christ as the Lord prophesied in the parable of the ten virgins (Matthew 25:6).

The dream felt like an URGENT warning, like I needed to be out on the street waving down cars and shouting out a warning to everyone who passed by. Yet, God gave His prophetic warnings as recorded in scripture with enough time to prepare for the prophesied events.

Because I am seventy-seven years of age at the time this book is being written, even if He grants me the spirit of Caleb so that I am still on the front lines dressed in battle armor at the age of ninety, this great wave of the Lord is coming very, very soon.

The assurance I received that I will be picked up and carried along with the wave and not destroyed by it applies not only to me, but to the entire company of the remnant elect of spiritual Israel, metaphorically identified by the Lord as the "wise virgins" of the end time church. Yet, the outcome for those identified metaphorically by the Lord as the "foolish virgins" of the end time church is decidedly tragic.

Therefore, the task I have been given by the Lord is to prepare the "wise" with the truth before this awakening event takes place.

As recorded in the book of Ecclesiastes certain events in the Old Testament concerning national, ethnic Israel are a prophetic forecast for events that have happened, or will happen, to spiritual Israel, the Israel of God in Christ.

"That which hath been is now; and that which is to be hath already been; and God requireth that which is past...(to be ultimately fulfilled in the future)...*"*   Ecclesiastes 3:15 KJV

When the Israelites, having been recently freed from their slavery in Egypt and miraculously delivered from Pharaoh's wrath by the parting of the Red Sea, sent spies from the twelve tribes into the land promised to them by God, only two men, Caleb and Joshua, came back with a "good," courageous, faith-filled report. The other ten came back with an "evil," fear-filled report.

According to Paul, Israel's experience was given to us by God for our instruction.

2

Now all these things happened unto them for ensamples: and they are written for our...(Christian believers)...*admonition, upon whom the ends of the world*...(age)...*are come.*
1 Corinthians 10:11 KJV (inserts are the author's)

What we see through this literal event in the history of national, ethnic Israel mirrors and foreshadows the greater event to be experienced in the future by spiritual Israel, the *Israel of God* in Christ.

National, ethnic Israel, believing the witness of the faithless spies and their "evil report," lingered in the wilderness until that generation passed away. These metaphorically represent the generation of spiritual Israel, identified by the Lord as "*foolish virgins.*"

These are "foolish" because they believe the false witness of various "blind guides" who have spied out the "promised land" of our immediate future, and returned with a non-revelatory message of both fear and false hope concerning the testing of our faith in the great end time conflict between the beast kingdom and the kingdom of God in the earth.

Yet, many who are currently "foolish" in regard to the prophetic truth of our immediate future will be awakened to the truth by the prophetically gifted and "wise" watchmen during the storm of the Lord, which is revealed to be an event in our immediate future.

This awakening of both the foolish and the wise, will be like the 4:30 a.m. wake up of new Marine Corps recruits as the drill instructor breaks through the door of the Quonset hut flipping on the lights, tossing bunks and lockers, and shouting, "*Wake up you sleepy heads! All hell is breaking loose and you are not prepared for it!*"

This wakeup event, though extremely unpleasant, will at least demonstrate to the "wise" that they have believed lies and are desperately in need of the truth.

3

The generation of national, ethnic Israel who followed the true, courageous witness of Caleb and Joshua represent the *"wise virgins"* of spiritual Israel who have received or will receive and believe the truth regarding the end time intent of the Father.

These, like Caleb and Joshua, will overcome the enemy in a time of great difficulty leading up to the glorious final days of the body of Christ before our last day resurrection on some future 1 Tishri Feast of Trumpets.

The foolish, falsely expecting a heavenly retreat before the final conflict between Satan's beast kingdom and the kingdom of God in Christ, will not overcome in this final conflict, as specifically prophesied by the Lord and recorded in Matthew 24 and 25, and theirs is the greatest tragedy imaginable, a tragedy that the blind guides of spiritual Israel will ultimately bear responsibility for.

Now, as I look back at the path that led me here, I realize that the Lord spent thirty-six years preparing me to receive this truth. In doing so, the falsehoods I adopted as a new believer were continually exposed with significant effort on my part as the Spirit of truth confronted me with the truth while exposing the lies.

In this regard, He made sure that the cornerstone and foundation stones of the Father's absolute, immutable, revelatory truth were in perfect alignment in my heart and mind. Then He built on that perfectly connected matrix of truth to reveal that which was previously "sealed" from both our understanding and Satan's understanding to warn and prepare this very generation for the GREAT ADVENTURE of the courageous, faith-filled *"wise virgins"* of the end time body of Christ.

What He has revealed and confirmed include two major end time prophetic events that will take place in the lives of the soon to be awakened body of Christ. The first is more tragic and the last more glorious than anyone, including this author, has perceived.

Many, out of fear and unbelief, deny that which is tragic, and their fearful denial, even of the possibility that it can happen, is a precursor to the tragedy itself.

At the same time that which will be the ultimate manifestation of the truth, power and glory of Christ manifested in and through the *"wise virgins"* of the end time church is almost unknown at the time this book is written, masked by elaborate deceptions and the intellectual speculations of men without revelatory insight.

The truth, though, is now unsealed and revealed by the Spirit of truth to those believers who have been given an unhindered ability to know the secrets and mysteries of the kingdom of God.

Yet, I recognize that this truth, obscured by erroneous and deceptive religious traditions and both manmade and demonically inspired doctrines of prophetic interpretation, will be new to many believers.

It is, therefore, important to recognize that traditional understanding based on false presumption and deliberate spiritual deceptions secretly introduced into the body of Christ by the father of lies is not the standard by which we are to judge the truth, promises, and commands of the Lord as we walk out our faith.

What we are told in Daniel 12 is that the prophecies given to Daniel concerning the time of the end were "sealed" (withheld from our revelatory understanding) until the literal time of the end.

And he said, Go thy way, Daniel: for the words are closed up and sealed till the time of the end. Daniel 12:9 KJV

It is safe to conjecture that many other prophetic passages concerning the time of the end were similarly "sealed," but like the book of Daniel, these are now being progressively unsealed for the benefit of the generation who will experience them.

Yet, a multitude of non-revelatory interpretations of end time prophecy injected into the body of Christ by previous generations who have unknowingly professed an intellectual understanding of both "sealed" and "unsealed" prophetic scripture without revelation, have now become strongholds (fortresses) of tradition opposed to the revelatory understanding intended by the Father at the appropriate time, which is exactly what the Lord encountered among the Pharisees at the time of His first advent.

5

In "Final Instructions," a Bible study guide I wrote based on the Lord's final instructions to His immediate disciples concerning how they would "hear" His voice and "see" His revelatory truth, promises, and commands after He was resurrected (John 13-17), the primary truth He gave them was that we must be supernaturally "guided" by the Spirit of truth if we are going to have "ears to hear" and "eyes to see."

But when He, the Spirit of truth, comes, He will ...(supernaturally)...*guide you into all the truth; for He will not speak on His own initiative, but whatever He hears, He will speak; and He will disclose to you what is to come. He will glorify Me, for He will take of Mine*...(the covenant promises)...*and will disclose it to you. All things that the Father has are Mine; therefore I said that He takes of Mine and will disclose it to you*...(so that you may participate in it by faith)...John 16:13,14 NASB (inserts are the author's)

Note the following truths revealed in this passage:

1. It is the Spirit of truth who guides us into the truth, not our mere intellects, no matter how studied;
2. It is the Spirit of truth who reveals the true meaning of prophetic scripture at the appropriate time, not our mere intellectual speculations, no matter how brilliant.

The resulting truth is simply stated. The intellect of man guided by the Spirit of truth unites believers and confirms the truth, promises, and commands of the Lord as the Father has intended. But the intellect not guided by the Spirit and potentially guided by spiritual deception, inaccurate intellectual presumption, or false tradition, like the Pharisees at the time of the Lord's first advent, divides believers and confirms the errors that have become strongholds assaulted against the absolute, immutable, revelatory truth of God.

It is these "strongholds" assaulted against the absolute, immutable, *rhema* truth of God that we are instructed to war against.

At the same time we must remind ourselves that our warfare is not against those believers deceived by the assumption of false traditions and inaccurate intellectual presumptions, or directly by the specific spiritual deception of the father of lies.

Our warfare is against the lies themselves in order to free those who are in bondage to the lies. Likewise, our warfare is not merely an intellectual battle, but one in which we are equipped by the Spirit of truth with the *rhema* word that proceeds out of the very mouth of God.

For though we walk (live) in the flesh, we are not carrying on our warfare according to the flesh and using mere human …(intellectual)…*weapons. For the weapons of our warfare are not physical [weapons of flesh and blood], but they are mighty before* …(through) …*God for the overthrow and destruction of strongholds,* …(described as)… *[In as much as we] refute arguments and theories and reasonings and every proud and lofty thing that sets itself up against the [true]* …(*rhema*)…*knowledge of God; and we lead every thought and purpose away captive into the obedience of Christ (the Messiah, the Anointed One)*

2 Corinthians 10:3-5 Amplified (inserts and emphasis are the author's)

Note that the intellect alone, no matter how brilliant and studied is not the source of the absolute, immutable, revelatory truth of God.

The fight described here is neither physical nor merely intellectual. Nor are we doing warfare against men, though men are divided by these issues.

It is the age-old fight between the spiritually inspired lies of the enemy assaulted against the spiritually revealed *rhema* truth of God.

For that reason, the Lord's primary warning for end time believers is, ***Do not be deceived***, because it is deception, not tribulation and persecution, that is the primary danger and dividing line for end time believers.

Daniel described this conflict between the "wise" and the "wicked" (or "foolish") concerning the revelatory end time intent of God.

Many shall be purified, and made white, and tried; but the wicked…(foolish)… ***shall do wickedly: and none of the wicked shall understand; but the wise shall understand.***
Daniel 12:10 KJV (emphasis is the author's)

"Wicked" in this passage obviously means something more specific than general sinfulness. "Wicked" implies the loss of their ability to know the revelatory secrets and mysteries of the kingdom of God so that these are unknowingly aligned with the purpose and intent of the father of lies and his beast kingdom.

It has nothing to do at all with their moral deportment. "Wicked" in this sense is entirely related to the fact that those who unknowingly teach doctrines that oppose the revelatory truth of God are unknowingly sinning against God by denying His absolute, immutable, revelatory truth, while, at the same time teaching doctrines introduced and promoted by demons.

Those believers, then, who continue in the comfort of various, conflicting group-think doctrines and theologies already received and believed after the truth has been revealed to them, are willfully ignoring the Lord's warning and are already defeated, but not yet unseated, in the warfare Satan is conducting against the end time body of Christ.

The tragic and unfortunate truth, as revealed by the Lord in the parable of the ten virgins, is that many believers in the spiritual body of Christ will not receive the truth because of heavy dependence on the false authority of various denominations and distinct theological traditions of institutional Christianity, including the false authority of their own intellects apart from the "guidance" and confirmation of the Spirit of truth, which is the same reason the Pharisees and other religious leaders, the intellectual giants of Judaism, rejected Jesus of Nazareth as "Messiah."

The rejection of Jesus of Nazareth as "Messiah" by the religious leaders of Israel, then foreshadows the rejection of the revelatory truth we have been given in the prophetic passages recorded by Old Testament prophets, as well as the prophecies given by New Testament apostles and prophets, and by the Lord, Himself, concerning the final days of the age immediately prior to His return, events that many in this current generation will experience whether they expect it or not.

Some, because of the multitude of conflicting doctrines concerning the future, play down the importance of prophetic scripture altogether as though God provided it for us without intending that we understand it.

Yet, prophetic scripture, once fulfilled, confirms the origin of the biblical text. No other source of prophecy even comes close to the biblical record of 100% accuracy. Just the multitude of biblical prophecies related to the genealogy, birth, life, death, and resurrection of Jesus of Nazareth, when computed mathematically, are so high that only an omnipotent God could have accomplished it.

However, the ultimate purpose of God in prophetic scripture, as is heavily demonstrated and confirmed throughout the Old Testament, is not to confirm the origin of biblical scripture, but to warn and prepare each generation for events in their immediate future.

For that reason, we can be certain that Satan is utilizing every weapon at his disposal to prevent this current generation's revelatory understanding of the Father's intent and purpose in and through the end time body of Christ.

In Matthew 24:3, The Lord's apostles, Peter, John, James, and Andrew asked Him, *"When will these things happen, and what will be the sign of your coming and of the end of the age?"*

After He gave them a lengthy prophetic revelation, not only of their own immediate future, but of the future of the church all the way to the last day resurrection of the saints of all time from Adam forward, He closed with the words, ***Behold, I have told you in advance*** ...(about both the truth of which you seek, and the deceptions to come of which you were unaware). Matthew 24:25 NASB (insert is the author's)

The word, "***Behold***," at the beginning of this statement by the Lord should be received by us as a shofar trumpet blast alerting us and warning us to pay attention to the lengthy prophetic revelation He gave them as recorded in Matthew 24 and 25, Mark 13, Luke 21, and, later, to John the apostle as recorded in "The Revelation of Jesus Christ," as well as a plethora of end time prophecies given to both Old Testament prophets and to the New Testament apostles and prophets.

Forty years ago at the age of thirty-seven, after spending six years involved in heavy New Age occult bondage, tripping on the so-called "deeper things of Satan," the Lord rescued me and immediately made me aware of the spiritual WAR between the kingdom of God and the beast kingdom.

The one I had unknowingly served as "god," was now the enemy, a furious enemy bent on my destruction and on the destruction of everyone and everything around me.

Unlike most Christian believers, the advantage I had was that I knew with absolute certainty that I was engaged in life and death spiritual warfare 24 hours a day, 365 days a year, and I knew with absolute certainty that I was entirely dependent on the Lord to deliver me safely all the way to the end.

As I recognized my true position, my intense love for the Lord and the need to protect myself, my family, my friends, and those He gave me responsibility for, motivated me to pursue the revelation of His truth, promises, and commands without compromise in spite of the resistance I experienced in the form of rejection from those in bondage to various forms of denominational and interpretational bias that had become strongholds assaulted against the absolute, immutable, revelatory truth of God.

What I have learned as a veteran of this warfare, is that Satan and his horde of subservient entities we call "demons," use their original, angelic spiritual powers to deceive mankind, with the primary objective being the deception of the *ekklesia* of Jesus Christ, the manifested presence of the kingdom of God in the earth.

It should not surprise us, then, that this same strategy of deception has been used throughout the centuries in the natural, but supernaturally influenced, wars of men against men and governments of men against governments of men.

Another undeniable proof that we have been significantly deceived and compromised by Satan's beast kingdom is the existence of many thousands of denominations (distinct belief systems) as well as cults (those who maintain extra-biblical beliefs and practices) within the institutional or professing "church" of Jesus Christ as this demonstrates a scattering of the sheep from one another and, subsequently, from the Shepherd Himself.

Yet, Paul tells us that us this was taking place in his own day, and we know by experience that it has multiplied exponentially in our day.

We have tried to solve this problem ourselves through ecumenicalism, through agreeing to "let the main thing be the main thing," while we argue and disagree about doctrine and practice in all other areas.

However, this ecumenicalism at the deepest level is a consensus to compromise, as though the absolute, immutable truth of God does not exist or cannot be discerned, and that He is okay with our multitudinous disagreements as long as we all agree that He is our Savior and Lord.

And it is this division that has become a perfectly plowed field for all of the subtle lies and deceptions of the enemy seeded into the spiritual body of Christ.

It is appropriate that we exhibit grace towards others with differing beliefs and practices in the body of Christ. Yet, peace without confronting the lies in order to prevent conflict is compromise, and compromising God's absolute, immutable, revelatory truth is not without consequences for the compromisers as is notably demonstrated by the Lord and recorded in Matthew 24 and 25.

Though the consequences for compromise may not seem substantial to us at this present time, the consequences in our immediate future will include the shocking apostasy of a large number of "born again" believers who will betray other believers during a time in which both the institutional church and individual believers are being persecuted without restraint by various demonically motivated and empowered authorities in the world.

Many of these who become apostate will even have been taught by their denominations that it is impossible to reject their faith through the unrepentant hardness of their hearts so that they no longer "hear" the Holy Spirit, which is the blasphemy of the Holy Spirit, leading to spiritual death.
(1 John 5:16)

"And then ...(at the time of the end)... *many* ...(of My people)...*will be offended and repelled* ...(because of intense demonic deception and trouble in the world)... *and begin to distrust and desert [Him whom they ought to trust and obey] and will stumble and fall away,* ...(from faith in Me)... *and betray one another and pursue one another with* ...(Satanically inspired and empowered)... *hatred."* Matthew 24:10 Amplified (emphasis and inserts are the author's)

We have read this passage in the past without concern, because we believed that it was related to some other generation or some other people, but as the certainty that we are the generation who will experience the painful and tragic spiritual polarity of Matthew 24:10 grows, the Lord's warning suddenly takes on meaning and importance.

Hence, the truth that this is a prophecy concerning the current generation of the body of Christ, a generation that includes our children and grandchildren, stuns us. And we do not want to believe it, though this warning from the Lord is impossible to deny.

Although we recognize and acknowledge the emotionally charged differences between denominations and theological interpretations present in the church today, this is not generally a great concern for us individually. The differences the Lord is describing as a future condition in the church includes the betrayal and persecution of a group that He describes in Matthew 24:10 previously quoted as those apostate, former believers who persecute those who have remained faithful.

This betrayal comes after the currently unexpected awakening of the entire body of Christ from our current state of spiritual somnolence by the Holy Spirit's announcement coming to us like the sound of a shofar blast from the watchtower, alerting the end time body of Christ that the final stages of Satan's beast kingdom warfare against the kingdom of God in Christ have begun:

"BEHOLD! The bridegroom is coming." Matthew 25:6 NASB

The obvious foreshadowing of the tragic event in which these future worldwide Spirit-awakened believers identified as the "foolish virgins" ultimately fall away from faith, and then persecute those who remain steadfast in their faith, is foreshadowed by the assault on the new, young, body of Christ by the faithless religious authorities in Israel.

Then we see it again in the corrupt Roman Catholic authorities as they persecuted those believers who broke away from the institutional church to follow Christ in spirit and truth.

Our own differences and divisions today, demonstrating a widespread disconnect from the Spirit of truth, is also a precursor to the ultimate future event described in Matthew 24 and metaphorically described in the parable of the ten virgins.

In the parable of the ten "virgins" (those who are innocent before God because they are in Christ) He describes that future condition as the result of the "foolish" failing to trim the wicks of their lamps (failure to respond to the Lord's demands of repentance after our awakening as revealed in Revelation 2 and 3).

This, then, ultimately results in the "foolish" having no oil whatsoever in their lamps (i.e. the Holy Spirit is no longer present - Matthew 25:1-12).

This is not evidence that God has rejected them from their covenant relationship with Him in Christ. It is evidence that they have blasphemed the Holy Spirit by continuously rejecting His voice, the voice of our Lord, to the point that they have become spiritually deaf.

This results in religion without active faith responses, which is the case of those who once responded to the Holy Spirit but are now blaspheming the Holy Spirit through spiritual deafness and have become apostate.

Strong's identifies apostasy as: "apostasia" – away from standing (away from covenant standing with God in Christ); defection from truth (properly, the state) ("apostasy"): falling away, forsake.

Thus the Father has not rejected them, but these, through their chronic rejection of the voice of the Lord, have rejected their true faith in Christ, and their ability to "hear" and "see" the truth, promises, and commands of the Lord by the Spirit of truth, though they may be actively continuing, and even leading, in some form of organized Christian religion.

Just as the Father frequently expresses His love to us through discipline, the prophetic gift used correctively to both expose deception and reveal truth is also a manifestation of the Father's love. Yet, it is not unusual for those who are "touched" by the prophetic voice of truth to respond in anger to the messengers, just as the ancient Israelites frequently responded to the prophets sent to them by the Father, even rejecting their "Messiah" when He came to them.

At the same time, I am aware that the absolute, immutable, revelatory, *rhema* truth of God in all things will not, and has not, come to any man born of the flesh, other than Jesus of Nazareth. Therefore, we are all, great and small, man, woman or child, only capable of receiving, responding, and communicating whatever *rhema* He has willed for the purpose to which He has anointed us.

My personal experience has been that the errors and deceptions I have either assumed or presumed to be true, errors that have become literal strongholds opposed to the truth of God, are questioned and examined in my own spirit and mind before I am able to receive and confirm the truth of God in their stead.

In the 2 Corinthians 10:3-5 passage previously quoted, the strongholds of deception and error must first be cast down in order to bring our thoughts and beliefs into the truth and obedience of Christ. However, let me be quick to add that for those noble Bereans who are hungry for the truth, the truth itself is often all we need to bring down the strongholds.

Yet, for those who are in bondage to, and heavily invested in the lies, i.e. large, well-known and established denominations, ministries, and individuals whose popularity and reputation (i.e. the status quo) would be damaged if the lies they teach are exposed, the spiritual, intellectual, and emotional chains of the lies must first be forcefully broken before the believer is able to receive the truth.

The difficulty of our flesh dominated souls in this process is represented metaphorically by the rich young ruler's encounter with Jesus when he asked the Lord what he must do in order to enter the kingdom of God.

What the Lord told him was to keep the commandments, and the rich young ruler's response, in my own paraphrase, was that he had a doctorate in biblical Hebrew and Greek, had authored half a dozen best-selling books, and was senior pastor of a church of 10,000.

In response, the Lord said, *Yet lackest thou one thing: sell all that thou hast, and distribute unto the poor, and thou shalt have treasure in heaven: and come, follow me.* Luke 18:22 KJV

This answer by the Lord, ultimately rejected by the rich young ruler, identified the fact that obedience to the religious expectations

15

and accomplishments of men is not enough. Only the willingness, desire, and commitment to pursue and obey the revelatory impartation of His truth, promises, and commands in all things, regardless of the cost, is truly "following Him."

Thus, following Him may include abandoning reputations unknowingly built on falsehood, as well as abandoning positions of authority in the institutional church, in order to follow Him in spirit and truth.

Unfortunately, for some, our adherence to denominational authority, the identity and personal reputations we have that are associated with certain schools of theological interpretation, and the Pharisaical confidence we have in our own prideful but inadequate intellects, will result in many believers and fathers of our faith making the same choice that the rich young ruler made.

"But the hour cometh and now is, when the true worshippers shall worship the Father in spirit...(by faith)...*and in*...(God's revelatory)...*truth: for the Father seeketh such to worship*...(hear and obey)...*him. God is a Spirit: and they that worship him must worship him in spirit and in truth."* John 4:23-24 KJV (inserts are the author's)

Worshipping in spirit and truth is not about spiritual gifts or great praise music that lifts the roofs off of our church buildings.

Worshipping in spirit and truth is seeking and obeying the Spirit-revealed truth, commands, and covenant promises of God in Christ no matter what the cost.

No matter what the cost.

Genuine praise, then, is not merely an emotional response. It is the natural and appropriate response of one who is in obedience to the revelation of our Lord's truth, promises, and commands.

Almost everyone reading this commentary has been through this process in coming to faith in Jesus Christ. The falsehoods and errors we once believed had to come into question in our hearts and minds before we could receive the absolute, immutable, truth of God in Christ. For some, like this author, the truth itself brought the falsehoods and errors into question.

This process continues to be the same throughout our lifetimes as we walk in Him by faith, because we have a spiritual enemy whose primary purpose is to separate the sheep from one another and separate the sheep from the shepherd through deception.

As we see in what we refer to as the "armor of God" passage (Eph.6:13-17), it is the absolute, immutable *rhema* truth of God that empowers all our defensive armor and all of our offensive weapons.

Simply stated, Satan's primary strategy in this warfare is to divide and conquer by corrupting the absolute, immutable, revelatory truth of God in Christ so that our defensive armor and our offensive weaponry is ineffective and we are divided from one another, which hinders our individual and corporate faith responses to the Lord's truth, promises, and commands.

What I have also learned in this continuous fight of faith to expose and reject error in order to receive truth is that no doctrine stands alone. All true doctrine, particularly eschatological doctrine, connects intricately to the entire matrix of revelatory truth.

What this means is that prophecy cannot be interpreted correctly on the basis of an intellectual understanding of the prophecy itself alone or by proof texts that do not mean what we want them to mean.

All prophecy must be interpreted as we are guided supernaturally by the Spirit of truth not only concerning the prophecy itself, but also concerning the entire context of revelatory biblical scripture.

In this regard we must not ignore the Lord's own instructions.

But when He, the Spirit of truth, comes, He will guide you...(supernaturally)...into all the truth; for He will not speak on His own initiative, but whatever He hears, He will speak; and He will disclose to you what is to come. John 16:13 NASB

This instruction from the Lord leaves no room for the possibility that the mere intellectual examination of prophecy, as well as the use of proof texts out of context, will result in our true understanding.

Though the Revelation of Jesus Christ has had some application to the church throughout the ages, the primary application is for the end time church who will experience the events prophesied by the Lord in metaphorical language that will only be fully revealed by the Spirit of truth to those for whom it is intended.

"I, Jesus, have sent my angel to testify to you about …(all)…*these things for* …(whom?)…*the <u>churches.</u>"* <u>Revelation 22:16 NASB</u> (inserts and emphasis are the author's)

Note, first of all, that the entire book of Revelation was written for the church, not for national ethnic Israel. Why, then, would the church be given detailed revelatory information concerning end time events if we are going to be whisked away in a secret (not disclosed in scripture) "rapture" before these events take place?

One of the proofs that the Revelation of Jesus Christ is intended primarily for the end time church is His promise to the Philadelphian church, a promise to "*keep*"…(protect them in the)… *"hour of trial that will come upon the whole world."* <u>Revelation 3:10 KJV</u>.

That "hour of trial," God's appointed time for the final 42 months or 3.5 years of the age, elsewhere referred to as the 7th seal of "*great tribulation*," (Matthew 24:21) has not yet taken place. Therefore, the promise is intended only for those believers who have overcome deception, remained steadfast in the Lord, and patiently endured persecution at the hands of the 7th and final beast kingdom during the 4th, 5th and 6th seal events of "*tribulation*."

Then, at that time, those who qualify as being participants in this end time Philadelphian identity are protected in the final 3.5

years of *"great tribulation"* rather than removed from *"great tribulation."*

"Keep" in this sense obviously does not indicate removal via a rapture event. Instead, the idea is that of protecting and preserving without removal.

This is exactly the same word used in the phrase, *"keep My commands,"* meaning to <u>protect</u> and <u>preserve</u>, not remove.

Strong's:
 I.to attend to carefully, take care of
  A.to guard
  B.metaph. to keep, one in the state in which he is

"Guarding" and "keeping one in the state in which he is" does not, therefore, suggest removal in any way.

Like most New Testament prophetic scripture, we see the foreshadowing of this event in the Old Testament.

The three Hebrew children, Shadrach, Meshach, and Abed-Nego (<u>Hebrew</u>: Hananiah, Mishael and Azariah) were protected in the fiery furnace after refusing to worship the golden image Nebuchadnezzar set up as his "god."

This is the same temptation and trial that will be experienced by the whole world during the appointed *"hour of trial,"* the 7th seal, otherwise known as the 3.5 years, 42 prophetic months, or 1260 days of *"great tribulation."*

This is, therefore, a perfect Old Testament parallel and foreshadowing of the event experienced by those qualifying as end time Philadelphian believers a.k.a. the "wise virgins." Instead of removal from the world, these are sealed and protected in the final 42 months or 3.5 years of the age, identified by the Lord as the 7th seal of *"great tribulation,"* to gloriously represent Christ in the world at the very same time that Satan is fully expressed through the final beast kingdom, and his false messiah, the "man of sin," whose world capital will be *Babylon the Great*, a.k.a. Jerusalem and the greatly expanded political nation of Israel.

19

The subject of this book, then, includes the prophetic events resulting in the tragedy of the "foolish," fearful virgins who do not endure and persevere during the 4th, 5th and 6th seal events of *"tribulation,"* but instead lose heart and grow weary as they fall prey to the intense trouble, persecution, and deception unlike anything we have experienced in the past. And the future of the remnant "wise" virgins after the awakening of the entire body of Christ, who continue to make obedient faith responses to the truth, promises, and commands of the Lord in the face of intense deception, trouble, and persecution, ultimately including persecution by the "foolish virgins" with whom they were once united by faith.

Because this storm of the Lord is coming like a gigantic wave to shake everything that can be shaken, a wave that will either destroy us or lift us up and carry us along in perfect unity with Him to experience the most tragic, and the most glorious days in the entirety of human history, I am charged by the Lord, along with many others, to engage in revealing this astonishing truth and confronting the deceptions that resist it, no matter what that may cost in personal pain and rejection by the Pharisees and "foolish" virgins of our faith...even by those closest to us.

The veil has been removed, and the wise will "see" and respond to the truth with joy and purpose. But the "foolish" will not "see" and will resist the truth to their own tragic, and everlasting dismay.

2 – The Tribulation Parables

The most important sources of truth concerning the end time events related to the spiritual body of Christ have been given to us by our Lord, Jesus Christ, who sent us the Spirit of truth to "guide" us supernaturally into all truth, including the truth about things to come.

Matthew 24 and 25 are the primary texts recording the Lord's direct response to His disciples' question immediately after He prophesied the destruction of the temple.

"Tell us, when shall these things be, and what shall be the sign of thy coming, and of the end of the world...(age)...*?"* Matthew 24:3 KJV (insert is the author's)

After giving them a straightforward synopsis in which He identified the four specific future timeframes (signposts) as being 1) *not yet the end*; 2) *the beginning of birth pains*; 3) *tribulation*; and 4) *great tribulation*, He gave them an outline of the entire future of the church followed by the metaphors of Noah and the ark, one taken and one left, and four illustrative prophetic parables.

Through these parables He has provided prophetic details for those end time disciples amongst us who have "ears to hear" and "eyes to see" the revelatory intent of God for the *ekklesia* of Jesus Christ.

In view of the birth metaphor used by the Lord in the Matthew 24 Olivet prophecy, His death, burial, and resurrection equate to conception, and *"not yet the end"* equates to the church's experience up to that period late in the third trimester identified as *"the beginning of birth pains."*

Prophetically we are in the latter part of *"the beginning of birth pains,"* corresponding with the 3rd seal of Revelation, but at some point in the very near future the birthing pains, increasing both in intensity and in the compression of time, will become *"tribulation,"* followed by *"great tribulation,"* followed by the birth event itself, the 1 Tishri "last day" resurrection of the saints of all time, and on the great and terrible day of the Lord, a.k.a. the 10 Tishri fulfillment of the Feast of Atonement as He returns to the earth with the saints of all time to destroy His enemies and establish His millennial kingdom.

We are, therefore, IN the end times, and have been in the end times for a significant amount of time.

< ------------------- the end times ------------------- >			
Matt 24:5-6	Matt 24:7-8	Matt 24:9-13	Matt 24:15-21
	1st-3rd seals	4th-6th seals	7th seal
not yet the end (times)	*beginning of birth pains*	*tribulation*	*great tribulation*

Strangely, the Lord left out the secret (not disclosed in scripture) "rapture" of the church prior to tribulation. What He told His disciples instead is illustrated in great detail in the typology of Noah and the ark, the one taken and one left, and in all four prophetic parables.

In Matthew 24 He identified *"tribulation"* as a time of serious testing ordained by God for the spiritual body of Christ, the true "church," with the shocking disclosure that many in the believing,

22

born-again, regenerated church would reject their faith during this time of testing.

This is the apostasy Paul said would take place before the day of the Lord.

Let no man deceive you by any means: for that day …(the "last day" resurrection on some future Feast of Trumpets, 1 Tishri)…***shall not come, except there come a falling away first, and that man of sin be revealed.***
2 Thessalonians 2:3 KJV (insert is the author's)

In this passage "falling away" comes from the Greek word transliterated as *apostasia* (Strong's G646), *apo* – away from, and *stasia* – standing, meaning to fall away from one's standing with God in Christ.

Thus, this has absolutely nothing to do with nominal, unregenerated "Christians."

What is specifically indicated instead is the apostasy of born-again, Christian believers during this time of extreme trouble.

Those who believe the doctrine of the unconditional, eternal security of the believer, or "once saved, always saved," based on a faulty and incomplete understanding of the doctrine of soteriology (covenant redemption) will have difficulty with this truth as I once did.

Having come out of the tradition of "once saved, always saved," I am aware that some will reject both the message and the messenger, because the tradition of "once saved, always saved," is more important to them than the truth.

That doctrine, then, has literally become a Satanically inspired and idolatrous stronghold assaulted against the truth of God in Christ, though it is considered by those who believe it as their most treasured doctrine.

I will quickly state, then, that the covenant between God the Father and God the Son cannot and will not fail. Our inclusion in that covenant as "joint heirs" of the covenant promises, though, is dependent on our remaining in Him by faith.

Thus, a synoptic understanding of our redemption in Christ is that the sealing of the Holy Spirit upon saving faith is the initial, but not final event of redemption:

In whom ye also trusted, after that ye heard the word of truth, the gospel of your salvation: in whom also after that ye believed, ye were sealed with that Holy Spirit of promise, which is the <u>earnest</u> of our inheritance <u>until</u> the redemption of the purchased possession, unto the praise of his glory. <u>Ephesians 1:13,14</u> KJV (emphasis is the author's)

The "earnest," our initial faith in Jesus Christ as Savior and Lord, is like a down payment on our redemption, but we do not receive the eternal blessing of our redemption unless we have remained "in Christ" by faith all the way to the end of our lives.

The word translated as *"earnest"* in this passage transliterated by Strong's as "arrabōn" has the following meanings:

1. an earnest
   A. money which in purchases is given as a pledge or down payment that the full amount will subsequently be paid

This is further demonstrated in John 15:6:

If a man <u>abide</u> <u>not</u> in me, he is cast forth... (meaning removed from his previous position)...*as a branch, and is withered; and men gather them, and cast them into the fire, and they are burned.* (insert and emphasis are the author's)

To "abide" in Him requires more than our initial faith response to the gospel truth. It requires an ongoing faith relationship in which we continue to respond in obedience to the revelation of His truth, promises, and commands as these are revealed and confirmed by the Spirit of truth, our Counselor, and the voice of the Lord.

Obedience to religious rules and the expectations of man is not "abiding" in Him. It is mere religion, and, in many cases, Christianity as a "religion" literally opposes the truth, promises, and commands of the Lord.

The warning in verse 6 is then juxtaposed against the promise in verse 7 for those who do abide in Him:

If...(the condition imposed by God)...*you abide in Me, and My words abide in you,*...(producing genuine faith and obedience)...*ask what you will, and it will be done for you.* John 15:7 NASB (inserts are the author's)

The promise for those who abide in Him reveals that those who do not abide in Him with His words abiding (producing His "life") in and through them will ultimately be reduced to a physical life of religion without genuine faith, which is apostasy.

If anyone does not abide in Me, he is thrown away as a branch and dries up; and they gather them, and cast them into the fire and they are burned. John 15:6 NASB

What is not in view here is our natural understanding of scripture. Natural understanding is a good foundation for receiving the *rhema* word of God, but it is not the *rhema* word of God itself.

If one starts a sentence with, "The Bible says...," then the next statement should be an actual quote from scripture, not our individual paraphrase, because the literal written word must be interpreted to us by the Spirit of truth. Then the word we have received becomes the anointed *rhema* word of the Lord that comes to us through the agency of the Spirit of truth by various means including scripture and is confirmed by our revelatory understanding of scripture.

Regeneration by grace through faith, then, is our status until the last day resurrection. On that future day, which will be some 1 Tishri, feast of trumpets on God's calendar of the appointed times for the redemption of fallen mankind in Christ, whether we are alive or have passed away and have been in the heavenly presence of the Lord, our redemption will ultimately be complete.

But our "full" and complete redemption requires us to remain in Him by faith during our entire physical lives as is demonstrated in numerous passages.

At the same time, those who are alive, and through the hardness of their stubborn, rebellious hearts, ultimately reject their faith in Christ (i.e. do not <u>remain</u> in Him), are not only lost, but become extremely susceptible to the influence and control of Satan.

For in the case of those who have once been enlightened... (received the "light" of the truth)...*and have tasted of the heavenly gift...*(experienced regeneration)... *and have been made <u>partakers</u> of the Holy Spirit, and have tasted the good word of God and the powers of the age to come, and then have fallen away,...*(*apostasia* – removed themselves from their standing with God in Christ through the rejection of their faith)... *it is impossible to renew them <u>again</u>* ...(a second time)...*to repentance, since they again...*(a second time)... *crucify to themselves the Son of God and put Him to open shame. For ground that drinks the rain which often falls on it and brings forth vegetation useful to those for whose sake it is also tilled, receives a blessing from God; but if it yields thorns and thistles, it is worthless and close to being cursed, and it ends up being burned.* <u>Hebrews 6:4-8 NASB</u> (inserts and emphasis are the author's)

If we cannot lose or reject our faith once we have it why warn us that regenerated, "born again" believers cannot come to faith again if they fall away from faith?

This passage makes it clear that it is possible for "partakers" of the Holy Spirit, who have experienced both regeneration by grace through faith, and the empowerment of the Holy Spirit to walk by faith, to remove themselves from their standing with the Father "in Christ."

This happens through the hardness of our hearts, which is the result of our chronic disobedience to the still small voice of the Spirit, our Counselor, and our spiritual conscience, (the law of God written on our hearts) who conveys the *rhema* word that proceeds from the very mouth of the Lord to us in numerous ways.

Then, because of the spiritual deafness and blindness of our disobedient and rebellious flesh, as well as the likely presence of demonic influence and controls, our faith is no longer real to us, and we experience degeneration.

This is the unpardonable sin, the blasphemy of the Holy Spirit (i.e. chronic rejection of the voice of the Lord).

In the parable of the vine and the branches the Lord emphasizes this truth.

"I am the true vine, and my Father is the vinedresser. Every branch in me that does not bear fruit he takes away, and every branch that does bear fruit he prunes, that it may bear more fruit. Already you are clean because of the word that I have spoken to you. Abide in me, and I in you. As the branch cannot bear fruit by itself, unless it abides in the vine, neither can you, unless you abide in me. I am the vine; you are the branches. Whoever abides in me and I in him, he it is that bears much fruit, for apart from me you can do nothing. If anyone does not abide in me he is thrown away like a branch and withers; and the branches are gathered, thrown into the fire, and burned. John 15:1-6 NASB (emphasis is the author's)

No one is a "branch" of the "vine" apart from regeneration by grace through faith, and the key to our understanding is that we must also "abide" in Him.

"Abiding" is an active, ongoing faith condition rather than a onetime faith experience.

This word translated as "abide" from the Greek is given the following meaning in Strong's in reference to state or condition: "to remain as one, not to become another or different." (i.e.

remaining as one = <u>regenerated</u>; becoming another or different = <u>degenerated</u>).

As long as a believer is "abiding" in Christ, receiving and obeying His truth, promises, and commands as revealed by the Spirit, he/she remains "in" Christ. But when the believer, because of the hardness of his/her heart, no longer hears, sees, or responds to the personally revealed truth, promises, and commands of the Lord, he/she is in danger of rejecting his faith.

This is not the believer's active intellectual decision to reject his faith. It is, instead, the accumulative result of chronic spiritual deafness, spiritual blindness, and lack of response to the still small voice of the Spirit.

If the believer is living a life of religious obligation without an active personal faith life in response to the still, small voice of the Spirit, our Counselor, who is the voice of the Lord, the ultimate result will either be religious obedience without faith, or, worse, an openness to respond to the voice of the father of lies.

It is no wonder, then, that Satan was able to introduce the deception of a secret "rapture" of church only saints prior to tribulation, because that "escape" with no possibility of rejecting our faith because of extreme trouble and deception during "tribulation" appeals to our flesh.

It should not surprise us, then, that he introduced this false hope of "escape" in order to prevent our preparation for this time of testing, which will lead to the despair and the shocking rejection of their faith in Jesus Christ by many.

If the reader is angered by this challenge to the popular pre-tribulation "rapture" theory or the doctrine of "once saved, always saved" by the thought that God would severely test the faith of the elect we only need to remember and reflect on James 1:2-4 KJV:

My brethren, count it all joy when ye fall into divers temptations; Knowing this, that the trying of your faith worketh patience. But let patience have her perfect work, that ye may be perfect and entire…(complete)…, ***wanting nothing***…(of the truth, covenant promises, and blessings of God in Christ)….

Strong's identifies "patience" in this passage as meaning, "**I. steadfastness, constancy, endurance**…" in the trials and testing of our faith that every, born-again believer faces throughout our lives.

Therefore, our entire walk of faith includes this testing, which, for the overcomer, results in spiritual maturity that glorifies the Lord. But the testing to come will exceed even the testing of the early church.

From my viewpoint it is apparent that the western church, at least, is not generally prepared for this testing, much less the possibility that scripture reveals that a majority of end time believers will ultimately reject their faith during the 4th, 5th, and 6th seals of tribulation.

And, not only reject their faith, but unknowingly become engaged with Satan as enemies of those who remain faithful.

Yet, Jesus revealed that "tribulation" (trouble) is normal in the everyday life of believers whether we are aware of it or not.

"These things I have spoken to you, so that in Me you may have peace. In the world you <u>have</u> tribulation, but take courage; I have overcome the world." <u>John 16:33 NASB</u> (emphasis is the author's)

Therefore, our individual "peace" (spiritual and mental calm) is the result of our deliberate and steadfast "abiding" in Him.

It shocks me how many believers I have known who are angry with God, because they have experienced worldly rejection and trouble, which rejection and trouble will increase dramatically in coming years. Yet, the apostle John clearly expresses the fact that "trouble" (tribulation), including constant spiritual warfare and demonic influence in the lives of numerous believers, is the natural lot for the redeemed of fallen mankind in the world, because we have an enemy bent on our destruction.

I John, who also am your brother, and companion in tribulation,...(both natural trouble and the trouble that comes from the warfare of the beast kingdom against us)... *and in the kingdom*...(of God manifested in the earth through the faith and obedience of believers)...*and patience of Jesus Christ*...(steadfastness and courage in the struggle and warfare against us)... <u>Revelation 1:9 KJV</u> (inserts are the author's)

In this passage John is expressing the truth that all of us who are brothers (male or female) in Christ experience "tribulation" (i.e. natural and spiritual "trouble").

In scripture if something is spoken twice, we know that it is really, really important, and the truth being revealed very, very crucial to our understanding. This theme of apostasy (rejecting our faith because of "trouble") is carried over into the Noah metaphor, the one taken and one left illustration, and three of the four illustrative parables.

It appears a total of six times in Matthew 24 and 25. The only other narrative recorded in scripture that gives this much emphasis to a single concept is the same threat of apostasy for those who do not overcome the testing of their faith through "trouble" given to five of the seven types of the church (applicable to individual believers) in the message to the seven churches (Revelation 2 and 3).

This tells me that the Father made certain that the generation who will experience the extreme trouble of end time *"tribulation"* receives this crucial warning so that we will prepare spiritually for the trials and testing of our faith immediately ahead of us.

At the same time we need to remember that the Lord's primary warning is to not be misled or deceived, and the obvious, observable fact is that the divided, somnolent church placing our hope in a false pre-tribulation "rapture," or believing that tribulation and the persecution of the church is historic, is deceived. And, because we are deceived, we are in desperate need of deliverance from deception before the testing of our faith begins in earnest.

30

As we will all ultimately realize, those fathers of the faith who will continue to teach the false, Zionist (national, ethnic Israel as the primary covenant intent of the Father), dispensational doctrine of a pre-tribulation resurrection-"rapture" of church only saints, Preterism, Historicism, or any other "ism" in denial of the very clear *rhema* truth of God concerning the great adventure of the end time church, are addressed specifically in the parable of the faithful and wicked servants. (Matthew 24:45-51)

The parable of the faithful and wicked servants reveals that the wicked servant (and one is not a "servant" unless one actually belongs to, and is serving, the Master) begins to beat his fellow servants (other believers) and to drink with the drunkards (the lost).

The word "beat" or "smite" in the original Greek uses this word metaphorically to mean to "wound" or to "disquiet one's conscience." The wicked servants (i.e. ministry leaders or "shepherds") accomplish this as they unknowingly wound the sheep with idolatrous, non-revelatory false doctrines as well as various flesh driven and Satanically inspired practices that divide and inflict spiritual impoverishment and disheartening pain on the sheep.

The end of the wicked servants, if they do not repent, is that they will suffer the same fate as the hypocrites where there is weeping and gnashing of teeth.

This is the future of the unrepentant "wicked" servants, who are not giving the sheep the food and supplies that the Lord has appointed and anointed them to administer, the "*hidden manna*" and "*unleavened bread*" of the absolute, immutable, revelatory truth of God, and are instead misleading and deceiving the flock held captive through the group-think fear of man.

For the "wicked servants" of our day repentance may include giving up ministries, denominations, false doctrines, false practices, and personal reputations in order to follow the Lord in spirit and truth.

Sadly, like the rich young ruler, many will not respond to this end time demand for repentance, as expressed succinctly in

Revelation 2 and 3, and according to the Lord, they, like the Pharisees and scribes of the Lord's own day, will experience the fate of all hypocrites.

The parable of the ten virgins (Matthew 25:1-12) is a synoptic view of the entire church age from the first Pentecost to the great white throne judgment, and this parable reveals that the early church was wide awake with their lamps (spirit-soul-mind connection) burning brightly and full of oil (the Holy Spirit), but when the Lord tarried all ten virgins became spiritually drowsy and fell asleep.

"Virgins" as it is used in this passage is also used metaphorically by Paul in 2 Corinthians 11:2, where he identifies these as those who are innocent before God because they are in Christ.

Thus, it has nothing to do with their natural virginity.

At the same time the number "10" metaphorically represents the entire corporate body of Christ, and, more importantly, represents the testing of the entire corporate body of God's people at a certain point in time.

Ten as a metaphor for "testing" is observed in the following events:

1. The 10 commandments as a test. Obey, or disobey.

2. The 10th plague in Egypt was a test resulting in the freedom of Israel from bondage in Egypt.

3. In Luke 19:12-26 we learn that the "nobleman" (Christ) gives each of his 10 servants (i.e. his complete staff of servants) a pound of silver. Then He tells them to occupy the kingdom of God in the earth until he returns, and when He returns those "servants" (believers) who used what he had given them to increase the master's estate (the

kingdom of God) were blessed by their obedient faith response to this test. Those who did not were cursed, demonstrating that His original orders were a kingdom of God test.

4. In Revelation 2:10 the church at Smyrna is told that they would have "tribulation" 10 days, not meaning ten literal 24 hour days but an ordained, non-specific time of testing.

5. In God's calendar of redemption, the appointed times and feasts of the Lord, the 10 literal days from 1 Tishri (the Feast of Trumpets) to 10 Tishri (the Feast of Atonement) is a time of testing and repentance.

The 50/50 split between the "wise" and the "foolish," though, is not an indicator of the number of believers who will fall away but of the fact that this will be a complete, polar opposite response to the testing of our faith during that time.

The "Bridegroom" is obviously Jesus Christ, and the groomsman who ultimately makes an announcement to the ten virgins (the entire living body of Christ) to prepare them for the bridegroom's soon arrival is the Holy Spirit.

In this parable, all ten grow drowsy and fall "asleep," and all ten wake up at the groomsman's announcement, ***"Behold! The bridegroom is coming."***

What is historically recognizable in this prophetic parable is that "all" of the virgins were wide awake in the beginning, but with the passage of time, and the increasing influence of the beast kingdom, "all" of the virgins became drowsy and fell asleep.

This status of somnolence identifies the overall general condition of the body of Christ at that time, but it does not identify the spiritual status of every single believer at that time or at this present time.

Yet, our general, relative somnolence, in comparison with the early church, will be changed very quickly at the time of the Spirit's "announcement," which comes to us like a shofar blast from the watchtower wall.

This awakening will include an event, or events, in the world that get our attention as they line up with prophetic scripture, identified by Jeremiah as *the storm of the Lord.*" (Jeremiah 23:19)

At this time the Spirit of truth will cause us to know with absolute certainty that we are the generation who will experience the final testing of our faith and the final conflict with the beast kingdom leading up to the return of our Lord, Jesus Christ.

It will also ultimately demonstrate the pre-tribulation "rapture" of church only saints as one of the enemy's most effective lies, introduced into the church by Satan for the purpose of defeating the end time kingdom of God in Christ.

And in the lengthy aftermath of this worldwide awakening of the body of Christ, identified as the 4th, 5th, and 6th seals of "tribulation," the "wicked servants" will wound the "foolish virgins," who spiritually represent a significant number of the corporate body of Christ. Then, because of the wounding, these are unable to respond appropriately to the Lord's demands of repentance from the idolatries of ungodly denominational traditions, false doctrine, false practice, and the pharisaical religiosity of the wicked servants who reverence denominational and doctrinal tradition over the absolute, immutable, revelatory Word of God.

Then these "foolish" believers eventually run out of oil (become apostate) resulting in their judgment at the second resurrection of the great white throne judgment when the Lord says, *"I do not know you,"* though He did know them at one time.

Even worse, many of these will ultimately become those of the harlot church, the ultimate "synagogue of Satan," drunk on the blood of the martyrs, who, believing that they are doing God a service, will persecute faithful believers during the 4th, 5th, and 6th seal events of tribulation.

These are the "foolish virgins," having become apostate, and subsequently empowered by Jezebellian religious demons, who will ultimately persecute the "wise."

In Revelation 2:9, the Lord literally identifies these as the *"synagogue of Satan,"* which was originally the synagogue out of which the Philadelphian church emerged.

Metaphorically this represents a future group of apostate former believers who say they are (spiritual) Jews but are not. These are those apostate former believers who, through various demonic entanglements, are motivated and empowered to persecute the end time Philadelphian type of believer identified in this parable as "wise virgins." Yet, these will believe that they are doing God a favor by persecuting those who have abandoned heretical doctrine and practice to follow the Lord in truth and love.

At the same time, I do not want to believe this, and most who are reading this testimony do not want to believe this. Yet, the record He has given us in scripture clearly reveals this truth.

In this regard, we need to remember how the Roman Catholic Church burned believers on the stake just for having a copy of the scriptures or remember and reflect on our own denominational enmities in order to recognize this possibility under extreme conditions.

Nevertheless, what causes my spirit to soar, in spite of my awareness that trouble is rapidly escalating in the world, is the knowledge that this present generation will soon be awakened from our somnolence to prepare for the great end time testing of our faith.

It is also this great end time fight, through which the "wise virgins" of the end time body of Christ will ultimately prevail to manifest the fullness of Christ in the face of the worst that Satan can do.

For that reason, I will refer back to this parable throughout this book as the details of this intensely hopeful and inspiring adventure of the heroic Joshua generation of "wise virgins" is progressively revealed.

In the parable of the talents, a biblical talent is a measure of weight, typically of precious metals, with the Roman talent at that time being the equivalent of 71 pounds. Talents are a money metaphor used to illustrate the gifts of the Spirit given to the Master's servants. In this parable (Mt. 25:14-30) the Master, Jesus Christ, is going on a long journey (2000 years), and He gives His servants (all Christian believers) charge of varying amounts of money or gold (spiritual gifts) to invest for Him while He is gone.

Two are faithful, investing what He has given them so that the Master receives a return on His investment. The third, receiving the smallest amount, a single talent, buried the talent instead of investing it for His Master.

What this represents is the believer, given the Holy Spirit and given specific spiritual gifts, attends church and lives up to the religious expectations of men but fails to exercise the gifts of the Spirit by grace through faith in genuine ministry.

His excuse when the Master returns is an accusation. He accuses the Master of reaping what he did not sow and gathering (the harvest) where he had not winnowed the grain. Therefore, the unfaithful servant feels justified in not sowing or gathering, as long as he is content just to be a "Christian," saved and going to heaven (the buried talent), but never allowing the seed planted in his spirit to grow and produce the "fruit" of a life of faith in service to the Master.

He did not even invest his faith in others (i.e. giving to ministries involved in sowing and gathering on behalf of the Master).

In the end, others who have been faithful are given this "good-for-nothing" servant's seed to sow, and they reap the reward that was meant for him. Then he not only loses the reward meant for him, but he rejects his salvation as well.

In all these parables we see a common theme with variations on emphasis. When tribulation comes both the faith of the shepherds and the sheep will be tested. The "wise" will wake up and manifest the faith the Lord has apportioned to them. The "foolish" will make a partial response, but will ultimately, through deception, and resentment against God because of tribulation, reject their faith in Jesus Christ.

In Matthew 24:37-39 the Lord tells us that these final days of the age will be like the days of Noah. Noah believed God and spent many years building the ark while everyone around him continued to live as if the flood would not come.

This bears an eerie resemblance to the majority of the church today, either believing that "tribulation" (the flood) will not come in their day or that they will be "raptured" away and escape the testing of their faith so adequately described by the Lord in Matthew 24 and 25.

When Noah entered the ark, a type of God's supernatural protection, the flood came and swept all of the apostate unbelievers away.

Noah was not removed from the flood but was protected in the flood (a type of the tribulation), while those who rejected the truth of God were swept away into apostasy.

In our case, this sadly includes many in the body of Christ today, who, because of deception or worldliness, are not prepared for the days immediately ahead of us.

But we have been warned:

"Behold, I have told you in advance." Matthew 24:25 NASB

3 – The Strong Delusion

Our emotive attachment to the nation of Israel and to the natural brothers of our Lord is appropriate, but we must not pervert the understanding of God's covenant intent based on our emotive attraction for the land and people of Israel. Any such perversion of the revelatory truth is a stumbling block for those other seeds of Abraham whom we intensely desire to be included in the "***Israel of God***" in Christ, as well as a stumbling block for us upon whom the fulfillment of the ages has come.

And I will make of thee a great nation…(the Israel of God in Christ)…, ***and I will bless thee, and make thy name great; and thou shalt be a blessing: And I will bless them that bless thee, and curse him that curseth thee: and in thee shall all families of the earth be blessed.*** Genesis 12:2,3 KJV (insert is the author's)

In this regard we have mistakenly applied the promise of Genesis 12:2,3 to national, ethnic Israel when, in fact, this promise now belongs exclusively to Christ through spiritual Israel in Christ.

This covenant blessing has been confirmed to Jesus Christ, the seed of Abraham for whom it was always intended, and for those who are covenanted in Him with the Father by faith.

The Zionist view is that Israel, as a nation, and ethnic Jews as a race, are still the apple of God's covenant eye, but what is clearly identified in scripture is that it is the *"Israel of God"* in Christ, that is God's covenant nation.

Thus it is those today who bless the nation of God, identified scripturally as the *Israel of God* in Christ who will be blessed in return, and it is those today who persecute the nation of God in Christ who will be cursed by God in return, and sadly this will include the deceived Jews who receive the antichrist "man of sin" as Lord and Savior.

The unfortunate immediate future for national, ethnic Israel, is that they will become home for **"Babylon the great"** as Satan, through the false prophet and the antichrist "man of sin," rule the world from Jerusalem for the final 3.5 years of the age identified as *"great tribulation."*

This future for Israel and all those, whether Jew or Gentile, who continue to believe the Zionist, dispensational, dual covenant pre-tribulation "rapture" of church only saints is identified as the *"strong delusion"*...(2 Thessalonians 2)...and it will result in the condemnation of the foolish who will eagerly take the covenant mark of the beast kingdom after the antichrist *"man of sin"* declares himself to be God and Messiah in the third temple, rebuilt by the Temple Mount and Land of Israel Faithful Movement or some other similar group of religious Jews.

It is entirely appropriate to desire the salvation of ethnic Jews and to support those ministries focused on bringing the truth of the gospel to Israel and to the Jewish people wherever they are today.

But the future for Israel as a nation, and for the majority of the Jewish people, is shockingly tragic.

As I examined the history of the Jewish people from the destruction of the temple forward a complex Satanic scheme was revealed.

The temple was destroyed in 70 CE (AD) by the Roman army under Titus on God's calendar day of 9 Nisan (9 Aviv), which, according to most Bible scholars is the same day and month that Jesus entered Jerusalem on a donkey, and on 10 Nisan Jesus prophesied the destruction of the temple and the judgment of the nation and people of Israel.

"For the days shall come upon thee, that thine enemies shall cast a trench about thee, and compass thee round, and keep thee in on every side, and shall lay thee even with the ground, and thy children within thee; and they shall not leave in thee one stone upon another; because thou knewest not the time of thy visitation. Luke 19:43,44 KJV

Nisan/Aviv is the first month of God's calendar as given to Israel for the very specific days and times for all the primary events of covenant redemption in Christ.

10 Nisan is also the day the Jewish people selected their lambs for slaughter on Passover, which occurs on14 Nisan.

Over time, 9 Nisan, historically identified by the Jewish people as "Tisha B'Av," has come to be a Jewish day of mourning, not only for these events, but also for later tragedies which occurred on or near 9 Nisan.

The First Crusade carried out by intensely corrupt aspects of the Roman Catholic Church, officially commenced on August 15, 1096 (24 Nisan), killing 10,000 Jews in its first month and destroying Jewish communities in France and the Rhineland.

We need to understand that the Roman Catholic "Christian" Crusades and later expulsions were NOT ordained by God, but by Satanically deceived leaders of the organized church of that day.

The Jews were expelled from England on July 18, 1290 (9 Nisan), from France on July 22, 1306 (9 Nisan), and from Spain on July 31, 1492 (7 Nisan).

Germany entered World War I on August 1–2, 1914 (9–10 Nisan), which caused a massive upheaval in European Jewry and whose aftermath led to the Holocaust.

On August 2, 1941 (9 Nisan), SS commander Heinrich Himmler formally received approval from the Nazi Party for "The Final Solution." As a result, the Holocaust began during which almost one third of the world's Jewish population perished.

On July 23, 1942 (9 Nisan), the mass deportation of Jews from the Warsaw Ghetto, on route to Treblinka began.

The AMIA bombing, of the Jewish community center in Buenos Aires, killed 85 and injured 300 on 18 July 1994 (10 Nisan).

The Israeli disengagement from Gaza began in the Gaza Strip, expelling 8000 Jews who lived in Gush Katif on 15 August 2005 (10 Nisan).

This is not coincidence. But these atrocities committed against Israel were not of God.

It was Satan, desiring to maintain Israel's rejection of God in Christ, and knowing that the nation of Israel no longer had God's covenant protection, who continued to assault the nation and people of Israel through his corruption of the Catholic Church and various associated organizations in order to set up his great end time deception, known as the "strong delusion," when Israel, and the religious Jews of that day, will receive the antichrist "man of sin" as "Messiah" in complete and total denial of Jesus of Nazareth as "Messiah."

We, then, mourn the atrocities committed against the Jewish people by intensely deceived organized Christianity, but, at the same time, we need to recognize that these atrocities, empowered by Satan, also hardened the hearts of ethnic Jews around the globe.

It then perfectly prepares Israel and the Jewish people in general for the "*strong delusion*" that will condemn many Jews and even more Christians.

Now we beseech you, brethren, by the coming of our Lord Jesus Christ, and by our gathering together unto him, That ye be not soon shaken in mind, or be troubled, neither by spirit, nor by word, nor by letter as from us, as that the day of Christ…(the great and terrible Day of the Lord or Day of Atonement on some future 10 Tisri)…*is at hand. Let no man deceive you by any means: for that day shall not come, except there come a falling away first, and that man of sin be revealed, the son of perdition; Who opposeth and exalteth himself above all that is called God, or that is worshipped; so that he as God sitteth in the temple of God, shewing himself that he is God.* 2 Thessalonians 2:1-4 KJV (inserts are the author's)

Then the Lord opens the 7th seal, and the final 3.5 years of "great tribulation" begins.

The continued persecution of Israel in the end times is not a manifestation of God's judgment. The judgment of God upon Israel for their rejection of Jesus of Nazareth as Messiah was completed by the destruction of the temple and the dispersion of the Jewish people into the nations.

Nothing that has happened to Israel or the Jews since their dispersion into the nations is a direct result of the will of God or His judgment of Israel for their rejection of Jesus Christ when He came to them.

The continued persecution of Israel is a deliberate act by Satan through the final forms of his beast kingdom in order to produce great empathy for the Jews not only in the world, but in the generation of spiritual Israel, the body of Christ, during the final days of the end times.

Satan's purpose in all this is for Israel, under the antichrist "man of sin," to rule the world for the final 3.5 years of great tribulation.

Many years ago in San Angelo, Texas, I was invited by a friend to attend a presentation by the Messianic ministry, "Prophecy Round-Up" out of Fort Worth, Texas. The presentation included a talk by Mr. Gershon Salomon, leader of the "Temple Mount and Land of Israel Faithful Movement," revealing how this group was preparing to rebuild the temple on the temple mount in

Jerusalem for the purpose of re-instituting the Levitical priesthood and temple worship in anticipation of the coming of their messiah, "mashiach Ben David."

After the presentation the leader of the Prophecy Round-Up group appealed to the Christians present for donations to support the Temple Mount organization in their preparation for rebuilding the temple and beginning temple worship and sacrifices again.

I was shocked when Christians all around the room, including members of my own fellowship, all dreamy-eyed with emotive empathy for Israel and the Jews, began to pull out their checkbooks.

When I stood up and protested that support of the Temple Mount Movement was a denial of the finished work of Jesus Christ and an antichrist stumbling block for the Jews, my protest was met with angry denials by the leader of the Prophecy Round-Up group, and I was quickly ushered out of the building.

That was my first encounter with Zionist, dual covenant, Jewish supremacist theology, and I recognize now that it was a divine appointment for my instruction.

I now subscribe to the Temple Mount and Land of Israel Faithful newsletter and watch their website regularly, and rather than explain this group's perfect alignment with Satan's schemes, I will present a copy of the page titled, "A Vision of Redemption" as it appeared on their website as authored by Mr. Gershon Salomon, allowing the author himself to reveal the antichrist influence of this intensely religious Zionist group to the reader.

Of interest is the fact that I copied this page from the website on January 3, 2015, and on January 6, 2015, when I went back to the page three days later, it had been significantly altered to remove some of the more provocative information on the page, though this webpage information was originally authored in 2004 and remained unchanged until Satan realized that I had read and recognized his antichrist deception.

In this regard we need to be aware that Satan knows what we are writing, saying, and doing, and whenever possible, he will attempt to circumvent any assault on his deceptive strongholds, especially the prophetically significant strongholds.

But he failed to remove page 29, middle column, of his "summer 5764/2004" magazine archive where this information also resides and is more difficult to remove, because it exists in print form.

My comments will be in parentheses and italics, and I will bold Mr. Salomon's most important disclosures:

A Vision of Redemption by Gershon Salomon:

The mashiach will be a great political leader descended from King David (Jeremiah 23:5). The maschiach is often referred to as "maschiach ben David" (maschiach, son of David). He will be well-versed in Jewish law, and observant of its commandments (Isaiah 11:2-5). He will be a charismatic leader, inspiring others to follow his example. He will be a great military leader, who will win battles for Israel. He will be a great judge, who makes righteous decisions (Jeremiah 33:15). But above all, he will be a human being, not a god, demi-god or other supernatural being.

It has been said that in every generation, a person is born with the potential to be the mashiach. If the time is right for the messianic age within that person's lifetime, then that person will be the mashiach. But if that person dies before he completes the mission of the mashiach, then that person is not the mashiach.

Before the time of the mashiach, there shall be war and suffering (Ezekiel 38:16).

The mashiach will bring about the political and spiritual redemption of the Jewish people by bringing us back to Israel and restoring Jerusalem (Isaiah 11:11-12; Jeremiah 23:8; 30:3; Hosea 3:4-5). **He will establish a government in Israel that will be the center of all world government, both for Jews and gentiles** (Isaiah 2:2-4; 11:10; 42:1). He will rebuild the Temple and re-establish its worship (Jeremiah 33:18). **He will restore the religious court system of Israel and establish Jewish law as the law of the land.** (Jeremiah 33:15).

Quotation break inserted here.

   By context Mr. Salomon is indicating that religious theocratic courts of justice throughout the entire world will be the means of the "maschiach's" control and the likely source for receiving his beast kingdom covenant "mark."

Quotation begins again.

Belief in the eventual coming of the mashiach is a basic and fundamental part of traditional Judaism. It is part of Rambam's 13 Principles of Faith, the minimum requirements of Jewish belief. In the Shemoneh Esrei prayer, recited three times daily, we pray for all of the elements of the coming of the mashiach: ingathering of the exiles; restoration of the religious courts of justice; an end of wickedness, sin and heresy; reward to the righteous; rebuilding of Jerusalem; restoration of the line of King David; and restoration of Temple service.

The Temple Mount and Land of Israel Faithful Movement understands the phenomenon of modern Israel as the beginning of the redemption of the world.

Quotation break inserted here.

   This is an obvious denial that Jesus Christ is the fulfillment of redemption.

Quotation begins again.

Two and one-half millennia ago, the Hebrew prophets spoke that in the "last days" G-d would regather His people from all the lands where He had scattered them (Isaiah 43:5-7). For the last 100 years the Jewish people have been returning to and rebuilding Zion. Today, Israel is again the dynamic center of Jewish life across the world. The regathering is not yet complete. Ezekiel prophesied that G-d would "leave none of them there any longer" (Ezekiel 39:28b).

It is the view of the Temple Mount and Land of Israel Faithful that the redemption will proceed in an orderly fashion according to G-d's plan.
•First is the foundation of the modern state of Israel and the miraculous victories that G-d gave the people of Israel in the wars against 22 Arab enemy states.
•Second is the regathering of the people of Israel from all over the world to the Promised Land.
•Third is the liberation and consecration of the Temple Mount.
•Fourth is the building of the Third Temple.
•The final step is the coming of the King of Israel, Messiah Ben David.

The existence of the state of Israel and the return of the people of G-d to the Promised Land is the biggest godly event and miracle in the history of mankind — ever. ...

Quotation break inserted here.

Meaning the life, death, and resurrection of Jesus Christ was NOT.

Quotation begins again.

This was predicted by the prophets of Israel. We are calling all the nations to link arms in support of this people and the State of Israel to help her complete this process of redemption. **We are not allowed to forget that the redemption of the people of Israel is a condition for the redemption of the earth.** Also, we remember what G-d said over 4,000 years ago to Abraham, the father of the

Israelites: "I will bless those who bless you and curse those who curse you" (Genesis 12:3).

Temple Mount and Land of Israel Faithful Movement
Gershon Salomon (*end of quote*)

Another common theme on the website, and an expectation of modern Jews in Israel and elsewhere, is that the Gog-Magog war (Ezekiel 38 and 39) will be the specific event that proves to the entire world that God has re-established His covenant with Israel.

Mr. Gershon's article demonstrates the primary view of religious Jews in Israel today, and it is shockingly identical with the view held by the Pharisees, rabbis, and priests of Israel at the first advent of our Lord, Jesus Christ.

These rejected Him as "Messiah" because of the lies that had become a tradition of "truth" assaulted against the absolute, immutable, revelatory truth of God.

The Lord prophesied to those who rejected Him at His coming that the future religious Jews, and all those who are in agreement with them concerning the supposed future redemption of Israel, (i.e. "Christian" Zionists) will be subject to the "***strong delusion***" coming upon all those who do not love the truth that Jesus Christ "***hath visited and redeemed his people.***" (Luke 1:68 KJV and Galatians 3:13) And these will receive the antichrist "man of sin" as their "mashiach."

I am come in my Father's name, and ye receive me not: if another shall come in his own name, him ye...(future Jews)... *will receive.* John 5:43 KJV (insert is the author's)

Let no man deceive you by any means: for that day shall not come, except there come a falling away...(apostasy of Christian believers)...*first, and that man of sin be revealed, the son of perdition; who opposeth and exalteth himself above all that is called God, or that is worshipped; so that he as God sitteth in the temple of God, shewing himself that he is God.* 2 Thessalonians 2:3,4 KJV (insert is the author's)

And then shall that Wicked be revealed, whom the Lord shall consume with the spirit of his mouth, and shall destroy with the brightness of his coming: even him,...(the antichrist "man of sin")...*whose coming is after the working of Satan with all power and signs and lying wonders, and with all deceivableness of unrighteousness in them that perish; because they received not the love of the truth,*...(that the redemption of Israel was completed at the first advent of Jesus Christ)...*that they might be saved. And for this cause* ...(the lie that God has not, yet, redeemed Israel)...*God shall send them* __strong delusion__*, that they should believe a lie:*...(THE lie as prophesied by the Lord in John 5:43)...*that they all might be damned who believed not the truth, but had pleasure in unrighteousness.* 2 Thessalonians 2:8-12 KJV (inserts and emphasis are the author's)

It is the Temple Mount and Land of Israel Faithful Movement who will build the third temple in anticipation of their "Messiah" with help from intensely deceived Zionist Christians all over the world to prepare the way for the antichrist "man of sin."

And, in this regard, those Zionist Christian believers will be, and have been, **tithing to Satan**. Likewise, many of these will ultimately be included "in Satan" as the future "synagogue of Satan" rather than included "in Christ."

There are, of course, many variations of this Zionist Jewish supremacy doctrine, but there are likely to be many Christian believers reading this book who were totally unaware that the popular theory of pre-tribulation "rapture" of church only saints is a prophetic distinctive that is only possible if the entirety of this Zionist, Jewish supremacy, dual covenant, dispensational model of God's covenant relationship with mankind is correct.

Hence the most important truth we need to examine about our covenant relationship with the Father in Christ is that it was, and still is, His intention (will) from before the foundation of the world, before the creation event itself, that a remnant elect of fallen mankind, from Adam forward, identified as spiritual Israel, the "*Israel of God*," made up of both Jews and Gentiles as "*one new man*" in Christ, would have an eternal covenant relationship with Him through His only begotten Son, the Son of God, Son of Man, Jesus of Nazareth.

This covenant, the New Covenant, was not an afterthought introduced like a chess move after Adam failed to uphold the original covenant and the sons of Abraham (other than Jesus of Nazareth) failed to uphold the covenant of Law.

The Father planned it from before the creation.

According as he hath chosen us in him before the foundation of the world, that we should be holy and without blame before him in love: Having predestinated us unto the adoption of children by Jesus Christ to himself, according to the good pleasure of his will, to the praise of the glory of his grace, wherein he hath made us accepted in the beloved. Ephesians 1:4-6 KJV (emphasis is the author's)

What Paul, the Hebrew of Hebrews, clearly reveals in this passage is that it was God's plan from before the fall of Adam, and before there was a racial distinction between Jews and Gentiles, to include the entire remnant elect of mankind in the New Covenant in Christ, which was obviously fulfilled on Pentecost on the 50th day after the crucifixion of Jesus Christ as the kingdom of God fell with power on the spiritual body of Christ, demonstrated afterwards to be made up of Jew and Gentile as "*one new man*" identified as the "*Israel of God*" in Christ.

It is the "*Israel of God*" in Christ that is demonstrated to be the ultimate covenant intent of God, not national, ethnic Israel.

Everything we believe by faith, having "heard" the truth with spiritual ears and "seen" truth through the eyes of our hearts, hinges on our understanding that it is now, and always has been, God's plan to include the entire remnant elect of mankind in this **ONE** redemptive covenant between God and man, the eternal covenant written in the blood of Jesus Christ, the eternal mediator and High Priest of this covenant.

This simple but profound truth is revealed progressively throughout scripture, but it is only revealed completely to those who have eyes to "see" and ears to "hear" what the Spirit is saying.

A confirming question we need to ask at this time is: "Was God's promise to Abraham a promise for national, ethnic Israel, or was it always, from before the creation itself, intended by God as a promise to the singular "seed" of Abraham, Jesus Christ, and through Him to all those from Adam forward, Jew and Gentile alike, who would be spiritually incorporated in Him either by God's sovereign election or by grace through faith?"

Now to Abraham and his seed were the ...(covenant)... *promises made. He saith not, And to seeds, as of many,*...(but to one)...*And to thy seed, which is Christ.* Galatians 3:16 KJV (inserts are the author's)

For all the...(covenant)... *promises of God in him are yea, and in him Amen, unto the glory of God by us.*
2 Corinthians 1:20 KJV (insert is the author's)

These two passages, among many others, clearly demonstrate that the covenant promise was always to Jesus of Nazareth, Son of God and Son of Man, and through Him to the entire remnant elect of mankind from Adam forward who would ultimately be identified as the "*Israel of God.*"

The resurrection of the saints, including Jews and Gentiles as *one new man* in Christ, will take place on the 1 Tishri feast of Trumpets.

This is the one and only resurrection of the saints as demonstrated in God's calendar for the redemption of fallen mankind in Christ from Adam forward.

No separate pre-tribulation "rapture" of living, born again Christian believers is demonstrated in any way by God's calendar, and the Zionist lie of a pre-tribulation "rapture" of church only saints is, therefore, a satanically inspired lie introduced into the body of Christ to keep us in a state of somnolence prior to the opening of the 4th seal to begin a time identified as "*tribulation*."

Likewise, the body of Christ's general ignorance where this prophetic, God-given calendar is concerned is one of Satan's greatest beast kingdom victories for setting up the "*strong delusion*" that will condemn many.

4 - God's Prophetic Calendar of Redemption

The appointed times and feasts of the Lord are God's prophetic calendar for all of the primary events of redemption, and is, therefore, the most important source of revelatory truth related to the primary events of redemption as those events relate to the body of Christ. This calendar also provides the chronological order for the core doctrine of covenant redemption with which all scriptural doctrine, and, specifically, prophetic doctrine, must comply.

This calendar identifies the specific dates of the "aviv" new moon calendar given to Israel for the seven primary events of God's covenant redemption of fallen mankind in Christ.

Yet, the vast majority of Christian believers presume, as I once did, that the appointed times and feasts of the Lord, first given to national, ethnic Israel and recorded in Leviticus 23, are not applicable to the New Testament body of Christ, because we are not required to celebrate these appointed times and feasts of the Lord.

We may choose to celebrate them, but we are not required to celebrate them. Yet, it is certain that we will celebrate them both during the millennial kingdom and the eternal age, but we are not required to celebrate them now.

Still, the requirement to celebrate and memorialize the appointed times for the redemption of an elect remnant of fallen mankind in pre-Christ Israel should convey to us just how important the revelatory understanding of the appointed times and feasts is for those upon whom the very fulfillment of this calendar has come.

Imagine the chaos in the world and in our individual lives if we had no specific calendar through which we could plan and organize both our societal and personal lives.

Those who believe that God's very specific calendar for all the primary events of redemption in Christ is no longer applicable, though it has not, yet, been completely fulfilled, are similarly confused in their various presumptions concerning "things to come."

We should also note that this calendar demonstrating God's plan of redemption for the remnant elect of fallen mankind in Jesus Christ has been, and will be, fulfilled exclusively to spiritual "born again" Israel, and not in any separate way to national, ethnic Israel.

This is, therefore, not now natural Israel's calendar. This is OUR calendar, the prophetic calendar of God's "eternal covenant," His foreordained plan for the redemption of an elect remnant of fallen mankind in Christ, in which the entire remnant He has identified as "*the Israel of God*," (Galatians 6:16) from Adam forward will be included.

This calendar of God's appointed times for the fulfillment of our redemption in Christ began to be fulfilled with the crucifixion of Jesus Christ on Passover, and it will end with the ultimate fulfillment of Tabernacles as we inhabit our eternal home in the New Jerusalem on the New Earth after it has been renovated by spiritual fire.

Therefore, any examination of end time prophecy, as well as the examination and revelatory understanding of the primary doctrine of redemptive covenant salvation (soteriology), must be viewed in the light of God's calendar of redemption presented metaphorically, but precisely, in the appointed times and feasts of the Lord.

It is surprising, then, to discover that the most popular schools of end time prophetic eschatology today do not comply with, or even acknowledge, this partially fulfilled calendar given to us for our revelatory understanding concerning things to come.

This failure to acknowledge the importance of God's calendar of very specific God "*appointed times*" for the redemption of fallen mankind in Christ is partially due to the fact that the continued practice of celebrating the appointed times and feasts of the Lord by early Christians was ultimately corrupted by the Roman Catholic Church.

There were various Greek and Roman calendars in use prior to the Gregorian Calendar introduced by Pope Gregory XIII in October 1582. But at that time the Roman Catholic Council mistakenly viewed God's very specific "aviv" new moon Calendar of the appointed times and feasts of the Lord as "Jewish" feasts rather than kingdom of God feasts. These then thought to change the times and laws of God by inventing a so-called "Christian" Passover.

So, instead of using the "aviv" new moon calendar given to us by the Creator to determine the date for "Passover," that event was no longer referenced as "Passover," but was called "Easter" (a derivative from "Ishtar," a.k.a. "Astarte," goddess of war and sexual love), and the date for this so-called "Christian" Passover is now determined by Catholics and protestants alike to be the first Sunday after the first full moon following the vernal equinox.

This heretical changing of God's appointed times by the 16th century Roman Catholic leadership has been fully adopted by Protestants, but it cannot be found anywhere in biblical scripture.

Nor can I find "Christmas," "Resurrection Sunday," or any of the numerous saints' days in scripture.

In this regard I am not arguing for the required celebratory observation of God's calendar for the seven primary events of redemption as God required of pre-Christ Israel so that they would be accountable for recognizing His incarnation, but for our diligent, Spirit-led examination and awareness of this calendar for the prophetic truth applicable to this current generation of spiritual Israel, the body of Christ.

Therefore, regardless of the supposed authority of the one expounding on his/her theories about biblical prophecy, or any long-standing and popular tradition of interpretation, if it does not and cannot conform to the truth revealed in the detailed prophetic calendar of God-appointed times for the seven primary events of covenant redemption in Christ, those theories are in error.

Likewise, we should note that if it was not important for the elect remnant of fallen mankind, which He has called *"the Israel of God,"* to have revelatory insight into *"things to come,"* He would not have given us the prophecies to begin with. Nor would Satan have set up so many elaborate deceptions concerning them.

That Satan was successful in blinding the spiritual eyes of the Pharisees, the intellectual giants of Israel who were intimately acquainted with every written word concerning the Messiah, and with the intricate details of God's prophetic calendar for the redemption of fallen mankind in Christ, is historic fact. That he has been successful in blinding the spiritual eyes of many of the intellectual giants of the body of Christ is also self-evident.

The interpretation of this calendar, like all biblical scripture, is only accurately perceived as we receive revelatory guidance from the Spirit of truth who wrote it.

From the Exodus story, we can see that the *Pesach* lambs were slain on 14 Nisan, the day of <u>Passover</u>. On 15 Nisan, the Israelites left Egypt in haste. On 16 Nisan, <u>Firstfruits</u>, the children of Israel crossed the Red Sea; and forty-nine days after Passover, on the <u>Feast of Weeks</u>, or <u>Pentecost</u>, God introduced Israel to the Torah (instruction or "Law") as the Law was written by the very finger of God on tablets of stone. (Exodus 31:18)

This is the historic prototype of the spring and summer feasts and appointed times, foreshadowing the complete spiritual fulfillment of these appointed times by Jesus of Nazareth, and their ultimate application to the newborn spiritual body of Christ.

In this regard, the author of Hebrews clearly reveals the Law as being only a "shadow" (foreshadowing) of the everlasting covenant to be fulfilled in Christ.

For the law having a <u>shadow</u> of good things to come, and not the very image of the things, can never with those sacrifices which they offered year by year continually make the comers thereunto perfect. Hebrews 10:1 KJV (emphasis is the author's)

For it is not possible that the blood of bulls and of goats should take away sins. Hebrews 10:4 KJV

It is, therefore, completely inappropriate for believers, including Messianic believers, to see the rituals associated with the Law as anything other than a foreshadowing (without power) of the substance of the promised covenant that has been fulfilled, as well as a foreshadowing of that part of the covenant promises yet to be fulfilled.

It is not a required celebratory sacrament of God for Christian believers, but, at the same time, it is the primary source for confirming prophetic truth and doctrine related to future God-appointed times for the redemption of the *Israel of God* in Christ.

And, it is certain that we will celebrate these "appointed times" throughout all eternity on the exact days and the exact manner foreordained by God.

In Leviticus 23 and Deuteronomy16 the Israelites were given the specific instructions for the appointed times and feasts, and the annual Sabbaths.

For them the appointed times and feasts of the Lord were to memorialize what was the historic natural fulfillment of the first four feasts (national Israel's deliverance from bondage in Egypt) with a forward view to the ultimate Messianic spiritual fulfillment, not only of the first four feasts, but of all seven feasts or "appointed times" for the redemption of a remnant of fallen mankind in Christ that He has called the ***Israel of God.***"

The elaborate celebration of God's calendar for redemption in Christ was a religious requirement for pre-Christ Israel so that they would be accountable for recognizing the ultimate time of their visitation by the Messiah, which, for them, was next on God's agenda.

Yet, because of non-revelatory religious traditions, not unlike many "Christian" religious traditions, all but a remnant of Israel missed the appointed time of their Messianic visitation resulting in the Lord's prophecy concerning the judgement of Israel.

For the days shall come upon thee, that thine enemies shall cast a trench about thee, and compass thee round, and keep thee in on every side, and shall lay thee even with the ground, and thy children within thee; and they shall not leave in thee one stone upon another; because thou <u>knewest</u> <u>not</u> the time of thy visitation (as prophetically foreshadowed in the appointed times and feasts of the Lord). <u>Luke 19:43,44 KJV</u> (insert and emphasis is the author's)

Paul made it very clear that everything that happened to national, ethnic Israel was written down for our instruction, upon whom the fulfillment of the ages has come.

Now all these things happened unto them for examples: and they are written for our admonition, upon whom the ends of the world are come. <u>1 Corinthians 10:11 KJV</u>

The lesson to be learned, then, is that we, too, must pay attention to the revelatory understanding of that part of the appointed times and feasts of the Lord that is yet to be fulfilled lest we also miss the time, and timing, of our visitation, the return of Christ, including future events to take place immediately prior to the return of Christ, resulting in the redemption of the "wise" and the judgment of the "foolish."

The prophetic judgment spoken by the Lord against the Pharisees and Scribes who missed the time of their visitation, as recorded in Luke 19:43-44, was fulfilled in 70 AD when Titus, the prince of Rome, invaded Israel. This was the deadly wound to the "head" (mountain kingdom) of Israel by the sword (war) when the temple was torn down with not one stone left on top of the other and the people of Israel were scattered among the nations.

Israel, from that date forward no longer existed as a nation-state until 1948 when the deadly head wound was healed for the purposes described in the author's companion book, UNMASKING The End Time Beast Kingdom.

Apostate Israel on some future date, believing that God is restoring the covenant promises given to Abraham, will rebuild the temple, destroyed because of Israel's rejection of the Messiah when He came to them.

Then this well-meaning, but antichrist body of religious Israel, will reinstitute the Levitical priesthood and temple sacrifices again under the direction of the "false prophet," who will appear in Israel with great signs and wonders following like prophets of old.

And many of those who are reading this book will witness this pivotal antichrist event.

Yet, these signs and wonders, like the signs and wonders of Jannes and Jambres, the magicians in Pharaoh's court, are manifestations of Satan's power, not God's power.

It is, therefore, this rebuilding of the temple and beginning of temple worship and sacrifices again that will pave the way for the ultimate manifestation of the antichrist "man of sin."

Some readers will emotively reject the author's assignment of the term "antichrist" to those religious Jews today who are in denial that Jesus of Nazareth is the promised Messiah. Therefore, please be aware that I only use the terminology already assigned to them by the Spirit of truth in scripture.

Who is a liar but he that denieth that Jesus is the Christ? He is antichrist, that denieth the Father and the Son. 1 John 2;22 KJV

"Denial" as it is used in this passage implies a choice by those who have been confronted with the truth.

Note that the denial of Jesus of Nazareth as "Christ" (Messiah) is the denial of both the Father and the Son. Therefore, the modern practice of Judaism is not a sister faith to Christianity, because the denial of Jesus of Nazareth as "Christ" is also a denial of the covenant intent of the Father.

Many of those Christian believers, then, who continue to be blind to the time of our visitation, will ultimately become those whom the Lord has identified as *"foolish virgins."*

The calendar given to the Israelites after the historic events of the exodus perfectly matched the dates of their historic natural fulfillment, and, as we will note, perfectly match the dates of their spiritual fulfillment. Those parts of God's calendar for the redemption of the elect remnant of mankind in Christ that have already been fulfilled are, then, our assurance that the remainder of this calendar will also be fulfilled on the exact dates and in the exact order and manner that God has foreordained.

I write this with the understanding that there are numerous intellectual interpretations of the details of this calendar without revelatory insight that are in disagreement with the revelatory truth contained in the same calendar. However, for those with ears to hear and eyes to see, God's calendar of appointed times and feasts is an amazing confirmation of past, present, and future truth, truth that the vast majority of Christianity is completely ignoring.

Yet, this is **OUR** calendar for all the primary events of the redemption of fallen mankind in Christ, and the primary source for both the revelation and confirmation of *"things to come."*

That part of the appointed times already fulfilled:

14 Nisan	15 Nisan	16 Nisan	6 Sivan
Passover	**Unleavened Bread**	**Firstfruits**	**Pentecost**
Natural fulfillment (national, ethnic Israel)			
Pesach lamb slain	Left godless Egypt	Red Sea crossed	Law given on Mt. Sinai
Spiritual Fulfillment (spiritual, born again, remnant Israel)			
Jesus crucified	Jesus sinless	Jesus resurrected	Law written on our hearts

What this calendar demonstrates in a powerful way is that the promised redemption of Israel took place two millennia ago as the one and only redemptive covenant was fulfilled to the "seed" of Abraham for whom it was always intended. This calendar also demonstrates that there is no second redemptive event to follow for national, ethnic Israel at the end of the age, though individual "survivors" of the 7th seal "great tribulation" who did not take the covenant seal of the antichrist "man of sin" or persecute Christian believers will receive Christ at that time. (Joel 2:23)

This one and only redemption of Israel manifested through the life, death, and resurrection of Jesus Christ was followed forty-nine days later by the coming of the kingdom of God with power on Pentecost as the promised Holy Spirit fell on the remnant, the 120 upper room believers who became "born again," spiritual Israel, the "Israel of God" in Christ, just as Joel prophesied.

And it shall come to pass afterward, that I will pour out my spirit upon all flesh; and your sons and your daughters shall prophesy, your old men shall dream dreams, your young men shall see visions: And also upon the servants and upon the handmaids in those days will I pour out my spirit. Joel 2:28, 29 KJV

What we note is that the covenant was fulfilled to the "seed," Jesus of Nazareth, for whom it was always intended, not to Israel as a nation, demonstrating that there is no possibility of some future fulfillment of the covenant promises to national, ethnic Israel apart from individual Jews coming to faith in Christ.

Now to Abraham and his seed were the promises made. He saith not, And to seeds, as of many...(Jews as a race or Israel as a nation)...; *but as of one, And to thy seed, which is Christ.* Galatians 3:16 KJV

What is clearly demonstrated here is that the New Covenant was always intended for Jesus Christ, and all those who are spiritually included in Him by faith or by the sovereign election of God.

It was never, at any time, intended for the geopolitical nation of Israel or exclusively for ethnic Jews.

And if it is not, therefore, clearly demonstrated in God's calendar of redemption, it does not exist.

What we also notice is that this calendar of the appointed times and feasts of the Lord is very specific. Furthermore, both the OT and the NT reveal numerous details by which the Spirit of truth confirms the redemptive covenant intent of the Father.

What we see here is that the miraculous events through which God delivered natural Israel from their bondage in Egypt were a foreshadowing of the spiritual fulfillment of those events to spiritual Israel, the body of Christ.

In this, natural deliverance from bondage became spiritual deliverance from sin, and the external Law became the internal Law, the perfect will of God, written upon our hearts through the indwelling presence of the promised Holy Spirit as the power of the kingdom of God fell on the new *ekklesia* of Christ.

From that specific point forward, every national ethnic Jew who has been or will be included, has and will only be included on the basis of their inclusion in the *Israel of God*, the spiritual body of Christ, by faith or by God's sovereign election.

A new heart also will I give you, and a new spirit will I put within you: (spoken to national, ethnic Israel, but fulfilled to spiritual, born again Israel, the Israel of God in Christ). Ezekiel 36:26 KJV (insert is the author's)

2 Samuel 7:10 is frequently quoted by Zionists to be intended for national, ethnic Israel, because Israel was re-established as a nation in 1948:

Moreover I will appoint a place for my people Israel, and will plant them, that they may dwell in a place of their own, and move no more; neither shall the children of wickedness afflict them any more, as beforetime...

However, the "children of wickedness" are afflicting national, ethnic Israel now, and the antichrist "man of sin" will *afflict them* in the future whether they submit their wills to him or rebel against him.

Likewise, it will ultimately be the "Israel of God," which includes Jews and Gentiles as "one new man" in Christ that permanently occupy the nation of Israel under the rule of the King of kings and Lord of lords, not ethnic Israel alone.

In 2 Samuel 7:10 the covenant promise to David is, therefore, clearly revealed to be for his "seed," Jesus of Nazareth, for whom the promises were and are intended.

From the resurrection of Jesus Christ forward, then, national, ethnic Israel plays no part in the fulfillment of God's redemptive covenant plan apart from individual Jews being included in Christ by grace through faith.

It is interesting to note that the Lord was crucified on 14 Nisan (Passover) at the same time that the *pesach* lambs were being slaughtered by Jewish families all over Jerusalem and the entire nation of Israel.

And on 16 Nisan (Firstfruits) the Lord was resurrected at the same time that the high priest, Caiaphas, in total denial that Jesus of Nazareth was the long-awaited "Messiah," waved a barley sheaf (without leaven) at the altar in spite of the curtain between the Holy Place and the Holy of Holies being torn from top to bottom as if slashed by a giant sword.

This "firstfruits" offering of the entire harvest, then, symbolized the ***"firstborn from among the dead"*** (Col. 1:18) harvest of Jesus Christ as the firstfruits of all mankind to be raised from the dead.

But every man in his own order: Christ the <u>firstfruits</u>...of redeemed mankind...; ***afterward they that are Christ's at his coming.*** 1 Corinthians 15:23 KJV (insert and emphasis is the author's)

His return, though, is in two parts. On 1 Tishri, the "last day" Feast of Trumpets, the Lord meets all the saints, those who have already experienced physical death and those who are still alive on that day, in the "air" (spiritual realm).

But on 10 Tishri, the Feast of Atonement, a.k.a. "the great and terrible day of the Lord," He returns to the earth with the saints of all time in their resurrection bodies.

On that day the "survivors" (Joel 2:32), including both Jews and Gentiles who have not taken the covenant mark of the beast kingdom and have not persecuted the spiritual body of Christ during the 3.5 years of 7th seal "great tribulation," will receive Him.

These, then, will enter into the millennial kingdom as regenerated believers, and it is these who will repopulate the earth during the millennial kingdom age.

All the rest of mankind at that time, in knowing or unknowing collaboration with Satan, will descend into hades, the region of the dead, to await their final judgment at the great white throne judgment. (Revelation 20:11,12)

Notice carefully that Paul does not leave room in his summary for any separate event for national, ethnic Israel as a whole. Those who are Christ's at His coming only includes Jews and Gentiles who have not taken the covenant mark of the beast kingdom and have not persecuted the body of Christ.

"Firstfruits" is the appointed time that the covenant first given to Abraham and his "seed" was fulfilled to Jesus of Nazareth, THE "seed" of Abraham, Son of God, Son of Man, and the "last Adam," who fulfilled all the Law and the prophets.

This, then, made it possible for an elect remnant of mankind, identified as spiritual, "born again," Israel, the *"Israel of God,"* to be included as joint heirs in the eternal covenant of God through their faith and spiritual incorporation in Jesus Christ, our great High Priest who upholds this covenant perfectly throughout all eternity.

Pentecost, the Feast of Weeks, is directly connected to Passover and Firstfruits in that this is the date upon which spiritual Israel, including both Jews and Gentiles as *"one new man"* in Christ, received the promised sealing of the Holy Spirit as a pledge of their complete redemption in Christ (inclusion as joint heirs in the covenant).

Most view the coming of the Holy Spirit on Pentecost as the complete and total fulfillment of this particular appointed time. But the coming of the kingdom of God with power through the indwelling presence of the Holy Spirit, as prophesied in Joel 2:28,29 is only the initiatory event of Pentecost, just as our sealing unto regeneration by the Holy Spirit at the moment of saving faith is the initiatory event of our redemption, not the completion of it.

The coming of the Holy Spirit on Pentecost (6 Sivan) was also the fulfillment of the Law being given on Sinai (which also took place on 6 Sivan). Thus, the perfect Law was written upon our hearts by the presence of the Holy Spirit, our Counselor and our spiritual conscience as promised to the remnant of Israel in Ezekiel 36:26-27 KJV:

A new heart also will I give you, and a new spirit will I put within you: and I will take away the stony heart out of your flesh, and I will give you an heart of flesh. And I will put my spirit within you, and cause you to walk in my statutes, and ye shall keep my judgments, and do them.

64

This covenant promise, first received by national, ethnic Israel, the temporary holders of the title-deed to this promise of God, was obviously fulfilled to the "*Israel of God*" in Christ on Pentecost, clearly demonstrating the covenant intent of God to be the believing remnant of national, ethnic Israel, not national, ethnic Israel as a whole.

Pentecost is the middle event between the first three events and the last three events yet to be fulfilled. Pentecost is, in reality, a feast to celebrate the redemptive plan of God in Christ as that plan is manifested in and through the spiritual, "born again" body of Christ as the sole representatives of the kingdom of God in the earth.

Although our redemption was initiated on that first Pentecost, it will not be completed for the majority of the elect until the resurrection of living and dead saints on some future 1 Tishri, Feast of Trumpets, also identified as the "*last day*" resurrection of the saints of all time.

But there is another event that will take place on some future Pentecost prior to the last day resurrection fulfillment of the Feast of Trumpets.

The wave offering of two wheat loaves containing leaven, representing both Jews and Gentiles as a **firstfruits** offering of the **wheat harvest** has not yet been fulfilled, because to date none from Adam forward have been fully redeemed (harvested), though the dead in Christ are now in the heavenly presence and cannot, therefore, reject their faith in Christ.

This is an important consideration. The first event of Pentecost was not a "harvest." It was a birth event as the kingdom of God fell with power on the believing remnant of Israel. Even these, though, will not receive the ultimate completion of their redemption until the 7th trumpet of the 7th seal on 1 Tishri, the Feast of Trumpets, which is the resurrection of the saints from Adam forward on the *last day*. (John 6:39-40)

Yet, there will be a glorious firstfruits of the wheat harvest unto God and the Lamb, to be fully explored in future chapters.

And, as we receive and confirm the revelatory covenant intent of God, our hearts will not be filled with fear because of the signs of the times, but will soar with joy at the promised glory to be manifested in and through the spiritual body of Christ in these last days of the end times.

5 – Paul's Unknown Prophecy

The Spirit from time to time over the years has shone a revelatory spotlight on certain passages of scripture, causing me to have an unusual and lasting interest in these passages as He opens them up, layer by layer over a relatively long period of time.

Each revelatory layer causes me to receive God's absolute, immutable truth as though that specific layer is the ultimate focus and truth in the passage, but each layer ultimately leads me into a deeper and more comprehensive understanding that connects perfectly to the entire matrix of scriptural truth.

Paul's letters contain numerous passages that are obviously prophetic, but most do not recognize Ephesians 4:11-16 as being prophetic. Still, as the Spirit of truth has opened my understanding to this passage an astonishing prophecy related to the wise virgins of the end time church has emerged.

It is important for us to acknowledge that the status quo of the deceived and divided church is not normal as God defines "normal" for the church (i.e. functioning perfectly as designed to function). It is also important to acknowledge that it is Satan, through deception, who has caused us to be in our present state.

At the same time, God has a plan for waking us up, taking back the spiritual ground the enemy has stolen, and bringing us to maturity to become the full manifestation of His glory and His purpose through Christ in the final days of this present age.

And this plan is already being manifested in the body of Christ, though it is intensely resisted by the Pharisees of our faith.

Yet, the shock wave to come will wake up even the sleepiest of the virgins.

Most of us, from Catholic to Charismatic, want to believe that we, individually, our particular fellowship, our denomination, and the spiritual body of Christ at large is what God has planned and purposed for us to be. Otherwise, we have to acknowledge the uncomfortable truth that we need a dramatic change, a change that we obviously cannot, or will not, make on our own.

We sometimes acknowledge this need for change as a need for revival, but our concept of "revival" is far below the standard of God's expectations for the church of Jesus Christ.

In the past, Ephesians 4:11-16 has been primarily viewed as an explanation of the purpose and function of the Lord's appointed ministry gifts of apostle, prophet, evangelist, pastor, and teacher, the "fathers" of our faith, for equipping the body of Christ for works of faith. In this, Paul notes that the ultimate result of these leadership gifts to the body of Christ will be complete unity and maturity in Christ.

Yet, most leaders and teachers in the church today deliberately explain this away, because it reveals that the spiritual body of Christ, as a whole, has not achieved this "unity" or complete "maturity" in Christ, and what leader-teacher in the church wants to confess this truth to those he is associated with and responsible for leading and instructing?

The identification of this passage as a prophecy is confirmed by Paul when he tells us that it is the Lord's <u>intention</u> (His will) to provide the body with the appointed ministry gifts of apostle, prophet, evangelist, pastor, and teacher, the "fathers" of our faith, until we *all* (the entire corporate body at some point in time)...*attain oneness in the faith and in the comprehension of the full and accurate* ...(experiential, relationship)... *knowledge of the Son of God; that [we might arrive] at really mature manhood – the completeness of personality which is <u>nothing less</u> than the standard height of Christ's own perfection – the measure of the stature of the fullness of Christ, and the completeness found in Him*...(while in the world). <u>Ephesians 4:13 Amplified</u> (inserts and emphasis are the author's)

Because we have not yet attained to this ultimate purpose for the body of Christ in the earth, this passage reveals that we will attain to this purpose at some point in the future.

Yet, I am not surprised that the concept of the body of Christ attaining to the completeness of personality which is nothing less than the standard height of Christ's own perfection, in perfect unity with the Lord and with each other, is either vigorously denied by delegating the fulfillment of this prophecy to either a heavenly or millennial event, or totally ignored as an unachievable goal.

I would not believe it myself if the Spirit of truth had not confirmed it to me in numerous ways, but the way in which the Lord will accomplish this has been a complete mystery until now. Moreover, we will not fulfill this mysterious transformation through our normal discipleship responses no matter how faithful we are. Yet, the Father will accomplish it at the time and in the manner He has foreordained.

It is important, then, just to acknowledge that it is God's intent, expressed prophetically by Paul, to bring the entire body of Christ, all of whom at that time will be "wise virgins," to full maturity by some mysterious means, while the body of Christ is still in the earth.

Just knowing that this is His revelatory intent and purpose, we can believe that it will happen, though our current condition (and tradition) screams, "**IMPOSSIBLE!**"

The entire world knows that the body of Christ has not, yet, attained to this specific intention of the Father. This event, and the completion of the purpose of apostles, prophets, evangelists, pastors, and teachers, is, therefore, a future fulfillment of Paul's prophecy.

The Pharisees of the institutional church embarrassed and condemned by our current state of somnolent division, claim that the fulfillment of this passage will only take place in heaven. Yet, we clearly will not need the offices of apostle, prophet, evangelist, pastor and teacher to bring us into complete unity in heaven.

It is, therefore, His intention (purpose, will) to bring us to complete maturity and unity in the faith in the world before the resurrection of the saints on the last day.

This is in agreement with the Lord's own prayer in John 17 in which He states that the purpose of the church manifesting His glory in **perfect unity** is to bear witness to the world.

"I do not ask on behalf of these alone, but for those also who believe in Me...(which necessarily includes the ultimate end time church)...*through their word; that they may all be one; even as You, Father, are in Me and I in You, that they also may be in Us, so that the world may believe that You sent Me.* ...(as opposed to our current witness of division with a limited manifestation of His glory)...*The glory which You have given Me I have given to them, that they may be one, just as We are one; I in them and You in Me, that they may be perfected in unity* ...(why?)... *so that the world may know that You sent Me, and loved them, even as You have loved Me.* John 17:20-23 NASB (inserts and emphasis are the author's)

The *doxa* glory He has given us, that makes us one with Him, even as He is one with the Father, is the indwelling presence of the Holy Spirit, but notice that He also said that the glory He has given us is for the purpose of causing us to be "*perfected in unity*" as a witness to the world.

70

The Greek word transliterated as *teleioo* means to make perfectly one. The Strong's outline of Bible usage demonstrates this:

1. to make perfect, complete
    a) to carry through completely, to accomplish, finish, bring to an end
2. to complete (perfect)
    a) add what is yet wanting in order to render a thing full
    b) to be found perfect
3. to bring to the end (goal) proposed
4. to accomplish
    a) bring to a close or fulfillment by event
        1) of the prophecies of the scriptures

This meaning is difficult for the divided, sin-conscious church to receive, but we cannot dis-acknowledge this truth found in the gospel of John, as well as in Paul's profound words in the letter to the Ephesians, whether we understand them or not. The fact that we cannot achieve this goal through normal discipleship responses, much less ecumenicalism, raises numerous questions.

What we do recognize, instead, is that the church as we know it falls shockingly short of the Lord's stated intention for His elect, and church leaders over the years have assuaged the knowledge of our shortcoming by denying the truth.

But RELAX. God neither planned nor expected the spiritual body of Christ, whether individually or as an entire body, to have a full and exact relationship knowledge of the Son of God, be "*perfected in unity*," or measure up to the perfection that is Christ, prior to the completion of our redemption. Yet, He did purpose that the body of Christ, His church, would experience this mysterious event during the final 3.5 years of "*great tribulation*" as a witness to the world of the glory and power of Jesus Christ in and through the body of Christ.

This mystery will be accomplished through the "wise virgins," spiritually identified as the end time "Philadelphian" identity, who will bring in the final harvest of an uncountable number of tribulation saints from every nation, tribe, and tongue during the 3.5 years of 7th seal events identified by the Lord Himself as "*great tribulation.*"

This is, truly, a great paradoxical mystery, but the mystery of this astonishing event has now been unsealed for those who will experience it and for those Fathers of the faith ministering in the spirit of Elijah to prepare the "wise virgins" for this GREAT ADVENTURE of the end time church, an adventure and a generation destined to be heralded and celebrated throughout all eternity as the ultimate fulfillment of Pentecost.

Keep in mind that Paul wrote this letter at a time after the first exemplary years of the church in Jerusalem, and he wrote it as a future expectation for the entire body of Christ. It also seems that he expected to personally see and experience this unified fullness of the truth, power, and glory of the Lord in and through the church.

What he experienced instead was a constant assault on the truth of God through the introduction of false doctrines and practices that divided and emasculated the church.

Paul's corresponding assessment of the corporate body of Christ as he knew it, even though they were still under the direct influence of the Lord's first apostles, was that they (the corporate body of believers) were still "children" (immature in the faith) and divided by "winds" of (false) doctrine introduced by evil men who were themselves unknowingly influenced by the spirit of Jezebel.

So then,...(at the time of the fulfillment of this prophecy)*...we may no longer be <u>children</u>, tossed [like ships] to and fro between chance gusts of teaching, and wavering with every changing wind of doctrine, [the prey of] the cunning and cleverness of unscrupulous men, (gamblers engaged) in every shifting form of trickery in inventing errors to mislead.* <u>Ephesians 4:14 Amplified</u> (inserts and emphasis are the author's)

Then, in his second letter to the church at Corinth Paul identified these wicked (spiritually adulterous) men introducing errors for the purpose of misleading the church as the unknowing "servants" of Satan.

For such __men__ are false apostles – spurious counterfeits – deceitful workmen, masquerading as apostles (special messengers) of Christ, the Messiah. And it is no wonder, for Satan himself masquerades as an angel of light, so it is not surprising if __his__ __servants__...(men, not demons)... *masquerade as ministers of righteousness. [But] their end will correspond with their deeds.* 2 Corinthians 11:13-15 Amplified (emphasis and inserts are the author's)

The diabolic cleverness of deception is that most of those who are deceived are unknowingly sowing the very deceptions by which they have been deceived. Thus, it is the deceived who are sowing deception in unknowing servitude to the father of lies.

Our examination of the history of deception begins with the constant corrections Paul and the other apostles had to make in the rapidly growing young church. This was followed by the unholy covenant between the church and the state of Rome from the Council of Nicaea in 325 A.D. all the way through the dark ages, which was Satan's greatest beast kingdom victory over the kingdom of God in the earth in the form of the spiritual body of Christ.

The Protestant Reformation did ultimately and effectively counter the ungodly authority of the Pope as the supposed inerrant "cleric of Christ," but it did not end Satan's assault on the truth of God through the corrupt aspects of institutional Christianity.

The development of numerous differing protestant denominations with various schools of doctrine and scriptural interpretation, including schools of eschatological doctrine, as well as the development of numerous "Christian" cults, reveals that the trend toward division has continued to expand dramatically for the past two millennia for the very reasons Paul identified in Ephesians and 2 Corinthians.

This should be seen by us metaphorically as the scattering of the sheep, separating us from one another and separating us from the Shepherd.

In the parable of the ten virgins the Lord specifically prophesied that the virgins (the unmarried kinsmen of the bridegroom – the church) all waited expectantly for His return. This was the "normal" church under its initial apostolic leadership. The oil of the Holy Spirit burned brightly in their souls, and they were unified and vigorous in their faith responses to the revealed will of the Lord as they manifested His truth, His love, His power, and His glory in a dark world that hated and persecuted them.

Paul's prophecy about the future of the church, which he wrote long after these first virgins became "drowsy" and began falling asleep (i.e. began to fall into a spiritual slumber because of deception and error), indicates an even more glorious future for the end time body of Christ than it was in the beginning.

Even in the first days of the church they were never "perfected in unity," nor did they have a full and complete relationship knowledge of the Son of God, much less attain to the "standard height of Christ's own perfection."

What Paul has prophetically described in Ephesians 4:11-16 and the Lord has prophesied in John 17:20-23 is, instead, a fulfillment of the Lord's prophetic parable of the ten virgins (Matthew 25:1-12).

Immediately prior to the opening of the 7th seal of "***great tribulation***" the "wise virgins" of the end time church who have persevered and endured the "tribulation" events of the 4th, 5th, and 6th seals of Revelation, are sealed upon the forehead with the name of God and of the Lamb immediately prior to the antichrist "man of sin" calling down fire from heaven and declaring himself to be "Messiah" and "God" from the secret chambers of the rebuilt temple, which is the very event that initiates the Lord's opening of the 7th seal and the beginning of 3.5 years of "***great tribulation***."

This promised sealing for protection (keeping them safe) in the 7th seal "*hour*...(appointed time)...*of trial coming on the whole world*," (Revelation 3:10) is the redemption of the metaphorical 144,000, the "*Israel of God,*", the "wise virgins" (a.k.a. Philadelphian believers) as "*firstfruits*...(of the wheat harvest)...*unto God and the Lamb.*" Revelation 7:2-8; Revelation 9:4; and Revelation 14:4 (inserts are the author's)

This is the ultimate fulfillment of Pentecost, the firstfruits of the wheat harvest, prefigured by the high priest making a wave offering of two wheat loaves (representing Jew and Gentile as "*one new man*" in Christ) over the altar in the holy of holies on 6 Sivan (Pentecost).

Jesus was the firstfruits of the entire harvest, symbolically represented by a barley sheaf containing no leaven (1 Corinthians 15:20), and these will be the firstfruits of the "wheat" harvest containing leaven.

These are also the final form of the "woman," spiritual Israel, who is "kept" (protected) in the wilderness, a place uncontaminated by the world, by the "*great eagle*," the Holy Spirit.

Wilderness in this instance metaphorically represents a spiritual place untouched by the world, and it is these who are in the world but not of the world who will manifest the full measure of Jesus Christ during the final 42 months or 3.5 years of the age.

These are those who will bring in the final harvest of an uncountable number from every nation, tribe, and tongue in the face of the full manifestation of Satan in the world at the same time.

So shall they fear the name of the LORD from the west, and his glory from the rising of the sun. When the enemy shall come in like a flood...(of intense demonic deception and persecution during the 7th seal)*..., the Spirit of the LORD shall lift up a standard*...(the "wise virgins" of the end time Philadelphian identity)...*against him* ...(which will cause him to flee [James 4:7])... Isaiah 59:19 KJV (inserts are the author's)

When this shocking but glorious prophetic truth is fully confirmed to us in our spirits and our souls, two things will take place. First, we will recognize why Satan, acting through that great demonic prince of religious deception, the spirit of Jezebel, has conspired for two millennia to keep this truth from the body of Christ, and especially from the body of Christ who will experience the awakening to take place in our immediate future.

Secondly, and simultaneously, we will realize why the Spirit of truth, according to Daniel 12:3, has sealed much of end time prophecy in order to reveal it fully only to those who will experience it.

Additionally, we will no longer be satisfied with the status quo as though deception and division is both "normal" and acceptable for ourselves individually, our church fellowships, or for the body of Christ as a whole.

Therefore, the balance of this book is dedicated to the confirmation of this astonishing mystery concerning the "wise virgins" a.k.a.:

1. the end time Philadelphian believers, those who have endured and persevered during the 4th, 5th, and 6th seals of "tribulation," those of the body of Christ who will receive the promise of being "kept" (protected without removal) during the 7th seal of "great tribulation";

2. the fathers (leaders) of the faith who will be responsible for preparing the awakened, wise virgins for their incredible adventure, an adventure that will glorify Christ as the final form of His end time *ekklesia*, perfectly one in truth and in the spirit of Christ, as they bring in the harvest of an uncountable number from every nation, tribe, and tongue in the face of the worst that Satan can do through his beast kingdom.

6 – Daniel's Seventy Weeks Prophecy

Although the pre-tribulation "rapture" view was not originally conceived by him, it was first popularized by Sir Robert Anderson, a Scotland Yard detective made famous by his part in the unsolved "Jack the Ripper" serial murders in London.

Sir Robert was associated with the preeminent leaders of the Plymouth Brethren, the Zionist popularizers of Dispensationalism, John Nelson Darby, along with Cyrus Scofield, whose study Bible, utilized by millions of seminary students, espouses the spiritually heretical Zionist, dispensational view.

In "The Coming Prince," published in 1894 by Sir Robert Anderson, he interpreted Daniel 9:24-27 (the 70 weeks prophecy) as meaning:

1. The antichrist "man of sin" will sign or confirm a seven year treaty with Israel and many other nations (the supposed 7 year "tribulation");
2. This treaty will initiate a seven year tribulation, during which God will discipline national, ethnic Israel and then bring salvation to "all Israel" (interpreted by Zionists to be national, ethnic Israel);

3. This will happen immediately prior to the Lord's
    millennial reign in Jerusalem in fulfillment of His
    promise to Abraham, and; The church, though
    commissioned to deliver the gospel message until *"the end
    of the age,"* has their commission <u>revoked</u> as they are
    removed from the "trouble" (the supposed seven year
    "tribulation") seven years before the end of the age, i.e. 7
    years before the "last day" resurrection, so that national,
    ethnic Israel can be judged (experience persecution) and
    then receive their covenant promise. Then the church will
    be grafted into that <u>superior</u> covenant.

This, of course, is a complete antichrist denial of the fact that
the one and only promised redemptive covenant has already been
fulfilled to the only seed of Abraham to fulfill all the Law and
prophets, and through Him to all those who are included "in
Christ" by grace through faith or by God's sovereign election.

*For <u>all the</u>...(covenant)... promises of God in him...(Jesus
Christ)...are yea, and in him Amen, unto the glory of God by us.*
<u>2 Corinthians 1:20 KJV</u> (emphasis and inserts are the author's)

"All" means all. Nor were the covenant promises of God ever
intended for the whole of national, ethnic Israel. They were always
intended for the singular seed of Abraham, Jesus of Nazareth, and
through Him, to the *"Israel of God,"* which is the entire redeemed
of God from Adam forward, whether Jew or Gentile. (Gal. 6:16)

In Daniel 12:4 we also learn that Daniel's prophecies are
sealed up, meaning that the revelatory understanding is not
available until the time of the end. During the time of the end,
however, the revelatory knowledge of God's purposes will be
increased and become great.

***But you, O Daniel, shut up the words and seal the Book
until**...*(when...***the time of the end. [Then]*** ...(which is
now)...***many shall run to and fro and search anxiously [through
the Book], and knowledge [of God's purposes as revealed by His
prophets]***...(all of His prophets, not just Daniel)...***shall be
increased and become great.*** Daniel 12:4 Amplified (inserts and
emphasis are the author's)

The obvious fact is that Sir Robert Anderson was not in the
ultimate end time generation, and the revelatory truth of Daniel 12
was not unsealed and not, therefore, available to him. It is
reasonable, then, to conclude that Sir Robert Anderson's
presumptive conclusions were in error, and when received by this
current generation as "truth," they become a stumbling block for
those who will experience the 4th, 5th, and 6th seal events of
"tribulation."

"The Book" in this passage is Daniel's book, but the sealing of
biblical prophecies concerning the end time include numerous end
time prophetic passages throughout the entirety of biblical
scripture, meaning all the prophecies as given by various prophets
concerning the final days of the age as seen in Daniel 12:4 quoted
above.

Knowing, then, that much of end time prophecy was sealed
from both our understanding and Satan's understanding, Satan has
been busy introducing false doctrine and false interpretations of
prophecy for the purpose of establishing long-standing traditions of
interpretation that have become strongholds opposed to the
revelatory intent of God for the generation who will experience
them. (This is the same scenario demonstrated by religious Israel
during the first advent of Christ).

This is specifically evident in Satan's corruption of a prophecy
that is intended by the Father to demonstrate the glory of Christ
that will be manifested through His spiritual body, the church, in
the final 3.5 years of "***great tribulation.***"

The Father's intent for the prophecies written down by His prophets is now, and always has been, to ultimately unseal and reveal the true meaning to those upon whom the fulfillment of those same prophecies will come.

Eschatologists attempting to understand biblical prophecy prior to the deliberate unsealing and progressive revealing by the Spirit of truth who was sent to guide us into all truth, including the truth about things to come, (at the appropriate time), were, and are, not only likely to misunderstand God's purpose and intent, but also prevent many who have accepted their non-revelatory, presumptive intellectual interpretations as "truth," from receiving the revelatory truth when it comes at the time the Father has ordained.

So here we are at the cusp of understanding. Will we stand on the popularly received tradition of a failed and divided church being whisked away in a "secret" (not disclosed in scripture) pre-tribulation "rapture" on the basis of a promise to the Philadelphian church who, instead, will demonstrate the full expression of Christ in the world during "***great tribulation***"?

Or will we allow the Spirit of truth to reveal the true, unsealed prophetic understanding of Daniel 9:24-27 as it was always intended for the "wise virgins" of the end time spiritual body of Christ?

Sir Robert's interpretation has now been so widely taught that a vast majority of Christians have accepted its premises as indisputable fact, though they are not even aware of the origin, or even the details, of this supposed "fact."

Yet, if we examine Daniel 9:24-27 without any predisposition toward the Zionist dispensational interpretation, we will note that the theme of the passage is the fulfillment of God's plan of covenant redemption in Christ.

We would then correctly presume that the covenant being confirmed is the New Covenant written in the blood of Jesus Christ, not some supposed covenant between the antichrist "man of sin," political Israel, and the "many."

80

In this instance Sir Robert denied the prophetic record that the Father gave us concerning how the Son would *confirm the covenant with many* as the only seed of Abraham to fulfill all the law and the prophets.

In doing so, Sir Robert Anderson, and all those who have believed and promoted his interpretation, an interpretation obtained prior to the unsealing of Daniel's book by the Spirit of truth, are in denial of the scriptural record that God gave of His Son: *"He that believeth not God hath made him a liar; because he believeth not the record that God gave of his son."* 1 John 5:10 KJV (emphasis is the author's)

That part of the record denied by Sir Robert Anderson and all who have accepted his false interpretation as truth is the record that the Father gave of His Son, the only seed of Abraham to fulfill all the Law and the prophets.

It is the Son, then, who will confirm this covenant to all who will believe, so that they will ultimately be incorporated into His spiritual body.

However, because this generation is thoroughly indoctrinated with the Zionist, dispensational interpretation introduced by Sir Robert Anderson, we will necessarily need to examine the passage more closely.

Daniel's seventy weeks prophecy is related to Daniel's people, the Israelites, but at the resurrection of Christ the prophecy no longer relates to national, ethnic Israel but to spiritual Israel, the *"Israel of God"* in Christ. It also relates to the "holy city," Jerusalem, which is not holy at this present time, and is described in Revelation 18 as *"the habitation of devils,"* and as *"Babylon the great,"* but will ultimately become holy again as the millennial capital of spiritual Israel and of the King of Kings.

The prophecy, part 1: *Seventy weeks are determined upon thy people and upon thy holy city, to finish the transgression, and to make an end of sins, and to make reconciliation for iniquity, and to bring in everlasting righteousness, and to seal up the vision and prophecy, and to anoint the most Holy.* <u>Daniel 9:24 KJV</u>

Pay attention: The entire seventy weeks of this prophecy are to fulfill the redemptive covenant purposes of the Messiah and have absolutely nothing to do with the antichrist "man of sin." The covenant being confirmed, then, must conform to the entire construct and purpose of the seventy weeks.

The seven covenant establishing purposes of the seventy weeks (of prophetic years – i.e. 490 years) as demonstrated in v.24 are to:

1. finish the transgression;
2. make an end of sins;
3. make reconciliation for iniquity;
4. bring in everlasting righteousness;
5. seal up the vision;
6. seal up prophecy;
7. anoint the most Holy (as King of Kings).

Does this look like a treaty between the antichrist "man of sin," Israel, and the many?

The covenant being confirmed is specifically related to the seven purposes, and the seven purposes of the seventy weeks are clearly related to God's redemptive covenant purpose in Christ. Therefore, the perversion of this prophecy to supposedly reveal a seven year "treaty" between the antichrist "man of sin", Israel, and the many is intended by the originator of that doctrine, Satan, to conceal the true meaning of the prophecy to those for whom it is intended.

Just this fact alone should end the argument, but it will be fruitful for the reader to press into the complete exegete of this passage.

1st purpose: *"finish the transgression"*

The "transgression" is Israel's covenant rebellion against God and their rejection of the full manifestation of God's presence among them in the person of Jesus Christ. Transgression is not merely rejecting God. Transgression is the rejection of God by those who are in a covenant relationship with Him. Therefore, if the fullness of this prophecy was about national, ethnic Israel, then the first purpose has not yet been fulfilled.

With few exceptions, the Jewish people are still in rebellion against God and still reject the manifestation of His presence in and through Jesus Christ.

The crucifixion and resurrection of Jesus Christ ended the rebellion of national, ethnic Israel by ending their possession of the title-deed to the covenant and establishing the New Covenant with spiritual Israel comprised of both Jew and Gentile as *"one new man"* in Christ, the one and only "seed" of Abraham for whom the covenant was always intended (Galatians 3:16).

The old covenant ended with the establishment of the new upon the fulfillment of the old to the One for whom it was always intended.

For if the inheritance be of the law, it is no more of promise: but God gave it to Abraham by promise. Wherefore then serveth the law? It was added because of transgressions, till the seed should come to whom the promise was made. Galatians 3:16,19 KJV (emphasis is the author's)

Notice that the promise was given to Abraham, but the fulfillment of the promise was for the "seed" of Abraham, Jesus of Nazareth, not national, ethnic Israel.

National, ethnic Israel's covenant transgression against God ended at the same time, resulting in the dispersion of national, ethnic Israel into the nations in judgment.

The covenant was fulfilled to Jesus Christ alone, and through Christ, to the initial remnant of Israel on Pentecost forty-nine days after His crucifixion.

It was on Pentecost, the specific appointed time given by God to the Israelites, that the promised Holy Spirit fell with power on the remnant of national, ethnic Israel baptizing them into Christ as spiritual, "born again" Israel, demonstrated afterwards to include both Jews and Gentiles as *"one new man"* in Christ, which God identifies as the *"Israel of God."* (Galatians 6:16)

This phrase itself, "the Israel of God" demonstrates that this body is not national, ethnic Israel as a whole, but "in Christ" the entirety of the redeemed from Adam forward are identified as spiritual Israel, the Israel of God, in Christ.

A quote from "Jesus Christ Immutable" by **Charles Spurgeon** puts this succinctly:

"These who saw Christ's day before it came, had a great difference as to what they knew, and perhaps in the same measure a difference as to what they enjoyed while on earth meditating upon Christ; but they were all washed in the same blood, all redeemed with the same ransom price, and made members of the same body. ***Israel in the covenant of grace is not natural Israel, but all Believers in all ages.***" (emphasis added by the author)

The kingdom of God in the earth was initially represented by Abraham, and through Abraham to national, ethnic Israel, but from the initial fulfillment of Pentecost it is the spiritual body of Christ, not national, ethnic Israel that is the *Israel of God* in Christ (i.e. covenant Israel).

With the transgression ended and "the" covenant now belonging to spiritual, "born again" Israel, the Israel of God in Christ, there is no imaginable purpose for removing the *ekklesia* of Christ so that God can restore the covenant once again to national, ethnic Israel.

2nd purpose: *"make an end of sins"* –
3rd purpose: *"make reconciliation for iniquity"* –
4th purpose: *"bring in everlasting righteousness"* -

The crucifixion and resurrection of Jesus Christ made an end of sins for those who receive Him by faith, and we who were once guilty of iniquity have been reconciled and forgiven. Additionally, at His resurrection everlasting righteousness belongs to those who are spiritually incorporated in Him.

This specific purpose was initiated at Pentecost but will not be completed until the last day resurrection of both the living and the dead saints.

Furthermore, the final three purposes of sealing up the vision and prophecy and anointing the Most Holy are yet to be fulfilled.

5th purpose: *"seal up the vision"*
6th purpose: *"seal up prophecy"*
7th purpose: *"anoint the most holy"*

The prophecy, part 2:

Know therefore and understand, that from the going forth of the commandment to restore and to build Jerusalem unto the Messiah the Prince shall be seven weeks,...(of years; 49 years)...*and threescore and two weeks...*(62 weeks of years, or a total of 483 years)....: *the street shall be built again, and the wall, even in troublous times.* Daniel 9:25 KJV

The coming of the Anointed One, "Messiah the Prince," at the end of 483 years of beast kingdom control over Israel is obviously not the event of His birth, or the years would already have been completed. The coming of the Anointed One, a Prince, to confirm the covenant with many after 69 weeks of years (483 years), is at the beginning of His earthly ministry shortly after being tested by Satan for forty days in the wilderness.

Based on God's calendar of the appointed times given to Israel, the forty days Jesus was tested by Satan in the wilderness began on 1 Elul and ended on 10 Tishri. This includes the thirty days of Teshuva and ten days of awe, also called ten days of repentance, and it was on 10 Tishri, which is *Yom Kippur* or the

Day of Atonement, an appointed Sabbath or feast day, and not a weekly Sabbath, that the Lord, at the end of His forty day fast and testing by Satan announced His ministry by reading Isaiah 61:1-2 (KJV) in the synagogue:

"The Spirit of the Lord GOD is upon me; because the LORD hath anointed me to preach good tidings unto the meek; he hath sent me to bind up the brokenhearted, to proclaim liberty to the captives, and the opening of the prison to them that are bound; To proclaim the acceptable year of the LORD, and the day of vengeance of our God; to comfort all that mourn;..."

Isaiah 61:1,2 as spoken by the Lord also perfectly and purposely reveals the seven purposes of the seventy weeks:

1. *finish the transgression*; (Jesus sent to preach good tidings to the meek);
2. *make an end of sins*; (Jesus sent to bind up the brokenhearted);
3. *make reconciliation for iniquity*; (Jesus sent to bring liberty to the captives);
4. *bring in everlasting righteousness*; (Jesus sent to free those that are bound in prison);
5. *seal up the vision*; (Jesus sent to proclaim the acceptable year of the LORD);
6. *seal up prophecy*; (Jesus sent to proclaim the day of the vengeance of our God upon His enemies);
7. *anoint the most Holy* (Jesus sent as King of kings and Lord of lords).

Therefore, 483 years or 69 weeks of years were fulfilled on 10 Tishri as the Lord read Isaiah 61:1-2. This is demonstrated as follows:

86

7 weeks (49 years): from the command to restore and rebuild Jerusalem by the King of Persia (Ezra 7) to the dedication of the second temple (at the beginning of a Jubilee year);

62 weeks (434 years): from the dedication of the second temple to the beginning of the Lord's ministry as the scroll is opened on *Yom Kippur* and He reads Isaiah 61:1-2.

This totals 483 years, leaving 7 years yet to be fulfilled.

Had the Lord fulfilled all the stated purposes of the seventy weeks of years, then His complete ministry would have begun on 10 Tishri (*Yom Kippur*) and ended seven years (1 prophetic "week" of years) later, completing the 490 years.

However, that is NOT what happened.

The prophecy, part 3, the final "week" of 7 years:

And after threescore and two weeks…(42 months or 3.5 years)…*shall Messiah be cut off, but not for himself: and the people of the prince that shall come*…(after Messiah the prince)…*shall destroy the city and the sanctuary; and the end thereof shall be with a flood, and unto the end of the war desolations are determined.* Daniel 9:26 KJV (inserts are the author's)

After the first 69 weeks out of 70 weeks, which ends on the day Jesus begins His earthly ministry, Jesus is "cut off," but His earthly ministry is not cut off immediately after the beginning of His earthly ministry. It is cut off in the "midst" of the God ordained seven year week, which coincides with 14 Nisan, Passover, the day of His crucifixion.

At His crucifixion 3.5 years of Jesus Christ confirming the covenant with many still remains, leaving us with an enigma.

How will He confirm the covenant with many in some future final time frame of 3.5 years?

He was "cut off" on 14 Nisan, not for Himself, but for the elect remnant of mankind who would be included in the eternal covenant planned by God from before the foundation of the world and fulfilled by the blood of His only begotten Son, Jesus of Nazareth, the Son of Man, the last Adam, and our Messiah.

"Cut off" would be a strange metaphor to use for the death of Jesus Christ if it did not mean that He was "cut off" from confirming "the" covenant with many, and completing the seven stated purposes of the decreed 70 weeks or 490 prophetic years.

Three years beginning on 10 Tishri (when He began His ministry by reading Isaiah 61:1,2 in the synagogue) plus that part of the fourth year beginning on 10 Tishri and ending on 14 Nisan is exactly 42 prophetic months or 3.5 years, leaving exactly 42 months or 3.5 years of Jesus confirming "the" covenant with many yet to be fulfilled in some future time frame.

Therefore, at the time this book is being written 486.5 prophetic years have already been fulfilled, and only 3.5 years remain to be fulfilled.

The "gap," then, is not between the 69 weeks and the last week (7 prophetic years during which "the tribulation" has been erroneously presumed to occur). The "gap" is between the earthly ministry of Jesus Christ prior to His resurrection and a final period of 3.5 years or 42 months of Jesus Christ confirming the covenant with many.

Yet, it seems unlikely that our Lord still has 3.5 years or 42 months of confirming the covenant left to complete. Surely, the final three events of confirming the covenant with many, 1) sealing up the vision, 2) sealing up prophecy, and 3) anointing the most Holy (as King of kings and Lord of lords) will not take three and a half years. So, how can we reconcile this truth?

What we note concerning this final three and a half years is that it is the same 3.5 years or 42 prophetic months that the antichrist "man of sin" is given to rule and reign on earth, so that Satan's full manifestation through the antichrist "man of sin" strangely coincides with the remaining 7th seal time of 3.5 years during which the Lord will complete His confirming of the covenant with many.

It also coincides with the sealing of the metaphorical 144,000, and with the opening of the 7th seal to begin that period the Lord identified as "**great tribulation**."

We are instantly alerted, then, that these events specifically relate to one another. But how?

Related events in the last 3.5 years or 42 prophetic months:

1. The 7th seal is opened by Jesus Christ (Rev 8:1);
2. "**great tribulation**" (Mat 24:21, Rev 2:22 & 7:14);
3. The 144,000 are sealed and redeemed, but not removed from the earth (Rev. 7:3-8);
4. The antichrist "man of sin" rules, after declaring himself to be "God" and "Messiah" in the third temple (2 Thess. 2:3-4);
5. The "woman" is protected and nourished in the wilderness (Rev 12:6);
6. The Philadelphian identity is "kept" from harm during the "hour" (appointed time) of trial (Rev 3:10);
7. The remainder of the seven purposes of the Lord are fulfilled (Daniel 9:24, Isaiah 61:1-2).

In the important detailed prophecy of Ezekiel 40-48, a prophecy concerning the millennial temple that follows immediately after the Gog-Magog prophecy (Ezekiel 38 and 39), it is the "prince" of Israel (Jesus Christ) who provides the daily burnt offering for the sins of the people.

On Passover, beginning on 14 Nisan, the same day on which Jesus of Nazareth was crucified, the "prince" makes both sin offerings and meal and oil offerings (provision) for the eight feast days of Unleavened Bread beginning on 14 Nisan, the day of Passover and the first day of Unleavened Bread, and ending at twilight on the eighth day, 21 Nisan. Thus, the firstfruits resurrection of Jesus of Nazareth was on 16 Nisan, and the Feast of Unleavened Bread ended five days later on 21 Nisan.

This also metaphorically represents both the seven appointed times and feasts of the Lord and seven literal years of the Lord confirming "the" covenant with many, as demonstrated by God's prophetic calendar of the appointed times and feasts of the Lord.

Of secondary importance, we should also note that the instructions given for the millennial temple worship and sacrifices follows after the Gog-Magog war (Ezekiel 38 and 39) indicating that the initial Gog-Magog war will take place prior to the second advent of the Lord as I have previously speculated. (The Gog-Magog war taking place at the end of the Lord's millennial reign on earth describes Satan's final revolt against the kingdom of God – Revelation 20:7-9).

Therefore, the events of the initial Gog-Magog war revealed in Ezekiel 38 and 39 are prior to the final 3.5 years or 42 months of the Lord confirming the covenant with many.

The 3rd seal is described by the Lord as the latter part of "*the beginning of birth pains.*" (Matt. 24:6-8) The 3rd seal corresponds with the 3rd horseman, the black horseman, representing the events that precede the entry of the 4th and final horseman, the pale green horseman.

It is likely that this Gog-Magog war will, then, be the event that is used by the Father to awaken the body of Christ as the 4th seal is opened and an unspecified length of time identified as "*tribulation*" begins (as compared to the specific 3.5 years of 7th seal "*great tribulation*" that follows "tribulation").

The events of that Gog-Magog war are both literal and spiritual in that it is Satan, identified as "Gog," who empowers and controls "Magog," identified as the natural forces, governments, and men led and controlled by Satan's demonic "princes" (i.e. the fourth horseman).

This war will be a spiritually controlled natural event at the end of the 3rd seal events, and we should note that most of the other wars in the world, after the resurrection of Jesus Christ, have been equally inspired by Satan.

We are near the end of the 3rd seal events at the time this book was written (2019) in which a deadly, but brief war, potentially including nuclear weapons, will throw the entire world into chaos.

In the aftermath, the entire political world will cry out for a one world government, and that one world government will likely be a revised form of the United Nations in which a ten nation ruling council will become the first form of a world government with a consensus vote rather than veto powers.

This event will also coincide with the opening of the 4th seal and the beginning of an unspecified and rather lengthy period of time identified by the Lord as *"tribulation,"* a time that includes the 4th, 5th and 6th seal events described in Revelation 7:7-17.

At the time that the seventy weeks prophecy was given to Daniel, the only literal, future seven year period associated with this prophecy was the seven years from the first day of the Lord's earthly ministry until the seven purposes of the seventy weeks of years are fulfilled.

However, because the Lord was "cut off" in the middle of the "week" of seven years, the manner in which the Lord will finish confirming "the" covenant during this final 42 months or 3.5 years, beginning on some future Feast of Pentecost, has been a huge mystery and has been sealed until now.

*And he...(Jesus Christ)... **shall confirm <u>the</u> covenant with many for one week**...(of years...i.e. 7 years)**...: and in the midst of the** ...(same)...**week he**...(Jesus Christ)**... shall cause the sacrifice and the oblation to cease, and for the overspreading of abominations he**...(Jesus Christ)...**shall make it desolate, even until the consummation, and that determined**...(as judgment)...**shall be poured upon the desolate**...(those who have rejected Christ.)* <u>Daniel 9:27 KJV</u> (inserts are the author's)

We note that in the midst of the week of seven prophetic years at His crucifixion and resurrection, He, Jesus Christ, causes the covenant sacrifice and oblations (the continual burnt offerings) to cease. This passage does not mean that the literal sacrifice and offerings ceased, but that the temple sacrifice and offerings ceased to have any relationship with the covenant He was confirming.

On 14 Nisan, appointed by God as the final day of the first 42 prophetic months of the Prince making literal burnt offerings for the sins of the people, the future, literal burnt offerings in the temple ceased to have any meaning or purpose. These same burnt offerings when practiced by the other "seeds" of Abraham from that day forward are, then, an idolatrous, antichrist abomination in denial of the Father's covenant intent in Christ.

At the moment of the Lord's death, the heavy curtain in the temple between the Holy Place and the Holy of Holies was supernaturally torn from top to bottom (Matthew 27:51), indicating that the temple worship and sacrifice system no longer had any function, because the title-deed to the promises of God was no longer held by national, ethnic Israel. It was fulfilled to the One for whom it was always intended, "the" seed of Abraham, Son of David, Son of God, Son of Man, Jesus of Nazareth and all those who are spiritually incorporated in Him by faith, which is spiritual, "born again" Israel, including both Jews and Gentiles as *one new man* in Him.

This also ended national, ethnic Israel's covenant transgressions against God, but not their judgment in the form of decreed desolations.

The "...*he shall make it desolate, even until the consummation*..." in Daniel 9:27 means that even if the temple is rebuilt after the Gog-Magog war by the Temple Mount and Land of Israel Faithful Movement and a new Levitical priesthood initiates temple worship and sacrifices again under the leadership of the false prophet, the temple will remain desolate and without the presence of God all the way up to the consummation.

The use of the word, "consummation," indicates that the full measure of judgment against the transgressors is complete. And this takes place on the coming *great and terrible* day of the Lord, THE ultimate day of atonement, on some future 10 Tishri.

There is no time whatsoever after the resurrection of Jesus Christ, including the final three and a half years of *"great tribulation,"* in which Jerusalem and national, ethnic Israel are not spiritually "desolate" all the way up to the great and terrible day of the Lord, when those "survivors" (Joel 2:32) who have pierced Him will look upon Him and grieve.

At this same time those "survivors" who have not persecuted the body of Christ and have not taken the covenant mark of the beast kingdom, will receive Him as previously demonstrated.

It is these "survivors," whether Jew or Gentile, who will enter into the millennial kingdom as regenerated, "born again" believers.

Referring back to Daniel 9:26, we see that the people of the prince who will come, a different "prince," one who will come after the original "Messiah the prince," shall destroy the city and the sanctuary. However, the "prince who will come" is not the antichrist "man of sin", and there will be no revived Roman Empire.

The crown prince of Rome was Titus, who later became Emperor of Rome, and it was his people who destroyed the city and the sanctuary in 70 AD. And, as the prophecy states, it was the people of this prince who continued the desolations until the end of the war.

There is, then, no prophetic projection of an end time event related to a revived Roman Empire ruled by the antichrist "man of sin."

The "man of sin" will, instead, rule over the "little horn," the nation of Israel, and the "head," nation whose deadly wound was healed when Israel became a nation again. This is also the nation whom God has identified during the final 3.5 years of the age as *Babylon the great.*

In referring back to Ezekiel 45:25, we see that the *"prince,"* Jesus of Nazareth, is to make exactly the same offerings for seven days during the Feast of Tabernacles, 15 Tishri to 21 Tishri. This is the initial spiritual fulfillment of the Feast of Tabernacles in which THE *"prince,"* Jesus of Nazareth, celebrates the fulfillment and completion of the seven purposes of the seventy weeks with spiritual Israel at the beginning of the millennial kingdom age.

Pray ye, therefore, that you will be in the presence of the King of kings and Lord of lords on that day.

Should it be a surprise to us that the final seven (7) prophetic years of Daniel's prophecy relate to the Lord confirming "the" covenant with many? Or that the desolations decreed upon national, ethnic Israel for their rejection of the Messiah will continue until the consummation on the great and terrible day of the Lord?

There is no dual covenant for the redemption of national, ethnic Israel. There is only the New Covenant planned by God from before the foundations of the world.

It is now, and has always been, God's plan from the beginning to include the entirety of an elect remnant of fallen mankind, Jew and Gentile as *one new man*" in a single covenant between Himself and Jesus of Nazareth, the only Israelite of the lineage of David to fulfill the Law and the prophets, and thus qualify as the sinless lamb of God who would take away the sins of the world.

Sir Robert Anderson and all those who have accepted his non-revelatory Zionist interpretation of Daniel 9:24-27 presume that a gap exists between the end of the 69th year and the beginning of the last week of years (7 years). Yet, the unsealed, revelatory understanding is that "the" covenant of Daniel 9:24-27 is God's covenant with Israel (fulfilled to spiritual Israel, the Israel of God), which the Lord begins confirming on the day He takes the scroll, and reads Isaiah 61:1-2 before saying, "*This day is this scripture fulfilled in your ears.*"

This was the beginning of the Lord's earthly ministry, and the beginning of His confirming of the promised redemptive covenant with "many" that would be written in His blood.

The presumption that the "he" who would confirm "the" covenant with many, as being the antichrist "man of sin" signing a treaty with Israel and many other countries, is completely false, and is a deception specifically designed by the father of lies to prevent the end time body of Christ from receiving the astonishing truth of Daniel's prophecy.

The subject of Daniel 9:24-27 is also supported by Nebuchadnezzar's statue kingdom dream (Daniel 2:31-42) with the statue kingdoms being the first four "mountain"/beast kingdoms assaulted against the kingdom of God, beginning with national Israel's return to Israel from the Babylonian captivity, then consecutively falling under the rule of the Medo-Persian empire, the Greek empire under Alexander, and the Roman empire under Titus. This is both historically and prophetically identified as 483 years followed by 3.5 literal and prophetic years (42 months or 1,260 days) of the Lord's public ministry until His resurrection.

This is then followed by the final, future 3.5 prophetic years (1,260 days) of the Lord confirming "the" covenant with many initiated by the opening of the 7th seal of Revelation. (Revelation 8:1)

The true revelatory "gap," is between the 483 years from the decree to rebuild the temple plus the time of the Lord's 3.5 years of earthly ministry confirming "the" covenant with many, and the final 3.5 years of His confirming of "the" covenant with many beginning with the opening of the 7th seal.

This is broken down as follows to simplify our understanding:

Seven (7) prophetic years equals 2,520 days:

Day 1: 10 Tishri (*Yom Kippur*) The Lord receives the scroll, reads Isaiah 61:1-2, and declares that the prophecy is fulfilled, which is the day on which His confirming of the covenant began.

The Lord announced the beginning of His ministry on the Feast of Atonement as the literal fulfillment of Isaiah 61:1,2a. What is interesting is the fact that He stopped in the middle of verse 2, because the rest of Isaiah's prophecy, vv.2b –11, were yet to be fulfilled by His ministry. (i.e. Isaiah 61:2a-61:1 describes the Lord's complete ministry, including things to come).

Day 1,260: (3.5 years or 42 months) The Lord is "cut off" from confirming the covenant with many on 14 Nisan (Passover).

Gap: unknown length of time between the crucifixion of Jesus Christ and some future 6 Sivan (Pentecost).

Day 1,261: The GAP between the first 3.5 years or 42 prophetic months and the final 3.5 years ends on some future 6 Sivan (Pentecost) after the wise virgins, a.k.a. the end time Philadelphian church, have endured and overcome persecution by Satan and the Babylonian world system during the 4th, 5th, and 6th seal events of *"tribulation."* These are then sealed upon their foreheads as the metaphorical 144,000 (Revelation 7:3,4). These Jewish and Gentile believers are completely redeemed as the firstfruits offering of the "**wheat**" harvest (Rev.14:4). Yet, they are not removed from the earth. The sealing of the metaphorical 144,000 takes place immediately prior to the opening of the 7th seal , which is specifically identified by the Lord as the beginning of *"great tribulation,"* lasting exactly 3.5 years.

Day 1,261 to Day 2,520 (Feast of Passover):
The metaphorical sealed and redeemed 144,000 (the "firstfruits" of the **wheat** harvest) bring in the *"great tribulation"* wheat harvest of an uncountable multitude from every nation, tribe, and tongue. Thus, this group, the metaphorical 144,000, minister in the earth in their redeemed and spiritually "sealed" bodies in the full, unmeasured spirit of Christ for 42 prophetic months or 3.5 years. And because the Lord is fully present in fellowship with them, this is the astonishing, previously unrevealed manner in which the Lord will fulfill the final 3.5 years of confirming the covenant with many (Daniel 9:27) as well as the fulfillment of Paul's prophecy as recorded in Ephesians 4:12-13: *For the perfecting of the saints, for the work of the ministry, for the edifying of the body of Christ: Till we all come in the unity of the faith, and of the knowledge of the Son of God, unto a perfect man, unto the measure of the stature of the fulness of Christ...*

This is also how the Lord prophetically announced His future fulfillment of Isaiah 61:2a-61:10 through the wise virgins of the end time Philadelphian identity.

I will greatly rejoice in the Lord, my soul shall be joyful in my God; for he hath clothed me with the garments of salvation, he hath covered me with the robe of righteousness, as a bridegroom decketh himself with ornaments, and as a bride adorneth herself with her jewels. For as the earth bringeth forth her bud, and as the garden causeth the things that are sown in it to spring forth; so the Lord God will cause righteousness and praise to spring forth before all the nations... (through the metaphorical 144,000, the ultimate representation of the kingdom of God in this age). Isaiah 61:10,11 KJV

On day 2,520: (Feast of Trumpets) The Lord appears visibly in the sky (spiritual realm) with His angels to gather the elect, living and dead, in the last day resurrection of the elect remnant of mankind, and the confirming of the covenant with many is complete.

< -------483 yrs-----> <--3.5 yrs--> gap < --3.5 yrs-- >
decree to rebuild
Jerusalem ↑ ↑ ↑

           Jesus   Jesus is "cut off"
           ministers   Jesus ministers
           for 3.5 years through the
                            144,000
                            (Rev. 14:4)

This revelatory truth concerning Daniel 9:24-27 was only gained by me because others pointed the way, and I deliberately and diligently sought the fullness of this truth until it was

97

confirmed to me by the Spirit of truth. In this He sent me a dream in which I shot an arrow at a target with a red bullseye, and the arrow hit the center of the bullseye. Then I looked down at my feet and found a Clovis point, a rare and treasured, pre-historic artifact. The Clovis point was beautifully crafted except for an unfinished point, which He caused me to understand was that sharp point of prophetic insight into Daniel's prophecy that He has not yet unsealed.

This great mystery has now been unsealed to the generation who will experience it, and the remainder of this book will be dedicated to the unveiling of this mystery to those for whom it is intended and to those who will be responsible for preparing the "wise virgins" of the end time church for their great adventure.

7 – The Awakening

"In our hearts, Lord, in this nation
Awakening
Holy Spirit we desire
Awakening"
(From "Awakening" by Hillsong)

Each time I hear "Awakening" by Hillsong I experience a deep angst and longing in my spirit for the awakening of the body of Christ at large, so that we might manifest the unified fullness and glory of Jesus Christ in an increasingly dark and dangerous world.

Yet, a general end time awakening of the entire body of Christ is highly improbable from a natural point of view because of our division into thousands of denominations and millions of rabbinic opinions concerning true doctrine and practice.

In forty years of seeking His absolute, immutable, revelatory truth, promises, and commands, I cannot recall hearing or reading a message by any prophet, pastor, or teacher confirming a partially fulfilled prophecy given by the Lord that reveals a unique spiritual awakening to be experienced by the entire regenerated body of Christ prior to His return.

Yet, that message in response to the disciples' question, ***"When will these things happen, and what will be the signs of your coming and the end of the age?"*** (Matthew 24:3) is clearly revealed in the parable of the ten virgins recorded in Matthew 25, and it is supported in many other passages. How, then, has this prophetic event in our immediate future been missed, and how and when will it be fulfilled?

What we have heard instead in the modern western church is that we must maintain our readiness because the Lord can come at any time.

That message taught for the last 150 years has not sparked a general revival in the body of Christ, much less a general awakening, because the Spirit of truth did not give it to us.

It is true that we should maintain our readiness, but not because the Lord can come "at any time." That specific part of the message is in complete denial of the truth revealed in the God-appointed times for the seven primary events of covenant redemption in Christ, as well as in the words of the Lord Himself detailing events that must take place before His return.

The true message, the message we have not heard, revealed by the Lord in the Olivet prophecy, and verified throughout both the OT and the NT, is quite different.

In the parable of the ten virgins, illustrating specific details of the Olivet prophecy (Matthew 24 and 25), the Lord gives us a synoptic view of the entire church age with emphasis on what will happen immediately prior to His return.

These details include a church-wide spiritual awakening that takes place at "midnight," the darkest hour of night, corresponding with the opening of the 4th seal (Revelation 6:7-8), and continuing all the way through the 6th seal, all of which are identified by the Lord as an unspecified length of time known as ***"tribulation."*** (Matthew 24:9-13).

The indication conveyed in this parable, then, is that the Father will awaken the body of Christ for the purpose of equipping us to overcome during the 4th, 5th, and 6th seals of ***"tribulation,"*** not for the purpose of removing us before the 4th, 5th, and 6th seal events of "*tribulation*."

Dispensational authorities, responsible for teaching and promoting the doctrine of a pre-tribulation "rapture" event, are in denial of both God's calendar and of the very specific, detailed words of the Lord Himself. And these, as well as all who accept their teaching as though it is the absolute, immutable, revelatory truth of God, do not expect an "awakening," because it is their belief that it will be an apostasy-ridden, failed church that will be taken out of the world so that God can restore national, ethnic Israel to covenant status.

And a "failed" church is not an "awakened" church.

What is coming instead of a pre-tribulation "rapture" is the spiritual awakening of every regenerated member of the body of Christ as the Holy Spirit arouses us out of our current state of relative somnolence with His announcement, at "midnight," an announcement shouted into our spirits like a shofar blast from the watchtower wall, "*And at midnight there was a cry made, Behold, the bridegroom cometh; go ye out to meet him.*" (Matthew 25:6 KJV)

"Midnight" is the darkest hour of night followed by continued darkness until the dawn brings light. Thus, the announcement shouted into the spirits of every regenerated believer in Christ will come at a time in which the status quo is interrupted by extremely dangerous events in the world.

"*Go ye out to meet him,*" is the Holy Spirit's instruction for the body of Christ to "come forth" from our somnolence in order to prepare ourselves for the rather lengthy fight of faith required in order for the "wise" to persevere during the 4th, 5th, and 6th seals of "*tribulation*."

Going out to meet Him is not a "rapture." It is simply tuning in to the Holy Spirit so that we clearly hear and respond to our Lord's truth, promises, and commands in a dangerous time in which our response to the Lord's commands of repentance as conveyed in Revelation 2 and 3, and our obedience to those spiritually conveyed commands, has become essential.

And it is those who respond appropriately to the alarm call of the Holy Spirit who will ultimately become the metaphorical 144,000 "wise virgins" who will bring in the harvest of the "multitude" in complete and perfect fellowship with the Lord. during the 3.5 years of the 7th seal of *"great tribulation."*

Our awakening is the next event to come for the true church prior to the return of the Lord, albeit, this major end time event is almost unknown, unrecognized, and unexpected by the very generation of the body of Christ who will experience it.

What the Father is doing in the body of Christ today, in preparation for the awakening of the entire body of Christ immediately after the opening of the 4th seal to begin that time identified as *"tribulation,"* is the restoration of revelatory truth through the leadership of a revived apostolic and prophetic ministry as well as a general anointing of revelatory awareness among "wise," already awakened believers, throughout the body of Christ.

In this regard, modern apostles and prophets, as well as the rest of the ministry gifts are not given the task of writing scripture or establishing new doctrine and practice. These "fathers" of our faith are, instead, appointed to the task of taking back the ground of truth that the enemy has already stolen from the body of Christ and revealing truth that has been "sealed up" by the Spirit during past generations but unsealed for the generation who will experience these events. (Daniel 12:4, 9,10)

These are also identified as "lamplighters," those who bring light where there is no light, and they do this at a time when complete darkness is rapidly approaching.

Ephesians 4:11-13 is the scriptural demonstration and evidence that it is the intention of the Father for the body of Christ to be under the influence and leadership of apostles, prophets, evangelists, pastors, and teachers until the end of the age, which takes place on some future 1 Tishri fulfillment of the feast of trumpets at the "last day" resurrection of the saints.

Because His intent is clearly demonstrated in Ephesians 4:11-13, the traditional explanation for the seeming absence of apostles and prophets is demonstrated to be a lie.

And he gave some, apostles; and some, prophets; and some, evangelists; and some, pastors and teachers; for the perfecting of the saints, for the work of the ministry, for the edifying of the body of Christ: till we all come in the unity of the faith, and of the knowledge of the Son of God, unto a perfect man, unto the measure of the stature of the fulness of Christ: that we henceforth be no more children, tossed to and fro, and carried about with every wind of doctrine, by the sleight of men, and cunning craftiness, whereby they lie in wait to deceive...(Ephesians 4:11-14 KJV (insert is the author's)

Have we all come in the unity of faith and the experiential knowledge of Christ?

Have we all attained unto the full measure of Christ?

Are we no longer tossed to and fro and carried about with every wind of doctrine?

The answer is a resounding, "NO!" demonstrating conclusively that we still need the leadership of apostles, prophets, evangelists, pastors and teachers.

Therefore, any claim that the offices of "apostle" and "prophet" have passed away is in direct contradiction with scripture, and we cannot base our spiritual understanding on the basis of our personal experiences, church tradition, or the body of Christ's current condition.

Yet, the "wise" virgins of the body of Christ, wherever they are in the world, and whatever denomination they currently identify with, will recognize and respond to the leadership of the Lord's chosen and anointed apostles, prophets, evangelists, pastors and teachers during the 4th, 5th, and 6th seal events just as the Father has prophetically revealed and intended.

No matter how the reader personally answers the implied "when?" question concerning our awakening, Ephesians 4 reveals that our deliverance from the current status of division and immaturity is a future event for the entire body of Christ prior to the resurrection of all the saints on some future 1 Tishri feast of trumpets.

A prophet, evangelist, and teacher I have known and respected for a considerable length of time, Chris Johnson, Director of Jubilee World Missions, intrigued his Bible study group with a specific word from the Lord that he received in regard to the beginning of intensified trouble and the awakening of the end time body of Christ.

What the Lord revealed to him was that the "trouble" i.e. *tribulation*, identifiable in scripture, was coming very, very soon.

He was even given the specific year, so that he would begin preparing those he is associated with for the "trouble," as well as our "awakening" that will occur as the 4th seal is opened by the Lord.

Surely the Lord GOD does <u>nothing</u> unless He reveals His secret counsel to His servants the prophets.
Amos 3:7 NASB (emphasis is the author's)

In this regard as recorded at the beginning of this book, and in UNMASKING The End Time Beast Kingdom, I have received numerous specific storm warning dreams concerning the coming storm of the Lord, indicating that the storm of the Lord is coming very soon, even in my lifetime. And I am seventy-seven years of age at the time that this book is being written.

Likewise, numerous others in the worldwide body of Christ are receiving similar dreams and visions, confirming the fact that God is warning His bond-servants, and His prophets concerning the coming spiritual "storm" for the benefit of the body of Christ entire, many of whom are falsely and dangerously expecting to escape the storm, though it is the Father's express intent that we be

104

tested by the storm in order to bring the remnant body of Christ to full maturity for the final conflict during the 7th seal of Revelation.

Though I am repeating what I have already recorded in the previous book, one dream He gave me, though metaphorical, is very specific and worth repeating concerning the events related to the awakening of the body of Christ.

On May 22, 2013 I was given a third spiritual storm warning dream. In this dream I was in Brad Kochis's LifePoint Church in Columbus, Ohio, where I have not, yet, been, with Brad issuing an emotional message of repentance to his congregation.

One third of the congregation came forward in repentance, but two thirds remained in their seats.

Outside, I walked along with an unknown witness, and we stopped to admire a marvelous, gigantic tree. It was tall and straight, like a eucalypt tree with smooth white bark, hundreds of feet tall and with a base at least six feet in diameter.

Suddenly the tree fell without warning, and what we saw was shocking to us. The inside of the tree was completely rotten except for a core of living heartwood through the very center of the tree.

And, though the tree itself was broken, the heartwood was only bent.

Moving further down the street followed by a group of children playing with a total lack of concern about the shocking events we were witnessing, we came to a tall, modern, high-rise federal building, and as we stood on the step we witnessed a glass-front bank building sliding down the street.

On the steps below us was a handsome, powerfully built, dark-haired man wearing a navy-blue blazer with a gold emblem on the right side.

As he looked up, I asked, "Is it going to be all right?"

He looked straight into my eyes and shook his head, "No."

Then when we turned and went up the stairs to the massive, heavily reinforced doors of the federal building, they were locked.

As I shook my head in disbelief I said, "I can't believe the post office is locked."

Like all of the previous storm warnings this dream contained unique specifics concerning the coming storm. The message Brad was preaching in Lifepoint Church was one of repentance related to the coming storm of the Lord and the shaking of all that can be shaken, which begins at the deceived, divided, and somnolent house of God.

The lack of response by two thirds of the congregation had nothing to do with Brad's own church but with the response of the universal true body of Christ once the storm hits and the church is awakened, as revealed in the prophetic parable of the ten virgins.

This response is specifically prophesied for the end time body of Christ by Zechariah:

And it shall come to pass, that in all the land,...(the entire body of Christ alive at the time)... *saith the Lord, two parts therein shall be cut off and die; but the third shall be left therein.*
And I will bring the third part through the fire,...(of tribulation)...*and will refine them as silver is refined, and will try them as* <u>*gold*</u> *is tried...*(see Rev. 3:18)...*: they shall call on my name, and I will hear them: I will say, It is my people: and they shall say, The Lord is my God.* <u>Zechariah 13:8, 9 KJV</u> (inserts and emphasis are the author's)

The one third that came forward in repentance represents the response of the wise virgins, and the two thirds that remained in their seats represents the response of the foolish virgins during the 4th, 5th, and 6th seal events of Revelation identified as "tribulation."

Zechariah 13:1 preceding this passage clearly indicates that this prophecy is specifically related to the spiritual body of Christ, the church.

In that day...(the time in which the prophecy will be fulfilled)...*there shall be a fountain opened to the house of David*...(those who are in Christ, the "son of David")...*and to the inhabitants of* ...(representative of the organized body of Christ)...*Jerusalem,*...(at the time the fountain is opened)...*for sin and for uncleanness.* Zechariah 13:1 KJV

Zechariah 13:1 was fulfilled on Pentecost two millennia ago as the Holy Spirit fell with power on the remnant of Israel in Jerusalem, establishing the kingdom of God in the earth through spiritual, "born again" Israel, the *"Israel of God"* in Christ, and a fountain was opened to the spiritual house of David through the indwelling Holy Spirit.

No other event in the history of national, ethnic Israel matches the fulfillment of this prophecy. It will then be the "wise" virgins who continue to drink from this fountain during the 4th, 5th, and 6th seal events of "tribulation," and it will be the "foolish virgins" of the end time church who are cut off and perish during the coming storm of the Lord, some of whom will continue to expect, but never experience, a pre-tribulation "rapture" of church only saints.

But the "wise virgins" who are drinking from the fountain that is Christ will be tested and refined by the fire of 4th, 5th and 6th seal *tribulation*, to ultimately become the end time Philadelphian entity who have the Lord's promise that they will be "kept" (protected in, but not removed from) the *"hour of trial that will come upon the whole world."* (i.e. the 3.5 years of 7th seal *"great tribulation"*)

The gigantic tree with the smooth white bark that we greatly admired is the United States of America. The tree, as we know it, will fall suddenly and without apparent warning, exposing the fact that, in spite of the magnificent appearance of the tree, the inside is rotten except for the core of living heartwood, representing the influence of the true *ekklesia* of Jesus Christ.

But, at the time that this tree will fall, the core of living heartwood, the spiritual body of Christ, will no longer be able to hold the tree in the upright position.

We will, therefore, be impacted and "bent" by the fall, but we will not be "broken."

The children following us and playing with no concern about the shocking events we were witnessing are the "foolish virgins" of the true church, the "two thirds" who are totally engaged in their "playing," which includes numerous false doctrines and false interpretations of prophetic scripture deliberately introduced into the church by the father of lies to keep us in a state of spiritual stupor and denial concerning our immediate future.

These "children" are those two thirds of Zechariah 13: 9 who will ultimately fall away from the faith because of the trouble and deception in the world, though most of these, without a revelatory understanding of the entire process of redemption from regeneration to resurrection, do not believe that it is even possible for a born again, regenerated believer to reject their faith in Jesus Christ through the hardness of their stubborn, rebellious hearts, the ultimate result of which is identified in scripture as the blasphemy of the Holy Spirit.

The glass front bank building sliding down the street needs little explanation. This is an indication that the fall of the United States of America will begin with a financial collapse that will hurtle us into a time of world-wide economic crisis corresponding with the black horseman carrying a pair of scales. (Revelation 6:5, 6)

Our knowledge that the financial prosperity and security that many of us enjoy in the United States of America will come to an end sooner than we hope or expect, putting us in the same state of crisis that much of the rest of the world has already experienced, is an unpleasant consideration to say the least. But I would rather be warned beforehand by a loving Father than to be surprised and shocked by it, leading to doubt and fear concerning the provisions and promises of a loving God and Father.

My shock that the federal building is locked indicates that at some point the true church, the spiritual body of Christ, will no longer have any influence on the federal government of the United States of America, although the United States of America was once the ultimate representative of the white horseman and a lion with eagle's wings (influence of the Holy Spirit).

But, at the point that the federal building is locked, the eagle's wings will have been plucked from the lion, and the lion will stand up and be given the voice of a man instead of the voice of the Lord. (Daniel 7:4)

This is an indication that the United States of America is likely to be the spokesman for the first form of a world government with the nations of the world surrendering sovereignty to a revised United Nations with a ten nation ruling council after a time of unprecedented danger, which almost certainly includes nuclear war and worldwide economic chaos, leading to famines and epidemic diseases all around the world.

I have noted that the ruling council of ten nations will have a consensus vote rather than a veto vote, and an elected President of the United Nations will have the deciding vote in the case of a tie.

The handsome, powerfully built, dark-haired man wearing a blue blazer with a gold emblem represents a messenger of the Lord, and when I asked him if everything is going to be all right, he answered by shaking his head, "No."

My question implied that I wanted to know if the fall of the United States of America, the foolish virgins continuing to "play" without spiritual awareness concerning the coming storm, the financial collapse, and the true church being locked out of any influence on the federal government of the United States, or the world government, is going to be restored to some former condition.

The answer is a firm, "No."

Then I hurried off to warn my family and friends concerning what I had witnessed, and, as usual, the Spirit awakened me one minute before my alarm was set to go off so I could write the dream down in my journal.

This is a conundrum for me as it is for most who are reading this testimony.

I served in the Marine Corps. I fly the American flag on the 4th of July, and I place my hand across my heart with the emotion of patriotic pride rising up in my heart as the pledge of allegiance is spoken and the national anthem is sung.

My presumption has always been that the United States of America and the kingdom of God were somehow synonymous.

But I am forced to acknowledge that no matter what country we live in or how strong our patriotism, our true citizenship is in the nation of God, the Israel of God in Christ, and not in whatever political nation we have our natural residence.

In this regard, for years I have heard the call to prayer for the nation of America in numerous churches as being a response to the promise of 2 Chronicles 7:14:

If my people, which are called by my name, shall humble themselves, and pray, and seek my face, and turn from their wicked ways; then will I hear from heaven, and will forgive their sin, and will heal their land.

The "land" in this passage though, is not the United States of America. It is the nation of God, the body of Christ, wherever we reside.

What that means to me is that the beginning of an unspecified length of time identified by the Lord as *"tribulation"* is very, very near. This will begin as the entire body of born-again believers are awakened by the Holy Spirit's announcement accompanied by significant events in the world including financial collapse, and potentially including nuclear war, with the ultimate result being a world government.

But at midnight there was a shout, 'Behold, the bridegroom! Come out...(of your somnolence)...*to meet him*...(and be instructed by Him)...' Matthew 25:6 KJV

110

The COMMAND spoken into the hearts of every single member of the body of Christ at that time is a command to respond appropriately to the prophetic message of the Lord's imminent, but not immediate, arrival to the generation who will experience it.

Strong's G1831 identifies this command of *"go ye out to meet Him."* as meaning to come forth from our current status of somnolence into an awakened or revived status of obedient faith responses to His truth, promises, and commands so that we are prepared to overcome during the 4th, 5th, and 6th seals of *tribulation*.

It does not indicate a pre-tribulation resurrection-rapture escape of church only saints from the trouble, and those who continue to expect this escape are the most likely to be wounded by the events that take place during the 4th, 5th, and 6th seals of *tribulation*.

All of this, of course, will be strongly denied by the Pharisees of our faith who feel personally and corporately threatened by the possibility of a move of God that will bring change to the status quo in order to prepare a generation for the serious testing to come, a change that condemns the current status and requires a significant amount of repentance throughout the body of Christ.

And, like the Pharisees of Israel during the first advent of our Lord under the influence of the spirit of Jezebel, these will oppose and deny the possibility that God is reviving apostolic and prophetic leadership to the church for this purpose immediately prior to the opening of the 4th seal and the time of testing that will ultimately separate the "foolish" from the "wise."

Yet, the "wise" of the body of Christ will respond by faith to this move of God as they prepare for the testing to come.

What cannot be denied is the Lord's prophetic description of the response of the entire body of Christ to the Holy Spirit's announcement immediately after the 4th seal is opened:

Then all those virgins rose and trimmed their lamps.
Matthew 25:7 NASB (emphasis is the author's)

PAY ATTENTION. "All" means all. Every single regenerated, "born again" believer in Jesus Christ will be awakened spiritually by the knowledge that the Lord's return is imminent but not immediate.

Even Zionists, Dispensationalists and pre-tribulation "rapture" theorists will be awakened at this time.

Therefore, if the truth presented in this book offends you, don't throw it away. You will want to give it another read after the awakening comes.

However, this announcement will NOT be heard in the spirits of nominal but unregenerate men and women of institutional Christianity who claim to be regenerated believers in Jesus Christ but are not.

What the parable, as well as the Lord's answer to the disciples' question, *"What will be the signs of your coming and of the end of the age?"* (found in Matthew 24 and 25, Mark 13, and Luke 21) demonstrates is that there will be an increasing division between the "wise" and the "foolish" virgins after all the virgins respond to the awakening in a time of intense world-wide trouble.

Consequently, this increasing division between the "wise" and the "foolish" virgins of the true church after our awakening will ultimately result in the apostasy (rejection of their faith) by the "foolish" because of the "trouble" in the world.

However, it does not result in the apostasy of the "wise."

The awakening will come during a MAJOR shaking of all that can be shaken, coinciding with the opening of the 4th seal, as the Lord prepares the body of Christ for this rather lengthy fight of faith wherein we might appropriately imagine the Lord speaking in a thunderous voice: *"Arise, My beloved, and hearken to My voice as I prepare you for the refining fires of tribulation so that My church will glorify Me in the midst of the greatest evil this world will ever know."*

112

Therefore, the question we should be asking is, "If this is true, why hasn't the body of Christ been generally aware of this astonishing event in our immediate future?"

The fact that most have not heard or received this message is strangely enough proof that it is true, and the obvious reason that we are not generally aware of it at the time this book is being written is that we are the somnolent virgins who became "drowsy" and fell asleep when He tarried.

"While the bridegroom tarried, they all slumbered and slept." Matthew 25:5 KJV (emphasis is the author's)

Another question we should be asking is, "Why is this event almost totally absent from the pulpits of our church fellowships and from the proliferation of books, articles, and websites adding daily to the weight of false presumption and deception concerning end time biblical prophecy?"

The deeply disturbing answer comes from the Lord in the parable of the sower and the seed after His disciples asked Him why He spoke in parables.

The answer He gave them applies directly to the numerous "blind guides" of the body of Christ at this present time: *And the disciples came and said to Him, "Why do You speak to them in parables?" Jesus answered them, "To you it has been granted to know the mysteries of the kingdom of heaven, but to them it has not been granted. For whoever has,...*(the truth revealed by the Spirit of truth)...*to him more shall be given, and he will have an abundance; but whoever does not have,...*(the *rhema* truth of God)...*even what he has shall be taken away from him....*(i.e. having the truth being taken away from these ultimately includes the truth concerning their redemption in Christ)...*Therefore I speak to them in parables; because while seeing they do not see, and while hearing they do not hear, nor do they understand* Matthew 13:11-13 KJV (inserts and emphasis are the author's)

In this passage spoken of the blind guides of national, ethnic Israel, the Lord is prophetically identifying the same condition as being applicable to "born again," regenerated believers of the end time generation, those who have received the Spirit of truth but whose "hearing" and "seeing" has grown dull through various influences, including their acceptance of the lies and deceptions of Satan introduced into the body of Christ through unknowing false prophets and lying shepherds.

And unless these overcome their spiritual blindness and deafness, they will ultimately lose their ability to "hear" and "see" at any level.

Behold, the days come, saith the Lord God, that I will send a famine in the land, not a famine of bread, nor a thirst for water, but of hearing the words of the Lord: Amos 8:11 KJV

Although the Lord's immediate disciples were still Old Testament believers at the time, it was the Spirit who was "given" to them so that they were enabled to know the secrets and mysteries of the kingdom of heaven.

In John 16:13 the disciples were told that the Spirit of truth would ultimately be "given" to every single regenerated member of the body of Christ from Pentecost forward so that we can be supernaturally "guided" into all revelatory (spiritual) truth, including the truth about things to come.

Howbeit when he, the Spirit of truth, is come, he will guide you...(supernaturally)...*into all truth: for he shall not speak of himself; but whatsoever he shall hear, that shall he speak...* (reveal)... *and he will shew you things to come.* John 16:13 KJV (insert is the author's)

Why is it, then, that the vast majority of the true church of Jesus Christ is totally unaware of the revelatory meaning of the parable of the ten virgins (Matthew 25:1-9) describing the great watershed event that will determine the fate of every believer who hears the wake-up call **SHOUTED** into our spirits by the Holy Spirit?

The unpleasant truth is that the majority of Christians are not "hearing" the Spirit of truth and have not paid attention to the Lord's primary warning concerning the end times:

Take heed that no man deceive you. Matthew 24:4 KJV

Instead, like the Pharisees of the Lord's own day, we have trusted in long-standing traditions devoid of revelatory truth with very little awareness that the "chess master," Satan, has been patiently working out his dialectical schemes on the chessboard of man's spiritually prideful intellect over a lengthy period of time.

This has even taken place among many in the spiritual body of Christ, just as he successfully did in national, ethnic Israel prior to the birth of our Lord, causing Israel to experience the judgment of God through the destruction of the temple and their diaspora into the nations.

Without the specific guidance of the Spirit of truth, we will be deceived, and the more deception we have received as "truth," the more we become deaf to the voice of the Spirit of truth.

While I was still under the dark cloud of Dispensationalism, and gave credence to the eschatological authorities at Dallas Theological Seminary, I was surprised by their inability to derive any meaning from this parable other than the need to maintain our readiness because "the Lord can come at any time."

These particular "authorities" in the church, trusting in their intellectual scholarship, have/had the power to "see" and the power to "hear" the absolute, immutable, revelatory truth of God in this parable, but through intellectual arrogance and non-revelatory tradition, they have not "seen" it or "heard" it. Therefore, the secrets and mysteries of the kingdom of heaven in this regard have not been revealed to them.

Yet, any believer with fresh, as yet unblinded eyes and spiritually open ears, can "see" it and "hear" it as many who are reading this text will confirm.

This partial blindness to the truth comes through powerful "strongholds" of deception deliberately and subtly introduced like addictive drugs into the body of Christ by the father of lies. And it comes to us through men and women who are or were, themselves, deceived.

Even though it includes my own confession of having been deceived in former years, I am sometimes cautioned by well-meaning friends that I should be gentler and more gracious in my exposure of those with godly reputations who promote and defend doctrines of demons.

Yet, I am already much gentler than Paul who says these men (and women) are hypocritical, pretentious "LIARS" who cause men to pay attention to and believe doctrines of demons that lead to spiritual death, which, according to the Spirit of truth will be two thirds of the body of Christ. (Zechariah 13:8,9)

But the [Holy] Spirit <u>*distinctly*</u> *and* <u>*expressly*</u> *declares*...(and WARNS)... *that in latter times*...(when?)... *some*...(Christians)... *will turn away from the faith*...(become apostate by)...., *giving attention to deluding and seducing spirits and doctrines that demons teach through the hypocrisy and pretensions of* <u>*liars*</u>...(the Pharisees and blind guides of spiritual Israel)...*whose consciences*...(spirit-soul connection)...*are seared (cauterized)*...(so that they no longer hear and respond to the Spirit of truth)...<u>1 Timothy 4:1-2 Amplified</u> (inserts and emphasis are the author's)

This passage has been delegated by many to only concern the end time church in the final years, but the warning by the Holy Spirit has been applicable to the latter times body of Christ for a significant amount of time.

The deceptive doctrine of Dispensationalism, as well as the doctrines of Historicism, Preterism, Amillennialism, and many other isms have dominated eschatological teaching in the modern church.

All of these spend an inordinate amount of time and effort to sell and confirm the lie they have believed to those who have believed other lies.

In doing so the truth has been veiled and hidden from most of the body of Christ so that we have not "heard" or "seen" the truth revealed in the parable of the ten virgins and in the Lord's straightforward synopsis of the events related to His return as recorded in Matthew 24 and 25, Mark 13, and Luke 21, much less the books of Daniel and the Revelation of Jesus Christ.

Yet, the Spirit is deliberately exposing the source of our blindness at this very time as he "guides" many into the truth concerning things to come in order to prepare a people for the return of the Lord.

In the parable of the ten virgins (innocent before God, because they are in Christ) we are told that all ten virgins, the unmarried kinsmen of the Bridegroom, with lamps full of oil and burning brightly, were waiting expectantly for the Bridegroom to come and lead them to His father's house for the marriage feast.

Nevertheless, when the Bridegroom tarried, all the virgins became drowsy and fell asleep.

This partially fulfilled parable is a perfect snapshot of the history of the church up to this present time.

If we had a heavenly perspective, we might see a bright light shining in Jerusalem on Pentecost, the fiftieth day after the Lord's crucifixion on 14 Nisan, which was His fulfillment of the Feast of Passover. Then during the historic days recorded in the book of Acts we would see bright lights spreading from Jerusalem throughout Israel and the Middle East, into Turkey, Greece, and, eventually, Rome.

This spread of the kingdom of God, though, was not unopposed. The spiritual forces of darkness, having usurped Adam's covenant right of dominion over the world, resisted the spread of the light of the kingdom of God in the world at every turn.

The early church's spearhead for this warfare against the spiritual forces of darkness in service to the great deceiver was the apostle Paul, and it is primarily through the instruction given to him by the Lord that we ourselves are instructed to carry on this spiritual warfare today (Ephesians 6:12-18 and 2 Corinthians 10:3-5).

Unfortunately, the kingdom ground of truth gained by Paul and the early disciples was largely taken back by the spiritual forces of darkness by the end of the 4th century.

Historically speaking, a major turning point in this warfare took place in 325 A.D. at the time of the Council of Nicaea when the Roman emperor, Constantine, ultimately decreed Christianity to be the state religion of Rome.

In doing so, he formed an unholy covenant between the church and the state of Rome, which was ultimately referenced as the "Holy Roman Empire."

Following this distinctly unholy covenant the syncretic worship of other "gods" was subtly instituted into church practice by establishing the Roman Catholic "holy" days of "Christmas" and "Easter" on days with pagan significance. Even the day of Christian worship, originally being the true Sabbath as determined by God's instructions in Leviticus and Deuteronomy, was changed from this "aviv" new moon calendar and true Sabbath days to the first day of the week as determined by the Julian calendar, and later adopted by the Gregorian calendar, which is the day Saturn, the sun god, was worshipped.

More importantly the "head" of the church, now joined in covenant with the state of Rome, became the "bishop of Rome," later identified as the "Pope," who was proclaimed to be the absolute authority over the church in direct denial of the Lord's own proclamation as recorded in Matthew 23:9 KJV:

And call no man your father...(absolute spiritual authority)...*upon the earth: for one is your Father,*...(absolute spiritual authority)... *which is in heaven.*

For those who are emotively disturbed by this charge against the early Roman Catholic Church I am only emphasizing the command given to us by the Lord Himself, but the proof of this charge has been historically demonstrated.

What ensued, because of the corrupt church coming under the rule of a politically, and spirit of Jezebel motivated papal authority, is what is now known as the "dark ages" as the church was led into idolatry and spiritual darkness, and from a heavenly perspective there were only tiny pinpoints of light appearing here and there until the 16th century.

This was the time of deepest spiritual "sleep" for the virgins as the Roman Catholic Church literally made the written word of God illegal for all but the clerics of the church, even burning at the stake any who dared oppose this rule, while Satan rejoiced with sadistic glee.

At the time of the Reformation in the 16th century, Martin Luther nailed his 95 Theses to the archbishop's door in the hopes of reformation from within the Catholic Church. However, Pope Leo X, received this challenge to existing practices in the Roman church as "rebellion" against the Pope's absolute authority, and he subsequently excommunicated Martin Luther.

Thus, division in the church occurred because of the Pope's actions; not because Martin Luther chose to break away from the Catholic Church rather than deny the truth of God in Christ.

The resulting reformation movement was led by men like John Wycliffe, Martin Luther and Jan Hus, and during this time numerous reformers were excommunicated by the Roman Catholic Church because they opposed the spiritually corrupt practices of the Roman church of their day.

The reformers further provoked the anger of Roman Catholic leadership by publishing Bibles in various languages as they put the written word of God back into the hands of the people, thus putting authority for what men believed back on the Spirit-illuminated, Spirit-guided understanding of scripture as intended by the Father.

From the heavenly perspective this could be seen as an awakening of sorts as lights began to come on all over Europe and into both the Middle East and Africa. It was not, however, THE awakening prophesied in the parable of the ten virgins, because THE awakening includes the astonishing event of an imminent, but not immediate, arrival of the bridegroom to the generation of virgins who literally hear the announcement in their spirits, *"Behold! The Bridegroom cometh."*

During the Reformation the pure gospel message began to be carried in earnest to the entire world, and in the 19th century, with points of light on almost every continent, a "Great Awakening" took place in America, Great Britain and parts of Europe during which time many spectacular events took place, including the dead being raised to life, demonstrating that the former and latter rains had not vanished, but had been suppressed through the somnolence of the body of Christ.

On one occasion the Holy Spirit fell upon a British navy ship passing twenty miles off the coast of Wales, and every man on board fell to his knees in repentance without a single word being preached to them.

Nevertheless, this was still not the awakening prophesied in the parable of the ten virgins, because that awakening will take place immediately before the opening of the 4th seal and the start of "tribulation".

Instead, it was a great international revival, and, from the heavenly perspective, bright lights came on in the eastern states of America, in Great Britain, Europe, and elsewhere before they began to fade away again.

In the early 20th century the lights of the Pentecostal movement began to appear, and the belief among many Christians that the manifestation gifts of the Spirit had passed away was ultimately demonstrated to be a lie, though Satan attempted to corrupt this truth through false manifestations.

As it concerns the manifestation gifts of the Spirit, Origen was a Christian theologian in Alexandria, Egypt, and in his book

"Against Celsus" written in 250 A.D., he described the manifestation gifts of the Holy Spirit still appearing, but he also noted that they were beginning to diminish.

This testimony corresponds perfectly with the Lord's prophetic parable of the ten virgins as He described the virgins, with lamps full of oil and burning brightly, becoming "drowsy" and then ultimately falling asleep when the Bridegroom tarried.

At the same time this testimony contradicts the false teaching that the manifestation gifts of the Spirit passed away with the death of the last apostle, or, as some claim, with the full canon of scripture being written, as though we no longer need the manifestation gifts of the Spirit, much less the leadership of apostles and prophets now that we have the Bible, though both the manifestation gifts and the leadership of apostles and prophets was given to us by the Lord until the end of the age, which takes place on the "last day" resurrection of the saints. (See Matthew 28:19,20)

Therefore, the seeming disappearance of the manifestation gifts from the Council of Nicaea up until the "Great Awakening," then subsiding again until the Pentecostal or Charismatic renewal, demonstrate that the manifestation gifts of the Spirit simply do not appear among those who are spiritually asleep or among those who are held captive by deception and unbelief.

Howbeit, when genuine revival takes place, as it did in Communist Russia after WWII and Communist China during Chairman Mao's regime, these gifts of the Spirit re-emerge.

Still, the Pentecostal and Charismatic renewal holding to the truth concerning the manifestation gifts of the Spirit but riddled with divisive false doctrines in many other areas, and particularly false doctrines where biblical prophecy is concerned, is not the awakening prophesied in the parable of the ten virgins.

The Pentecostal and Charismatic renewal has been, and continues to be, a revival of the truth concerning the manifestation gifts of the Spirit and faith for all things. But, at the same time, many Pentecostals and Charismatics remain deceived concerning "things to come" as well as various other doctrines and practices.

What is apparent is that the church at large, divided into thousands of denominations and millions of rabbinic opinions concerning doctrine and practice, is not "hearing" and "seeing" the unifying secrets and mysteries of the kingdom of God that the Spirit of truth brings.

Yet, instead of yearning to seek the empowerment of the Lord and the absolute, immutable, revelatory truth of the Lord whatever the cost, we presume incorrectly, that we, individually, or we and our group-think denominations, hold to the truth while all others are in error.

We also believe that this is the norm and the intent of God for the remnant elect of Israel instead of confessing that what the majority of the body of Christ is experiencing at this present time is not the full manifestation of the Lord's will.

Watchman Nee, the primary apostle of the underground house church movement in China, a widespread body of believers more awake than most, wrote a book titled, "The Normal Christian Life." In this brilliant book he described "normal" as being the life of Peter, John, James, and Paul, and most of us are aware that our particular denomination, sect, fellowship, or ourselves individually, are not, yet living up to that standard of "normality," (i.e. functioning as designed to function).

At the same time, we rationalize our failure to walk in the manifestation gifts, pointing the finger at those practitioners of false gifts as though their presence in the body of Christ proves the absence of true manifestations of the power of God through believers.

However, we are told that "tares" (a weed resembling wheat) will be present among the true wheat of the body of Christ until the end of the age. (Matthew 13:24-30)

The Lord's instructions given to us to the end of the age, which obviously includes this present generation, are to make disciples by bringing them to faith in Christ, and teaching them to obey all things whatsoever He commanded His original disciples to obey all the way until the "last day" resurrection.

Go ye therefore, and teach all nations, baptizing them in the name of the Father, and of the Son, and of the Holy Ghost: Teaching them to observe all things whatsoever I have commanded you: and, lo, I am with you always, even unto the end of the world...(age)... Amen. Matthew 28:19,20 KJV (insert is the author's)

If we are NOT teaching them to observe (obey) "*all things whatsoever*" He commanded His original disciples to do and obey we are in disobedience to the revelation of His will expressed in scripture (i.e. what we call the "great commission").

"*All things whatsoever*" includes God's appointment of apostles, prophets, evangelists, pastors, and teachers, the fathers of our faith.

It also includes the delegated "*dunamis*" power and authority of Jesus Christ to cast out demons as well as the laying on of hands to heal the sick (Mark 16:17,18) as well as the entire list identified by Paul and recorded in 1 Corinthians 12 and 14.

To deny this is on the basis of our own experience is to deny both the spoken command of the Lord and the written Word of God.

Our present general, church-wide condition is then demonstrated to be subnormal, and both direct and persistent disobedience to the command of the Lord as recorded in Matthew 28.

On Pentecost when the kingdom of God fell with power on the remnant of Israel, our standing orders included all that He commanded His original disciples through the apostles.

This list includes the leadership of apostles, prophets, evangelists, pastors and teachers. It also includes authority over evil spirits, special faith, healing, miracles, prophecy, prophesying, discerning of spirits, tongues and interpretation of tongues among many others, and there is nothing whatsoever in scripture indicating that believers today are to walk out their faith in any lesser way.

Yet, the vast majority of the somnolent church, the "sleeping" virgins, denying the leadership of apostles and prophets, are not manifesting the full array of the gifts of the Spirit or the command of our Lord.

They are, instead, excusing themselves by denying both the truth and the command of our Lord applicable to us until the "*end of the age*."

In the very near future, this denial of the Lord's specific command to teach and practice (obey) all of the commands and instructions He gave His original disciples, will identify the "foolish virgins" of the generation who will be tried and tested in the fire of the 4th, 5th, and 6th seals of tribulation.

Yet, the "wise" will awaken to rise up and walk in the fullness of God-appointed leadership as well as the entire list of Spirit-anointed empowerments for ministry.

In this regard the parable of the ten virgins reveals that the wise "virgins" (innocent before God, because they are in Christ) will overcome the assault of the beast kingdom during the 4th, 5th, and 6th seals of "*tribulation*."

The foolish "virgins," though, will fail to overcome, and theirs is the most tragic fate imaginable. A fate that I have wept over as the Holy Spirit confirmed the future of these men and women, all of whom were at one time "born again" believers, many of whom were taught that they could not reject their faith through the hardness of their stubborn and rebellious hearts.

And I, for one, do not want to stand before the Lord in judgment as He shows me the many who ultimately rejected their faith in Him because I taught and confirmed that it was impossible for a born-again believer to reject his or her faith because of the hardness of their stubborn and rebellious flesh dominated hearts.

After Jesus explained to His disciples why He spoke in parables, He quoted a prophecy given to Isaiah (Isaiah 6: 9-10) as the reason why the Israelites, other than the Lord's immediate disciples, did not have a revelatory understanding of the parables.

124

Although the quote from Isaiah's prophecy was directly related to national, ethnic Israel at that time, the Spirit of truth makes application both to national, ethnic Israel in the Lord's own day, and, by implication, to the future nation of God, spiritual Israel, who would become spiritually drowsy and fall asleep when He tarried.

For this nation's...(the nation of God)... *heart has grown gross*...(fat and dull)..., *and their ears heavy and difficult of hearing, and their eyes they have tightly closed, lest they see and perceive with their eyes, and hear and comprehend the sense with their ears, and grasp and understand with their heart*...(spirit-soul connection)..., *and turn*...(away from their somnolence)... *and I should heal them.* Matthew 13:15 Amplified (inserts are the author's)

What other reason can we give for the fact that the nation of God, the "Israel of God" in Christ, to whom the Spirit of truth was given for the purpose of "guiding" us into all truth, including the truth about both the assignment of administrative authority and the empowerment of God for ministry, as well as the discernment of things to come, than to confess that the majority of the body of Christ is not manifesting the unity and the uncompromised truth and delegated *exousia* power that is ours in Christ.

Yet, we fail to recognize that the Lord specifically prophesied the current status of the church in the parable of the ten virgins and in His straightforward discourse recorded in Matthew 24. Yet, because we have been "given" the ability to "see" and "hear" and "understand" the secrets and mysteries of the kingdom of God through the presence of the indwelling Spirit of truth, it is almost impossible to misunderstand this parable or misunderstand the Lord's very specific prophecy as recorded in Matthew 24 and 25.

Nevertheless, because of the deceptions and lies of the enemy introduced into the body of Christ over a long period of time, these deceptions have been established as strongholds of tradition opposed to the very clear absolute, immutable, revelatory truth of God.

As a result many in the nation of God today have become "deaf" and "blind," not to all truth, or they would not still be participants in the body of Christ, but blind to certain areas of truth and, particularly, the truth about the manifested power and glory of the Lord through His *ekklesia* as well as prophetic truth concerning both our present condition and His future intent for the body of Christ.

In the parable of the ten virgins, the lamps represent the believers' souls filled with the oil of the Holy Spirit, burning brightly with their faith-filled response to the revelatory truth, promises, and commands of the Lord.

Historically, this is a picture of the first days of the early church.

Then the Lord tells us a prophetic fact, currently fulfilled in the body of Christ today. Yet, because this shocking fact is a condemnation of our current status almost no institutional, denominational, theological, or pastoral authority in the church today will dare teach it though they will someday be rebuked for their disobedience, disobedience that will ultimately lead to the shocking apostasy of the "foolish" during the trouble to come.

Then shall the kingdom of heaven be likened unto ten virgins, which took their lamps, and went forth to meet the bridegroom. And five of them were wise, and five were foolish. They that were foolish took their lamps, and took no oil with them: But the wise took oil in their vessels with their lamps. While the bridegroom tarried, they <u>all slumbered</u> and <u>slept.</u> Matthew 25:1-5 KJV (emphasis is the author's)

"All" means that both the wise and the foolish virgins ultimately began to slumber and fall asleep spiritually.

Thus, verses 1-5 of the prophecy have been fulfilled. Furthermore, we know this is the present general, but not individual, status of the spiritual body of Christ, because the next specific event of this parable has not yet taken place.

The kingdom of heaven (a.k.a. kingdom of God) in the earth is the church (*ekklesia*) allegorically depicted as all ten virgins…(innocent before God, because they are in Christ)…which is the entire corporate body of Christ, expectantly awaiting the arrival of the bridegroom with their lamps burning brightly.

Then we are told that a divisive influence separating the "wise" from the "foolish" entered into the body of Christ, and this divisive influence among the ten virgins is described as the failure of the "foolish virgins" to make provision to maintain the oil of the Holy Spirit in their lamps.

And without the oil of the Holy Spirit we have no light, (i.e. no light = religion without revelation, which ultimately results in apostasy, or, at the very least, a lack of faith for all things.)

When the Lord tarried, the entire body of Christ, not just the "foolish virgins," became spiritually drowsy and fell asleep.

Collectively, the institutional church has been unwilling to admit and subsequently teach that we are now and have been for some time, prophetically speaking, "drowsy" or even "asleep" by comparison with the church body of the first century when the believers were wide awake with lamps full of oil, wicks trimmed, and the flame burning brightly (manifesting the truth, love, and power of Jesus Christ in a dark world).

Our present state of general somnolence, though, thankfully, not equally applicable to the entire body of Christ, is a shocking parallel with the somnolence of national, ethnic Israel during the first advent of Jesus Christ when the Pharisees, believing themselves to be in perfect accord with the truth and will of God, rejected their "Messiah" when He came to them.

As modern Pharisees unwilling to confess our true status, we are also unwilling to receive the truth that there will be a universal awakening of the church as all ten virgins, whether "wise" or "foolish," hear the Holy Spirit's announcement, ***"Behold! The*** *bridegroom cometh,"* (Matthew 25:6) prior to the second advent of our Lord.

The reason we have failed to recognize this is that the deceived and divided institutional church is unwilling to receive or confess the truth of our present condition.

In today's spiritual climate I cannot imagine the senior pastor of some televised mega-church confessing to his audience that they are spiritually "drowsy" and that he is, in part, responsible for allowing them to remain in this condition.

Yet, we will all experience this ultimate wakeup call at some point in our immediate future, which the Lord has given me, at the age of seventy-seven, reason to believe I will personally experience.

I have speculated elsewhere that this announcement will be accompanied by startling events in the world, triggering a world-wide response.

Yet, regardless of the external events in the world, the announcement itself will be heard in the spirits of every single born-again, regenerated believer in the body of Christ no matter what level of faith they are experiencing at the time, and the external events, demonstrable in scripture, will confirm what we receive in our spirits.

I have also compared this awakening blast of the Holy Spirit's shofar to the 4:30 am wakeup call for new U.S. Marine Corps recruits on the first day of boot camp as the drill instructor shouts, "ATTEN-HUT!" and then begins tossing bunks and lockers like a tornado of starched olive drab mayhem shouting, "Wake up you sleepy-heads! All hell is about to break loose, and you are NOT ready for it!"

The vast majority of sleeping virgins in complete denial of their current status will not expect this event. It will shake us to the core, and as we scramble to our feet, fully alert in whatever emergent events are taking place in the world at the time, we will begin to trim the wicks of our lamps so that we are prepared, not only to meet the Bridegroom and go with Him into the Father's house for the marriage feast, but, more importantly, be prepared for the rather lengthy fight of faith that will take place during the 4th, 5th, and 6th seal events of Revelation, i.e. *"tribulation,"* a fight that the majority of the protestant church, having believed the enemy's lies concerning a pre-tribulation "rapture," in total denial of God's very specific "appointed times" and of the Lord's own words in Matthew 24 and 25, is expecting to escape.

This announcement event and its repercussions will cause the virgins to doubt the leadership of those Christian leaders who proclaimed various lies as "truth," including the aforementioned and intensely dangerous lie of a pre-tribulation "rapture" of the saints. (i.e. If they have lied to us about this important truth what else have they lied to us about? And can we trust them now to lead us through tribulation?)

What we are told in the Olivet prophecy and the parable of the ten virgins is that during this lengthy time of tribulation the "foolish" will ultimately reject their faith in Jesus Christ because of trouble, persecution, and intense deception by satanically deceived false prophets and lying shepherds.

After this awakening the response and ensuing fate of the "foolish" is the most tragic imaginable, and I tremble at the thought that members of my own family, members of my local fellowship, and those brothers and sisters in Christ who are known to me throughout the world today, will experience this unparalleled testing of their faith during a time of great difficulty.

Having been given the warning by the Lord that I, along with many others who have been given responsibility for restoring truth to the body of Christ, will be persecuted by leaders currently serving in the body of Christ who will remain in bondage to the lies, I, like the awakened "wise" virgins, have no choice but to continue pressing into the Lord regardless of personal pain, rejection, and persecution, even by those that I love and serve.

In this regard, the "wise" virgins will repent of worldliness, repent of false doctrines, and false, idolatrous practices as they endure, persevere, and remain steadfast in their faith, overcoming the 4th, 5th, and 6th seal events of tribulation through Spirit-filled faith (i.e. lamps filled with oil and wicks neatly trimmed).

These will also respond appropriately in Spirit-guided obedience to the Lord's commands as given to the seven churches in Revelation 2 and 3 and intended primarily for the awakened end time church.

These seven churches were literal churches in Asia Minor (Turkey) at that time, but they represent seven types of the church throughout history.

The proof that the message of Revelation, chapters 2 and 3, is primarily, and specifically, intended for the end time church undergoing tribulation is found in the Lord's promise to the "wise virgins" of the Philadelphian church, the church of brotherly love, who will endure, persevere, and remain steadfast in their faith during the intense trouble and persecution to come.

Because thou hast kept the...(rhema)...word of My patience,...(holding fast to your faith during tribulation)...*I also will keep thee from...*(being harmed by)... *the hour ...*(God's appointed time)...*of temptation, which shall come upon all the world,...*(the 3.5 years of 7th seal "great tribulation")...*to try them that dwell upon the earth.*

Behold, I come quickly: hold that fast which thou hast, that no man take thy crown... (by leading you into apostasy).

Him that overcometh will I make a pillar in the temple of my God, and he shall go no more out: and I will write upon him the name of my God, and the name of the city of my God, which is new Jerusalem, which cometh down out of heaven from my God: and I will write upon him my new name. He that hath an ear, let him hear what the Spirit saith unto...(all)... *the churches.* Revelation 3:7-13 KJV (inserts are the author's)

Philadelphian believers, then, will not escape the 4th, 5th, and 6th seal events of "*tribulation,*" during which they are instructed to keep the word (revelatory command and promise) of His patience.

This word, "patience," does not mean to merely endure. Strong's expands and portrays the meaning as being the characteristic of a man who is not swerved from his deliberate purpose and his loyalty to faith and piety by even the greatest trials and sufferings.

Likewise, the word, "keep," in this passage does not indicate a removal of believers from tribulation. It is the same word used in "keep My commandments," meaning to carefully guard and protect IN tribulation.

The indication here is that those who are identified as "Philadelphian" believers (regardless of denomination or geographical location) will clearly "hear" and respond to the Lord's truth, promises, and commands during a lengthy period of time in which they will not only experience the worldly problems, but will also be targeted for persecution, not only by the world systems controlled by the beast kingdom, but by those who were once "brothers" and "sisters" in Christ.

The apostate believers persecuting the "wise" virgins are identified as "foolish" virgins. These are those who have unknowingly rejected their faith and are led by false prophets and lying shepherds who themselves are unknowingly led by demons masquerading as angels of light. (2 Corinthians 11:13-15)

Proof that this promise of protection during "great tribulation" is for the end time Philadelphian church and Philadelphian type of believer that I refer to as the "Philadelphian identity" is revealed in the promise that they will be "kept" (protected and guarded) IN the "hour of trial," (the 3.5 years of a God-appointed time of testing identified as *great tribulation*") not removed from that "hour of trial."

That "hour of trial" (God appointed time of trial) is described in Revelation 8 as the events that take place after the Lord opens the 7th seal, identified in Matthew 24:21 as *"great tribulation."* This is clearly distinct from *"tribulation,"* identified as the 4th, 5th, and 6th seal events, during which the Philadelphian believers steadfastly overcome the testing of their faith by keeping and acting on the Lord's revelatory word without losing heart during the trials.

It is worthwhile, then, to examine both the testing of the Philadelphian "wise virgins," and the traits they are commended by the Lord for manifesting, because out of the seven types of churches and believers it is ONLY the Philadelphian type of believer who has the promise of being "kept" (protected) in the final 3.5 years of "*great tribulation.*"

At the same time, remember that the promise to this church is obviously not to the original Philadelphian church who, along with all the original churches addressed in the Revelation of Jesus Christ, would not be tested by the appointed 7th seal "hour" of testing identified as "*great tribulation.*"

And to the angel...(primary apostolic messenger)... *of the church in Philadelphia write; These things saith he that is holy, he that is true, he that hath the key of David, he that openeth, and no man shutteth; and shutteth, and no man openeth; I know thy works: behold, I have set before thee an open door,*...(to complete the works assigned to you as "faithful bond-servants")... *and no man can shut it: for thou hast a little strength*...(moral power and excellence of soul)..., *and hast kept*...(protected, cherished and obeyed)...*my* ...(*rhema*)...*word, and hast not denied my name. Behold, I will make them of the synagogue of Satan, which say they are Jews, and are not, but do lie;* ...(initially the synagogue from which the Philadelphian Jews originated; ultimately the apostate "foolish" believers who will persecute "wise" believers)...*behold, I will make them to come and worship before thy feet, and to know that I have loved thee.* Revelation 3:8-9 KJV (inserts and emphasis are the author's)

It is the response to the tribulation and spiritual warfare of the 4th, 5th, and 6th seal events after our awakening that will determine the fate of the ten virgins (i.e. the entire body of Christ).

132

Those who are "wise" will endure, persevere, and overcome during that time. The "foolish" will ultimately reject their faith during that same time, and, though claiming to be "Christian," they will be empowered by demonic religious spirits as they persecute the faithful Philadelphian believers during the final days of "tribulation."

What the western church in general does not recognize is that the concept of an "escape" from tribulation via a rapture event, is contrary to the specific will of God.

It is the specific will of God for believers to be tested through trials, tribulation, and various assaults of the beast kingdom for the purpose of refining us in the fire that we might also glorify Christ while in the fire.

This is succinctly demonstrated in my favorite daily devotional book by Oswald Chambers:

"The surf that distresses the ordinary swimmer produces in the surf-rider the super joy of going clean through it. Apply that to our own circumstances, these very things—tribulation, distress, persecution, produce in us the super joy; they are not things to fight. We are more than conquerors through Him in all these things, not in spite of them, but in the midst of them. The saint never knows the joy of the Lord in spite of tribulation, but because of it. *"I am exceeding joyful in all our tribulation,"* says Paul. Undaunted radiance is not built on anything passing, but on the love of God that nothing can alter. The experiences of life, terrible or monotonous, are impotent to touch the love of God, which is in Christ Jesus our Lord."

(Chambers, Oswald. My Utmost for His Highest, Classic Edition p. 48. Discovery House Publishers. Kindle Edition.)

We also notice that the "wise virgins" of the Philadelphian church are promised that they will escape being harmed by the 3.5 years of *"great tribulation"* that follows *"tribulation,"* but not by removal from the earth.

These, having endured the trials and testing of the 4th, 5th, and 6th seals of "*tribulation*," will be sealed and redeemed as "*firstfruits*...(of the "wheat" harvest)...*unto God and the Lamb*" (Revelation 14:4) immediately prior to the opening of the 7th seal.

These are also metaphorically identified as the 144,000, the perfection of spiritual Israel, the "Israel of God" in Christ to be fully examined in future chapters.

The literal number of those who are sealed and experience the completion of their redemption at that time, though, are potentially in the millions.

These are the entire company of spiritual Israel who have endured the fiery trials and testing of their faith during "*tribulation*," and it is these identified as having been "*bond-servants*" of the Lord during the 4th, 5th, and 6th seals of "tribulation" who will ultimately bring in the harvest of an uncountable number from every nation, tribe, and tongue during the 3.5 years of 7th seal events identified as "*great tribulation*."

It is also these who will manifest the fullness of Christ in the earth in perfect unity with Him and with one another during the 7th seal. (Ephesians 4:11-13)

You can imagine, then, why Satan does not want the body of Christ to receive this truth and why he has been working diligently for almost two millennia to keep it hidden from us as he discourages us by scattering the sheep into denominational sub-flocks, all of whom disagree with the other sub-flocks in doctrine and practice.

"Wise" or "foolish," the awakening announcement spoken into the heart of every member of the body of Christ by the Holy Spirit and accompanied by the shaking of all that can be shaken, which the Spirit of truth revealed to Jeremiah as "*the storm of the Lord*," (Jeremiah 22: 3:19) is close at hand.

The "foolish" and the unbelievers will be unprepared for both the storm and the awakening, and their response to both will be inadequate. However, the "wise" will repent as directed in the

Lord's message to the seven churches as they seek His wisdom in preparation for both.

Be therefore, "wise," because dark storm clouds are gathering on the prophetic horizon. And, as a body entire, we are NOT ready.

And at midnight there was a cry made, Behold, the bridegroom cometh; go ye out to meet Him. Then all those virgins arose and trimmed their lamps. Matthew 25:6-7 KJV (emphasis is the author's)

What we notice first is that the announcement occurs at midnight, suggesting deep darkness and slumber (somnolence) before the day brings light. Secondly, we notice that all of the virgins (believers) "hear" the Holy Spirit's announcement, and all of the virgins awaken from their slumber and begin trimming their lamps, which represents the heart (soul and spirit) of born-again believers.

What this indicates to me, as confirmed both in scripture and in the storm warning dreams given to me and to many others at this time, is that our spiritual awakening will be accompanied by worldwide conflict and disaster that we will all recognize as being the beginning of the end.

All of the virgin's lamps contain the oil of the Holy Spirit at that time, but it is apparently necessary for the awakened virgins to "trim" the wicks of their lamps (cutting away the sins and falsehoods that so easily beset us, i.e. Revelation 2 and 3) so that our lamps provide as much light as possible. It is also necessary to maintain (continue to be filled with) the oil of the Holy Spirit as the source or fuel for the living flame of light in a dark and dangerous world.

The key regarding our individual response to this event is whether or not we respond in repentance and obedience to the instructions of the Lord, instructions that will come through those fathers of the faith anointed with the spirit of Elijah for this purpose.

Speaking of John the Baptist preparing a people, national, ethnic Israel, for the first advent of Christ, and applying metaphorically to those who will minister in the spirit of Elijah a.k.a. "Elias", to prepare a people, the Israel of God in Christ, for the return of the Lord:

It is he...(those "lamplighters" anointed with the spirit of Elijah)... *who will go as a forerunner before Him in the spirit and power of Elijah, to turn the hearts of the fathers* ...(leaders of the faith)...*back to the children,*...(of the faith)...*and the disobedient*...(of the faith)...*to the attitude of the righteous,*...(of the faith)... *so as to make ready a people*...(the wise virgins)...*prepared for the*...(return of the)...*Lord."* Luke 1:16-17 NASB (inserts and emphasis are the author's)

Amen. Come Lord Jesus.

8 – The Former and Latter Rains

Though the coming storm itself does not seem like good news, there is an aspect of the coming storm that is undeniably good news.

The GOOD NEWS is that after our awakening, and the beginning of the 4th, 5th, and 6th seal events of "tribulation," faithful believers will receive help from God to overcome the assaults of the beast kingdom.

In the prophetic parable of the ten virgins (Matthew 25:1-13), we notice an unusual encounter between the "wise virgins" and the "foolish virgins" after the awakening in which the foolish virgins recognize not only that they are running out of oil (the apparent presence of the Holy Spirit), but that the wise virgins obviously have an abundant manifestation of the oil of the Holy Spirit.

The conflict between "Charismatic" believers and "Cessationist" believers over the manifestation of certain gifts of the Spirit, as well as the offices of "apostle" and "prophet," has not generated this open church-wide recognition of the manifestations of the Holy Spirit. This future event, then, must represent a significant change in the status quo. Yet, even now the remnant "wise" among the body of Christ are moving toward those fellowships where the full manifestation of both the leadership appointments and the manifestation gifts are present in their fellowships for the mutual benefit of all.

What believers in America today are beginning to desire more and more is what the original believers of the first century experienced, which is the full manifestation of all the gifts and all the ministry assignments.

Religion without the presence of Christ in the form of the Holy Spirit's empowerment is not the will of God for the body of Christ.

This is evidenced by the words of the Lord Himself in what we have termed as the "great commission."

And Jesus came up and spoke to them, saying, "All authority has been given to Me in heaven and on earth. Go therefore and make disciples of all the nations, baptizing them in the name of the Father and the Son and the Holy Spirit, teaching them to observe all that I commanded you; and lo, I am with you always, even to the end of the age." Matthew 28:18-20 NASB

What we clearly recognize here is that the "all" He commanded His original disciples included laying hands on the sick (with the expectation of instantaneous healing), casting out demons, prophesying, prophetic utterances, and spiritual dreams and visions.

"All" He commanded us also includes teaching believers how to respond to the *rhema* voice of our Lord through the Spirit of truth in scripture, instead of authoritatively telling those whom we are responsible for what to believe and practice without leading them into a Spirit-revealed, Spirit confirmed understanding of the truth, promises, and commands of the Lord (i.e. denominationalism).

Likewise, in the early church, new believers spontaneously spoke in unknown tongues or prophesied as soon as they received the Holy Spirit. In some cases, believers did not receive the Holy

Spirit until hands were laid on them,…(initiating their faith)…but as soon as they did receive the Holy Spirit many of them spoke in tongues and prophesied without ever having heard of "tongues" or "prophesying." This sign will flourish again during an end time outpouring of the Spirit on "wise" believers.

New believers will speak in tongues, and prophesy even in traditional churches as the Spirit enables them. This will confound many traditional believers and some Charismatic believers as the power of the Spirit manifests through believers at the moment of salvation.

This outpouring of the Spirit spoken of by the prophet Joel, and commented on by Peter and James, has been referred to as the combined former and latter rains. Nevertheless, certain areas of confusion need to be addressed in order to understand the prophetic fulfillment of Joel's prophecy as it relates to the church both today and after our awakening.

"Be glad then, ye children of Zion, and rejoice in the LORD your God: for he hath given you…(past tense)…the former rain moderately, and he will cause to come down for you the rain, the former rain, and the latter rain in the first month." Joel 2:23 KJV (insert and emphasis is the author's)

This prophecy initially spoken to national, ethnic Israel by Joel, but ultimately delivered to spiritual, "born again" remnant Israel on the initial fulfillment of Pentecost, states that God had already given them the "former rain" moderately.

This "moderate" (i.e. limited) former rain came to national, ethnic Israel in the form of God's spiritual anointing of His prophets, priests, and kings, but not on the entire body of corporate Israel.

The "former rain" is also known in Israel as the seed germinating rain.

The "latter rain" is the harvest producing rain, and this rain from the fulfillment of the initial event of Pentecost forward is the presence of the Holy Spirit in all of His functions, gifts, and manifestations in and through the body of Christ entire.

Then Joel tells them that the prophecy related to the church includes a promise of both the former and the latter rains in the first month to the future *"children of Zion,"* which is the spiritual body of Christ made up of both Jews and Gentiles as *"one new man"* in Him.

In this regard, there is no known old covenant event revealed in scripture from Joel forward that could potentially be a fulfillment of this promise.

In addition, we note that Peter claimed the day of Pentecost as the *"beginning"* of the fulfillment of this promise. We must presume, then, that Joel's prophecy was for "spiritual Israel," the *"Israel of God,"* as the true *"children of Zion"* for whom the promise was intended just as Peter proclaimed.

Joel also identified the month of Nisan, the "first month" of the Jewish calendar, as the time in which this promise would begin to be fulfilled. Nisan is the same month in which Passover occurs. It was on 14 Nisan that the Lord was crucified, and on 16 Nisan He was resurrected. Therefore, it is the death, burial, and resurrection of the Lord that initiated the ultimate fulfillment of this prophecy in the first month.

Pentecost, though, takes place during the month of Sivan and is forty-nine days after Passover. Therefore, the prophetic promise of Joel 2:23 was initiated by the death, burial, and resurrection of Jesus Christ in the month of Nisan (the first month), and literally fulfilled on Pentecost.

Pentecost takes place on the 49th day after Passover (i.e. day 50). Thus, Passover is the first day, and Pentecost is the 50th day and is viewed as the ultimate result of Passover.

This is also the day that the kingdom of God fell with POWER on the new believers.

Hence, the promise prophesied by Joel was initiated (made possible) by the resurrection of Jesus Christ, and the church, the true *"children of Zion,"* received the full package of both the restoration of the former "moderate" rain falling on the Lord's prophets and the latter rain falling on "all flesh" (all believers, not just prophets) on Pentecost.

We note, then, with absolute certainty that God specifically appointed this day for the fulfillment of this promise.

Nor can we ignore the importance of the fact that the "former," limited outpouring of the Spirit on the prophets, priests, and kings of Israel included spectacular, special faith events like raising the dead to life, which have taken place only in a very limited manner in the history of the spiritual body of Christ.

The most important purpose of the outpouring of the Spirit in fullness is to manifest the power, glory, and presence of the Lord through the spiritual body of Christ.

This was thoroughly demonstrated in the early days of the church as believers cast out demons, laid hands on the sick, and raised the dead to life, manifesting the love, power and glory of Christ as they preached the gospel of Jesus Christ with signs following.

And my speech and my preaching was not with enticing words of man's wisdom, but in demonstration of the Spirit and of power: That your faith should not stand in the wisdom of men, but in the power of God. 1 Corinthians 2:4,5 KJV (emphasis is the author's)

What Paul clearly stated is that the revelatory, *rhema* word of God spoken through believers as the Spirit "guides" will result in the manifested power of God as confirmation for that same spoken *rhema* word.

But this confirmation will not accompany mere intellectual presentations, even if the intellectual presentations are accurate.

Joel's prophecy also demonstrates that this promise was exclusively intended for the spiritual body of Christ from the initial fulfillment of Pentecost all the way to the "last day" resurrection of all the saints from Adam forward on some future 1 Tishri feast of atonement.

Therefore, the kingdom of God was ultimately demonstrated to be the spiritual body of Christ, the *"Israel of God"* in Christ.

This prophecy, therefore, has nothing whatsoever to do with national, ethnic Israel.

"Therefore say I unto you, The kingdom of God shall be taken from you, and given to a nation bringing forth the fruits thereof." Matthew 21:43 KJV

I need to quickly explain that this is NOT "Replacement Theology," a derogative term deliberately but erroneously applied by dispensationalists to those who teach Covenant Theology.

The body of Christ did not replace Israel. National, ethnic Israel was never at any time intended to be the ultimate geopolitical covenant nation of God in this present age.

The covenant, even before the foundations of the world, was exclusively intended for THE "seed" of Abraham, Jesus of Nazareth, and all those who would be included in Him as joint heirs, identified as spiritual Israel, the *Israel of God* in Christ.

Wherefore then serveth the law? It was added because of transgressions, till the seed...(Jesus of Nazareth)...*should come to whom the promise was made; and it was ordained by angels in the hand of a mediator.* Galatians 3:19 KJV (inserts and emphasis are the author's)

Any false charge that this is "replacement" theology is claiming that Jesus of Nazareth, the seed of Abraham for whom the promise was always intended, replaced Israel in the covenant intent of God.

But the obvious truth is that the promise was never intended for national, ethnic Israel as a whole. The Israelites were temporary "tenants" of the kingdom of God in the earth, carriers of the bloodline of THE "seed," and therefore subject to both the promises and judgments associated with the covenant.

However, when He (THE "seed" of Abraham, the "last Adam," the Son of God and Son of man), to whom the promises were always intended, came, the temporary "tenants" and title-deed holders to the kingdom of God in the earth were removed from their tenancy.

From that point forward individual Israelites could only be included in the New Covenant through their spiritual incorporation in Jesus Christ, the Messiah, by grace through faith.

Our participation, whether Jew or Gentile, in the covenant is not direct. The covenant is between God the Father and God the Son, the only seed of Abraham to fulfill the Law and inherit the Covenant. Our participation in the covenant and in the kingdom of God, whether Jew or Gentile, is a result of our spiritual incorporation in Christ by grace through faith in Him. Matthew 21:38-43 NASB:

> *But when the tenants...* (national, ethnic Israel)... *saw the son, they said to themselves, 'This is the heir...*(to whom all the covenant promises of God belong).... *Come, let us kill him and have his inheritance.' And they took him and threw him out of the vineyard...* (the kingdom of God in the earth)...*and killed him. When therefore the owner of the vineyard comes, what will he do to those tenants?*
>
> *They...* (the Pharisees)... *said to him, "He will put those wretches to a miserable death and let out the vineyard to other tenants who will give him the fruits in their seasons."*
>
> *Therefore I tell you, the kingdom of God will be taken away from you...* (national, ethnic Israel)... *and given to a people...* (the true *children of Zion* including both Jews and Gentiles as "one new man" in Christ)... *producing its fruits.*

The "people" in reference here are those who are "in" Christ spiritually. The covenant is between the Father and the Son, Jesus

143

of Nazareth, not between the Father and those who have received Christ.

To claim, then, that the body of Christ replaced Israel is false. It is Jesus of Nazareth, THE "seed" for whom the promises were always intended, and the covenant of God the Father with national, ethnic Israel (i.e. the Law) was always intended for Him, and for all those who would ultimately be included in the spiritual body of Christ from Adam forward.

The Lord's presence in the midst of spiritual Israel, as promised, was evident on the day of Pentecost and in the early years of the church, but as the Lord tarried the evidence of His presence in the form of the Spirit's outpouring and manifestations as both the former "moderate" rains falling on prophets and the latter rains falling on all believers, began to fade.

This turn of events was identified and prophesied by the Lord in the parable of the ten virgins as the entire spiritual body of Christ becoming "drowsy" and "falling asleep," which, according to this parable, is our present general condition, with obvious differences in the degree of our somnolence.

This present condition is also confirmed by our division into thousands of denominations and millions of rabbinic opinions concerning the truth, promises, and commands of God in Christ.

Apart from the specific revelation of the Spirit of truth, Peter would not have been able to discern the application of Joel 2:23-32 to the church, but after the outpouring of the Spirit on the 120 upper room believers, Peter did reveal the application of Joel's prophecy to the church:

But this is that which was spoken by the prophet Joel; "And it shall come to pass ... (afterward)...in the last days," ...(a.k.a. "latter days")...saith God, "I will pour out of my Spirit upon all flesh: and your sons and your daughters shall prophesy, and your young men shall see visions, and your old men shall dream dreams:

"And on my servants and on my handmaidens I will pour out in those days of my Spirit; and they shall prophesy…"

(A break is inserted here for expository purposes as Joel jumps forward from the beginning of the "last days" / "latter days" on that first Pentecost all the way to the day of the Lord on some future 10 Tishri Feast of Atonement.)

And I will shew wonders in heaven above, and signs in the earth beneath; blood, and fire, and vapour of smoke: The sun shall be turned into darkness, and the moon into blood, before the great and notable day of the Lord come: And it shall come to pass, that whosoever shall call on the name of the Lord shall be saved." Acts 2:16-21 KJV (quoting from Joel 2:28-32)

Review the following observations from Joel's prophecy as Peter related it to the church:

1. Joel identifies the time in which the prophecy would come to pass as "the last days" (a.k.a. "latter days" identified as the entirety of the New Testament all the way to "the last day" resurrection);

2. Peter makes the application of this last days prophecy to the church by saying, *"This is that which was prophesied by the prophet Joel."* Therefore, from that first Pentecost until today is all included in the term, "last days" or "latter days" compared to the "former days" of the Old Testament;

3. We then note that the promise first given to national, ethnic Israel is fulfilled, not to national, ethnic Israel, but to spiritual Israel, the *ekklesia* of Christ, consisting of both Jew and Gentile as *"one new man,"* which is consistent with the fact that all of the covenant promises of God belong to Jesus of Nazareth, the only Israelite to fulfill the

145

Law and the prophets and qualify as the inheritor of the covenant promises of God (2 Corinthians 1:20). These covenant promises still belong to the spiritual body of Christ though they are not fully manifested at this present time because of our somnolence;

4. The promise of the restoration of natural former and latter rains to literal Israel points to and illustrates an outpouring of the Spirit on spiritual Israel (the church) as both the former "moderate" rains on prophets and the latter rains on "all flesh" for the purpose of bringing in the complete "wheat" harvest;

5. "All flesh" obviously does not mean all men and women whether believers or not, because the outpouring began with only 120 in the upper room. The inclusive "all," therefore, means both Jews and Gentiles who receive Christ by faith, not just ethnic Jews. It also means all believers, not just prophets, but it does include the former "moderate" rains that fell specifically on prophets in the former days with NO indication that the "moderate," limited rains on prophets would cease;

6. We know by context that it is a progressive outpouring initiated in the first month of Nisan with the death, burial, and resurrection of Jesus Christ, and first manifesting on Pentecost with the birth of spiritual Israel as both a former and a latter rains event. Yet, it will not conclude until the resurrection on the last day, which exposes the cessationist view as being an erroneous lie used to excuse our somnolence and unbelief;

7. We note, however, that the prophecy itself does not reveal or explain a time of lesser rainfall in which the manifestation of the Spirit and the glory of the Lord was to be less than it was in the beginning.

What this means is that there is no specific discontinuance of this outpouring from the first Pentecost until the last day resurrection of the saints in Joel's prophecy or in Peter's explanation of the fulfillment of Joel's prophecy.

Yet, experientially and historically we recognize that the body of Christ as a whole seems to be in a period of drought, not only where unity in doctrine and practice are concerned, but also where the "rain" of the Holy Spirit and the manifested glory of the Lord are concerned.

Neither the supposed absence of apostles and prophets or our possession of the full canon of scripture can be supported as an explanation for any absence or minimization of the manifestation gifts of the Spirit or the leadership of apostles, prophets, evangelists, pastors and teachers.

But the Lord provides the clear explanation for this period of lesser rainfall in the prophetic parable of the ten virgins given to Peter, Andrew, James and John as a part of His prophetic response to them when they asked Him, *"What will be the signs of your coming and of the end of the age?"*

The Lord's clear parabolic explanation is that the vigorous faith of the early church began to wane when He tarried, and the entire body of Christ became spiritually "drowsy" and fell asleep. "Sleep" in this instance does not mean death, but rather a loss of vigorous faith and a subsequent decline in the manifestations of the Spirit, which is spiritual somnolence.

Yet, throughout church history, there have remained remnant pockets of Christian believers revived from spiritual slumber in various places at various times among whom the manifestations of the Spirit have glorified the Lord.

How do we, then, account for the historical fact that there has been a drought of this outpouring on the church at large? Or that the corporate church, in spite of the Charismatic renewal, has not generally manifested the signs of this outpouring of the Spirit, either as a continuance of the former "moderate" (limited) rains on prophets, or as the heavy latter rains on all believers?

Our observation of historical reality demonstrates that wherever denominational bureaucracy, including Charismatic denominational bureaucracy, has institutionalized the church, "winds of doctrine" have continued to divide us and limit our response to the Lord's truth, promises, and commands as these are conveyed to us by the Spirit of truth.

It is also important to note that the institutionalization of Christianity is basically non-existent in the underground persecuted church wherever it is found in the world today. Additionally, and most notably, the power gifts and spoken gifts of the Spirit frequently manifest in the persecuted underground church whereas much of denominational Christianity is devoid of both the spoken, prophetic gifts as well as the power gifts that the Lord has intended for the body of Christ until the end of the age.

Conformation to the institutional church was largely ignored in the great revivals of 18th and 19th centuries, as the spoken prophetic gifts and the power gifts of the Spirit, including raising the dead to life, were demonstrated to still be the intent of God for the body of Christ.

It is likely, therefore, that the future restored fullness of this promise in Christ will be hindered in those who cling to ungodly or deceptive denominational and institutional traditions (i.e. the "foolish virgins").

Conversely, it will be increasingly manifested in those "wise virgins" during a time of increasing trouble in the world who will abandon false doctrine and false practice in order to follow the Lord in Spirit and truth. (John 4:24)

In Israel, the former or early (fall) rains come in November and December preparing the soil and germinating the seed of grain crops like barley and wheat, and the latter rains (a.k.a. spring rains or the "heavy" rains) cause the crops to mature for harvest. The outpouring of the Spirit on the holy remnant of the kingdom of God, the church, on the day of Pentecost, is presented as an outpouring of both the "early" fall rains for the purpose of germinating the seed of the newborn church of Jesus Christ (spiritual Israel) and the heavy "latter" rains for maturing the crop for harvest.

Our experience of a generally decreased outpouring of the Spirit as the combined former and latter rains, because of the somnolence indicated by the Lord in the parable of the ten virgins, suggests the possibility that there will be a remarkable increase or restoration of this combined outpouring of the Spirit after the church receives the groomsman's wake up call, *Behold! The bridegroom cometh*.

But what additional scriptural proof of this restoration of the fullness of the combined former and latter rains outpouring of the Spirit do we have?

James reveals the purpose of the outpouring of the Spirit as the combined former "moderate" or limited rains and the heavy latter rains on spiritual Israel as being the New Covenant harvest beginning on Pentecost and ending with the resurrection on the last day.

Additionally, he instructs believers to be patient while they wait for the coming of the Lord for His church, which is on "the last day" (1 Tishri, the Feast of Trumpets) nine days prior to the great and terrible day of the Lord on the first day of the Feast of Atonement (10 Tishri).

Therefore, be patient, brethren, until the coming of the Lord.... (the day the harvest will be complete)...*The farmer*...(Jesus Christ)... *waits for the precious produce of the soil, being patient about it, until it gets the early and late rains. You too be patient; strengthen your hearts, for the coming of the Lord is near.* James 5:7-8 NASB (inserts and emphasis are the author's)

The promise of the fullness of the combined former "moderate" rains that fell on the prophets of national, ethnic Israel and the latter "heavy" rains together (the combined rains) in the first month has been ours from the day of Pentecost forward, because this covenant promise is to Christ and those who are in

149

Christ all the way until the harvest is complete. There is, therefore, no scriptural rationale for a drought in the church apart from our somnolence and our loss of vigorous faith, which the Lord has described prophetically as the church (the virgins) becoming drowsy and falling asleep.

Even so, we are in expectation of an awakening event that will cause the combined former and latter rains to fall again in an ever-increasing manifestation of the outpouring of the Spirit and of the glory of the Lord for the purpose of maturing the crop for the harvest. And this will take place among the "wise" after we hear the clarion call of the Spirit, like the sound of a shofar from the watchtower.

Behold! The bridegroom cometh. Come out to meet Him.
Matthew 25:6 KJV

The command, "**Come out to meet Him,**" is not a reference to the resurrection or the non-event of a pre-tribulation "rapture," because the awakened virgins, innocent before God because they are in Christ, go through a rather lengthy period of "tribulation" that includes the 4th, 5th, and 6th seal events of Revelation.

Coming out to meet Him is our awakened response to Him during the 4th, 5th, and 6th seal events of "tribulation" during which the "wise" virgins respond to both the corrections and instructions of the Lord as revealed in the message to the seven churches. (Revelation 2 and 3)

The "foolish," though, do not respond to the same message, and these ultimately reject their faith because of the "trouble."

A period of lesser rainfall between the initial fulfillment of Pentecost and a future manifestation of the heavy spring rains corresponds perfectly with the natural rainfall patterns in Israel. It also corresponds with the prophetic revelations of Joel (Joel 2:23), Peter, James, and Jesus (Matthew 24 and 25), and with the historical fact that the church has generally been somnolent and sub-normal with only intermittent "rains" in various places at various times as parts of the body of Christ have been revived.

150

The revived outpouring of the Spirit as the combined former and latter rains will be preceded and accompanied by our experience of the accelerated and intensified "birth pains" in Matthew 24, Mark 13, and Luke 21, and that prospect is frightening even though we know that it must take place.

What this means practically for end time believers is that both the world and the spiritual body of Christ, will be subjected to a time of great difficulty. At the same time it will be during this time of shaking that our faith will be tested and revived as the "wise" virgins begin to *"come out"* in repentance to the issues that the Lord has identified in His letter to the seven churches (Revelation 2 and 3).

This awakening will be accompanied by a notable increase of the harvest producing "former" and "latter" rains of the Holy Spirit through the awakened "wise virgins" who respond appropriately to the Lord's commands of repentance.

And these latter rains will equal and even exceed the early seed germinating rains of the first years of the body of Christ in the earth.

But it will NOT be manifested through the "foolish" virgins who will not respond appropriately to the instructions of the Lord for our repentance.

The failure of the "foolish" to respond to the Lord's commands at that time, and the ultimate rejection of their faith, as well as their persecution of the "wise" virgins who do respond to the Lord's commands is the most tragic event in the entire history of the body of Christ, even the entire history of mankind.

The Lord's instructions for the awakened virgins is, therefore, worthy of considerable evaluation, and those who are in denial of this event are the most likely to experience it.

9 – The "Naked" Church

In the previous book, "UNMASKING the End Time Beast Kingdom," the seven seals of Revelation opened in order by the Lord are clearly demonstrated to be: 1st-3rd – *"the beginning of birth pains"*; 4th-6th – *"tribulation"*; and 7th – *"great tribulation."*

The awakening of the entire true body of Christ, as described in a previous chapter, takes place at the opening of the 4th seal and the beginning of that unspecified length of time identified by the Lord as *"tribulation."*

As demonstrated elsewhere, we are currently experiencing 3rd seal *"beginning of birth pains"* events leading up to the shocking (but awakening) events that accompany the opening of the 4th seal, as these are prophesied to take place in our immediate future.

This was confirmed to me through a progression of seven (7) storm warning dreams, and it is evident that many, many others are receiving similar dreams and visions in order that the "wise" might be prepared for *"things to come."*

What we desperately need to recognize is that it is God's eternal intent and purpose for mankind from Adam forward to be tested during this brief time of physical life on planet Earth. This testing is also contested by a God-ordained enemy, that fallen archangel, Lucifer, who is now known as "Satan" (meaning "enemy"). And this testing will either result in our eternal spiritual life in Christ, or our eternal spiritual life separated from the life and covenant blessings of God, the Father.

Though our flesh fears and wants to avoid tribulation of any kind, it is **IMPORTANT** for us to recognize and openly acknowledge that it is God's intention for the *ekklesia* of Christ to be seriously tested, and through testing, ultimately arrive at the fullness of His divine appointment for the body of Christ in the earth as we overcome the final manifestation of the enemy during the 7th seal events.

It is also important to note that He has provided us with specific instructions for the repentance and obedience that will be required at the ordained time of our testing during which the "wise" will persevere, endure, and overcome.

But, at the same time, the "foolish" will not overcome, and their fate is the most tragic imaginable, though many falsely believe that it is impossible to reject our faith through our chronic disregard of the covenant truth, promises, and commands of the Lord spoken through the still, small voice of the Spirit.

It is also at this time that there will be a noticeable increase in the former and latter rains manifestations in the world wide body of Christ, and it is through the prophetic ministry of the true fathers of our faith walking in the spirit of Elijah, that the Lord will bring the "wise" to repentance so that we are able to walk by faith in the trials to come.

Though specifically applicable to the seven original churches in Asia Minor, the message to the seven churches (metaphorically represented by the seven candle lampstand) are prophetically intended for those same seven types of believers throughout the ages, but with emphasis on the awakened body of Christ for whom "The Revelation of Jesus Christ" was primarily intended.

In particular, the message to the church at Laodicea will be the general message to which the awakened body of Christ will be required to respond, but the message to all seven types of the church will be applied by the Spirit to the awakened body of Christ as needed for our instruction and correction in order to prepare us for the intense time of testing during the 4th, 5th, and 6th seal events.

Over the years I have received personal correction and instruction from the Lord through spiritual dreams and visions. These typically take place early in the morning and end just before my alarm is set to go off.

As I awaken from the dream, I rehearse the details in my mind before getting up to write down the details in my journal. Then I meditate, pray, and respond to the correction, instruction, or warning I have received.

The metaphors He uses in the dreams and visions He has given me correspond with the metaphors He has used in scripture, and when I dream that I am naked in public the Lord is telling me that my sinful man is exposed to others, and I quickly repent of whatever it is that I am doing or have done in that regard.

This metaphor was first used scripturally in reference to Adam and Eve after the fall when they "saw" (understood by revelation) that they were "naked" (i.e. their sinful, fallen nature exposed), and in response attempted to cover their exposed sinful nature with their own (religious) works.

This same response is evident throughout the body of Christ today as the NAKEDNESS of the corporate church of Jesus Christ is exposed to the entire world by our division into thousands of denominations and millions of rabbinic opinions concerning the truth, promises, and commands of the Lord.

It is also evident as the leadership of the institutional church from Catholic to Charismatic is embarrassed by the "nakedness" of those "shepherds" whose nakedness is exposed by gross sexual sin that even the un-regenerated masses abhor.

This is both deliberately instigated by the enemy and allowed by the Lord for the purpose of awakening the body of Christ concerning our "nakedness" in all its forms and manifestations.

At the same time the vast majority of believers are in denial of the Lord's intent that we be unified in our faith and doctrine when, in fact, He has given us the Spirit of truth for that express purpose. (John 16:13)

As we acknowledge the truth of our condition, though we are secretly convinced that "we" and our own "group-think" associations and denominations hold to the truth while all others are deceived and in error, there is only one correct response. That correct response is the steadfast and passionate desire to know and respond by faith and obedience to the absolute, immutable, *rhema* truth of God, even if the truth contradicts what we have believed and proclaimed to others, even if it destroys the reputations and ministries we have built for ourselves around unknown and undetected falsehoods, even if our proclamation of the truth, as He compels us, causes us to be rejected, persecuted by fellow believers, and even ridiculed as a "fool" by the blind guides of spiritual Israel.

For the one who seeks to know and respond to the absolute, immutable, *rhema* truth of God at any cost, the reward is a "treasure" that cannot be compared with any loss experienced by our prideful, flesh-driven souls.

Yea, if thou criest after…(rhema)… knowledge, and liftest up thy voice for…(revelatory)… understanding; If thou seekest her as silver, and searchest for her as for hid treasures; Then shalt thou understand the fear of the Lord, and find the…(true)… knowledge of God. Proverbs 2:3-5 KJV (inserts are the author's)

The Pharisees, rabbis, and priests of Israel prefigured this current condition of division in the body of Christ at the time of the Lord's first advent.

Israel had been without a prophet for four centuries, and the leaders of Judaism in that day had established a complex array of denominational, non-revelatory, and demonically inspired doctrine and practice. Then, at the coming of their Messiah the vast majority failed to recognize the time of their visitation because of their non-revelatory religious conditioning and were eventually both judged and condemned by their unbelief.

We should not let their example escape us upon whom the fulfillment of the ages has come.

For the "*Israel of God*" in Christ nothing is more misunderstood than the prophetic message contained in "The Revelation of Jesus Christ," though this is the MOST IMPORTANT message that the awakened church will be required to respond to in order to remain steadfast in the faith, and overcome the assaults of the beast kingdom during the 4th, 5th, and 6th seals of "tribulation."

"The Revelation of Jesus Christ" is the Lord's letter written primarily, <u>not</u> for the seven churches in Asia Minor, but for the end time church whose response will literally determine each individual believer's eternal fate.

The epitome of this letter is a call to repentance, endurance, and perseverance by the awakened but "naked" church.

That the seven churches addressed in Revelation 2 and 3 were literal churches in Asia Minor at the time the Lord gave this message to John is confirmed fact, but these were not the only congregations of believers in existence at that time.

Because seven (7) is the specific metaphorical number for Christ, we may accurately presume that these seven types of congregations represent seven universal types of the church and universal types of believers throughout the age.

Likewise, because He addressed these seven specific congregations as a prelude to the prophetic revelation of future events involving the church, we may also accurately presume that His commendations and condemnations have their greatest prophetic application for the end time "wise" and "foolish" virgins of the awakened church (Matt. 25:1-9) who will be required to face and respond to those future events.

PROOF that the most important application of this message is for the end time church is His message to the church at Philadelphia (the church of *agapeo* brotherly love), in which He promises to "keep" them from being harmed by the "*the hour*...(appointed time)...*of temptation, which shall come upon all the world, to try them that dwell upon the earth.*" Revelation 3:10 KJV

That "hour," or appointed time, is the final 3.5 years of "*great tribulation*" after the opening of the 7th seal by our Lord.

The temptation they (the Philadelphian believers) will not have to face during the 7th seal events of "*great tribulation*" is the demand by the antichrist beast kingdom to worship and obey the antichrist "man of sin" as "Messiah," and as the "head"/king of the 7th and final beast kingdom.

This "head"/king is also identified as the ruler of the mountain empire of Israel, the "little horn" that controls a one world government with ten horns (demonic principalities) and ten crowns (political authorities) whose capital will ultimately be Jerusalem, identified by the Father as "*Babylon, the great*". (Daniel 4:30 and Revelation 14:8)

That "hour" (appointed time) has not yet come, and all believers of all time have escaped that dangerous and terrifying "hour" or appointed time up to now.

At the same time only one type of the church and only one type of believer, out of all other types, has been promised to be kept from being harmed or tested by both the "temptation" and the six trumpet judgments of the 7th seal (a.k.a. "*great tribulation*" - Matthew 24:21)

The word translated as "keep" in this passage is the Greek word transliterated as "tēreō," and it is given the following meaning in Strong's:

I.to attend to carefully, take care of
    A.to guard
    B.metaph. to keep, one in the state in which he is
    C.to observe
    D.to reserve: to undergo something

This is the same word used in the Lord's command, *"keep My commandments"* (John 14:15). It has nothing to do with removal by a so-called "rapture" event, but is instead, about preserving and protecting Philadelphian believers in the "hour" (appointed time) of trial ("temptation"), identified as the 3.5 years of the 7th seal of *"great tribulation."*

Intelligent, scholarly men unknowingly manifesting all the characteristics of the Pharisees, Scribes, and priests of Israel at the time of the Lord's first advent, have presumptively claimed that the Philadelphian church will represent all believers, or the so-called "universal church" at that time.

And because we are attracted to the concept of end-time believers escaping tribulation by being "raptured" at some point prior to the opening of the 7th seal, and preferably before the 4th seal, we eagerly embrace their pharisaical speculations as "truth."

However, when we examine the passage with spiritual insight we note that the promise only applies to one type of church and one type of believer, a church and believer who has endured, persevered, and overcome both the general tribulation (trouble) and the specific persecution of the beast kingdom during that time.

We also note that the great persecution of the end time *ekklesia* of Christ begins with the opening of the 4th seal, and that even if a "rapture" event were to take place after the 6th seal, those being "raptured" would not have escaped the lengthy 4th, 5th, and 6th seal events defined by the Lord as *"tribulation."*

Likewise, we need to remember that the Lord has instructed the church from the very beginning that His church WILL experience "tribulation" (trouble and testing) from the day of Pentecost all the way to the last day resurrection. <u>John 16:33 KJV</u> (emphasis is the author's):

These things I have spoken unto you, that in me ye might have peace. In the world ye shall have tribulation: but be of good cheer; I have overcome the world.

Our flesh-driven FEAR concerning this time of great difficulty, requiring a much greater level of faith and obedience than most of the body of Christ is currently experiencing, inhibits our revelatory understanding of *"things to come."*

Yet, Paul and James clearly reveal the will of God for His elect:

…but we glory in tribulations also: knowing that tribulation worketh…(produces)…*patience; and patience, experience; and experience, hope: and hope maketh not ashamed; because the love of God is shed abroad in our hearts by the Holy Ghost which is given unto us.* Romans 5:3-5 KJV (insert and emphasis are the author's)

Consider it all joy, my brethren, when you encounter various trials, knowing that the testing of your faith produces endurance. And let endurance have its perfect result, so that you may be perfect and complete, lacking in nothing… (of the truth, faith, POWER, and righteous obedience of Christ)… James 1:2-4 NASB (insert is the author's)

Knowing that it is the will of the Father for all believers in all ages to experience the refining fires of "tribulation" …(i.e. testing by fire)… we can understand why it is necessary for the Father to allow us to experience an intensifying increase of tribulation in order to prepare the "wise" of the end time generation for "things to come."

It is also important for us to note that the Lord's letter to the churches is the entirety of the Revelation of Jesus Christ as He gave it to John, an apostle of the church, not just Chapters 2 and 3. Therefore, the entire book of "The Revelation of Jesus Christ" was passed around to the churches so that each noted the Lord's commendations, condemnations, and required repentance as well as the Lord's warnings about the prophetic future of this present generation.

The purpose of the commendations and condemnations at the beginning of the letter is to warn and prepare the church, not only for the persecution of their day, but for the intense events that the church will experience in the years immediately prior to His return on the "last day."

The response of these various types of churches and corresponding types of believers has been important throughout the ages, but the most important response is that of the end time church who will experience the actual events of Revelation 4 through 22.

For that reason, "reading" or "preaching" and "heeding" this letter is much more relevant for the church today than it was for those first seven types of the church in Asia Minor to whom the letter was sent.

It is so IMPORTANT that the Lord commanded a curse on those who either "add to" or "take away from" the revelatory intent of His missive given to the church in what we have named, "The Revelation of Jesus Christ."

He also commanded a blessing on those who read and heed (obey) the message with revelatory insight.

__Blessed__ is he that readeth... (with revelatory insight)...*and they that hear*...(with spiritual ears)...*the*... (*rhema*)...*words of this prophecy, and keep*... (preserve and treasure God's revelatory Word and obey it by faith)... *those things which are written therein: for the time*...(appointed "hour" of testing)...*is at hand*. Revelation 1:3 KJV (inserts and emphasis are the author's)

For I testify unto every man that heareth the words of the prophecy of this book, If any man shall add...(his own interpretation or adds words the Author did not originally intend)...*unto these things, God shall add unto him the plagues*...(of the curse)...*that are written in this book: And if*

160

any man shall take away from...(either by omitting words originally given by the Author or masking the revelatory understanding of)...*the words of the book of this prophecy, God shall take away his part out of the book of life, and out of the holy city, and from the things which are written in this book.* Revelation 22:18-19 KJV (inserts are the author's)

This is a **SERIOUS** warning, and those who continue to teach that only the first three chapters of Revelation apply to the church are "taking away" from the words of this book. Yet, I believe that the curse does not and will not apply in any permanent way until the body of Christ is awakened from our general state of somnolence. At that time, however, it will apply to the false prophets and lying shepherds of the awakened spiritual body of Christ who are unwilling to respond to the truth and the corrections the Lord will bring to us at that time.

In spite of the fact that we each think the Laodicean definition belongs to some other group, almost all modern Christian ministry leaders, authors, and teachers believe that the Laodicean definition specifically defines the materialistic, non-committed, legalistic, ho-hum church of America and the western world, but not ourselves individually or our own church fellowship and denomination.

A closer examination of His message reveals exactly what His condemnation of this church is really about so that we might respond appropriately to Him, and it is not what we have thought, taught, and preached without unction.

"I know thy works, that thou art neither cold nor hot: I would thou wert cold or hot. So then because thou art lukewarm, and neither cold nor hot, I will spue thee out of my mouth....(unless you repent)...*"* Revelation 3:15-16 KJV (emphasis is the author's)

The Lord modifies this promised threat only by the implied condition, "unless you repent." Yet, I am only personally acquainted with a handful of believers who are concerned about this threat of judgment. And these are those who are already exhibiting traits characteristic of Philadelphian believers.

Yet, it is the Lord's intent that those who are participants of, and defined by, His scathing rebuke of the Laodicean identity, respond in repentance in order to become participants in the Philadelphian identity.

But those who continue in the unrepentant Laodicean identity will ultimately experience degeneration as they harden their hearts to the Lord's demands for repentance and obedience to the revelation of His truth, promises, and commands during the trials to come.

This is the **MOST IMPORTANT** revelatory awareness that believers in this current generation can have.

What, then, do we Laodiceans need to repent of if we desire to be identified as "Philadelphian" believers?

The presumption that the metaphorical use of "hot" means "on fire for Jesus" and the metaphorical use of "cold" means "no religious fervor whatsoever" is totally erroneous, and is proof that we are currently guilty of the errors the Lord exposes in His letter to the Laodicean church.

What we have generally concluded is that being "lukewarm" means a materialistic, lackluster enthusiasm for things of the Lord, which is what the condemnation of the church at Ephesus, the church that has lost its first love, is all about.

JESUS specifically defines "lukewarm" as believing that we are spiritually rich (lacking nothing of the character of Christ and the power of the Spirit) when we are actually lacking in Christian character, lacking in true righteousness, lacking in revelatory insight, and lacking in the resurrection power of Christ without any apparent ability to discern our true condition.

Because you say,...(and falsely claim)...*"I am rich, and have become wealthy, and have need of nothing," and you do not know that you are <u>wretched</u> and <u>miserable</u> and <u>poor</u> and <u>blind</u> and <u>naked</u>, I...*(strongly and urgently)...*advise you to buy from Me gold...*(the righteous characteristics of Christ)...*refined by* *fire*...(testing)... *so that you may become*...(truly)... *rich, and white garments*...(of genuine righteousness)...*so that you may clothe yourself, and that the shame of your nakedness*...(exposed sin nature fostered by false demonically inspired doctrine and practice)...*will not be revealed; and eye salve to anoint your eyes so that you may see*...(the revelatory truth, promises, and commands of the Lord). <u>Revelation 3:17,18 NASB</u> (insert and emphasis are the author's)

The simple implication is that the lukewarm church is a church that thinks it's "hot" but is not. Neither is it "cold."

Laodiceans are those who believe that their church fellowship, or their denomination, is manifesting the mature fullness of the Lord's truth, promises, and commands when, in fact, they are not.

"Cold" is a metaphor for the complete absence of truth and a complete absence of corresponding faith responses, while "hot" is a metaphor for the complete presence of God's absolute, immutable, revelatory truth and the corresponding faith responses (i.e. the original church in Jerusalem under apostolic leadership).

Therefore, "lukewarm" is the metaphor for blending faith with unbelief and truth with error without the ability to distinguish the difference between the two, which is exactly what the dialectical deceptions of Satan for the past two millennia have produced in the "lukewarm" church.

Laodicean believers, who yet lack awareness of the truth of our condition, say they are rich in the spirit and lack nothing of the manifestations of the Holy Spirit or the character of Christ, and they DO NOT KNOW that they are actually "wretched" (afflicted by troubles they cannot overcome), "pitiable" (defeated), "poor" (not manifesting an abundant faith life), "blind" (lacking the ability to "see" by revelatory insight), and "naked" (revealing the sinful man in what they think, say, and do).

It is easy to see in this passage that "rich" and "wealthy" and "have need of nothing" is a metaphor for something other than material wealth, because it is juxtaposed against "wretched, pitiable, poor, blind, and naked."

163

The church at Laodicea at the time the letter was written was a wealthy church, and by telling them that they were in reality "wretched," "pitiable," "poor," "blind," and "naked," He alerted both them and us that His message has nothing to do with their material wealth. By comparison, the Lord told the church at Smyrna, a poverty-stricken church, that they were "rich," confirming that His use of the word is not in reference to worldly wealth but to the "gold" and "riches" of Christian character.

Keep in mind that the Lord addressed the churches as a whole, because they manifested, as a group, certain attributes either contrary to the will of God or in agreement with the will of God.

Yet, the response demanded by the Lord, is, and will be, required of each individual believer.

His condemnation of the "lukewarm" Laodicean church and believer is that they believe they are spiritually rich, and, like the rich young ruler, they do not know that they are actually spiritually wretched, pitiable, poor, blind and naked. Therefore, at this present time Laodicean believers do not recognize the need for repentance.

But after our awakening at the opening of the 4th seal, we will all recognize our true condition, and the "wise" will either repent of whatever the Spirit reveals as "sin" (missing the mark of the Lord's revealed truth, promises, and commands) so that they are ultimately associated with the "Philadelphian" identity, or they will fail to repent and ultimately fall into the apostasy of the "foolish virgins" who do not believe that the apostasy of born again Christians is possible. (Matthew 25:11,12)

As will be demonstrated clearly in future chapters, those who are aligned with the Philadelphian identity will escape the greater trial of "*great tribulation*," which is the final 3.5 years, 42 months, or 1260 days of the 7th seal.

Yet, as is also clearly demonstrated in scripture, this escape has nothing to do with a pre-tribulation "rapture" event.

"Escape" for the wise virgins is demonstrated to be a 3.5 year time of glorious victory over the ultimate beast kingdom as these bring in the harvest of the multitude in the face of the worst Satan can do through his beast kingdom.

Many believers will die or be killed prior to the opening of the 7th seal without rejecting their faith, and these, like all believers, will be in the heavenly presence of the Lord as they await resurrection on the "last day."

At the same time, as revealed in the parable of the ten virgins, many "foolish" virgins will not repent as directed by the Lord and will ultimately reject their faith because of the hardness of their hearts during tribulation. And theirs is the most tragic future imaginable.

In this regard, I have wept with the Lord on various occasions as He confirmed that there will be a MASSIVE "falling away" or apostasy of believers in the trying years immediately before us, and that I MUST teach the truth concerning "things to come" though I will suffer rejection and, even, persecution, from both friends and strangers for teaching the truth.

The repentance required of Laodicean believers is not about religious zeal. If we attend a mega-church with great music, a church that immediately adopts all the popular Christian fads, a church that does not come behind in any of the spiritual gifts, a huge building that shakes with the fervent praise of its participants, a large professional staff, televised services, and a senior pastor known far and wide as a televangelist and author of numerous books, our response to the Lord is still an individual responsibility.

Conversely, if we attend a cold, dead, traditional church with narrow pews and narrow views, a church with nary a "Hallelujah!," it is our individual response that counts with the Lord.

"Rich" in Revelation 3:18 is the Greek word transliterated as *plouteo*, meaning rich in outward possessions, with a secondary metaphorical meaning of being rich in the spirit. And it is in this context that He urges (strongly commands with an implied penalty for failing to respond) the Laodicean believer to become "rich in the spirit" through "buying" gold refined in the fire of testing from Him.

I counsel thee...(sternly)...*to buy of me gold*...(Christian character)... *tried* ...(purified)...*in the fire,* ...(of tribulation and testing)...*that thou mayest be rich*...(in the Spirit)...*; and white raiment*...(of genuine, faith-filled righteousness)..., *that thou mayest be clothed, and that the shame of thy nakedness*...(the exposed sin nature)...*do not appear; and anoint thine eyes with eyesalve, that thou mayest see*...(by revelation).... <u>Revelation 3:18 KJV</u> (inserts are the author's)

What He tells the Laodicean church, and all believers of all ages, is that they need to "buy" from Him the gold of spiritual riches (paid for through the testing of their faith in the "fire"), the white clothes of true righteousness (paid for through genuine repentance and obedience by faith), and salve for their blind eyes (paid for by seeking the truth at all costs) so they can "see" by revelation as originally intended by the Lord (John 16:13).

At ALL costs.

The most important "counsel" of the Lord that we need to notice and respond to is that the "gold" of Christian character is only produced through the "fire" of testing, not meaning the testing of our faith in Christ as Savior, but meaning the testing of our obedient faith responses to the truth, promises, and commands of the Lord in the trials and warfare that Satan and the beast kingdom continually wage against us, even through brothers and sisters in the faith as well as those we love the most.

Therefore, the historic church in Laodicea, a church that was wealthy in material goods, like much of the Laodicean "type" of church prevalent today, is not being admonished for believing that they have all that they need in material wealth, or even for their obsessive pursuit of wealth through various faith "techniques," but for their belief that they are rich in spirit (manifesting an abundant,

Spirit-filled faith life) when they are, in reality, wretched and poor in spirit and do not recognize their true condition.

Being poor in the spirit may produce a lack of religious zeal, but it is not a lack of religious zeal that He is addressing.

The danger of ignoring the Lord's stinging condemnation is greatest for those individuals who presume that they are spiritually rich and lacking nothing of the truth, character, gifts, and delegated authority (*exousia*) of Jesus Christ (i.e. evangelical believers, and, even, Pentecostal and Charismatic, "Spirit-filled" believers, among whom I count myself).

This is the modern church in America and the western world, united only in our basic faith in Jesus Christ as Lord and Savior but divided by winds of doctrine, including doctrines of demons and pagan practices, with very little ability to distinguish the truth of our condition or the willingness to change. Therefore, His specific charge against OUR denomination, OUR church, and numerous individual believers, is that we believe that we are spiritually rich, but we are, in reality, spiritually poor, and don't know it.

It is, then, a great mistake to compare our walk of faith with others in the body of Christ today. For that reason, it is my suggestion that we do not compare ourselves with other contemporary denominations, fellowships, or individual believers, but compare ourselves with the first years of the body of Christ in Jerusalem.

Theirs was the "normal" (functioning as designed and ordained to function) corporate body of Christ and "normal" individual faith responses to the truth, promises, and commands of the Lord.

Ours, corporately or individually, if anything less, is "subnormal."

If we are, then, operating at their level of faith, glory, and the corresponding manifestations of the Spirit, then we can proclaim ourselves to be "Philadelphian" believers who have no need of correction.

More importantly we need to acknowledge the fact that our Lord instructed His disciples, which now includes this current generation of believers, to instruct their disciples to obey **ALL** of His commands and instructions.

>*Go ye therefore, and teach all nations, baptizing them in the name of the Father, and of the Son, and of the Holy Ghost: Teaching them to observe*...(hear and obey)... *__all__ things whatsoever I have commanded you: and, lo, I am with you always, even unto the end of the world*...(age). Matthew 28:18-20 KJV (inserts and emphasis are the author's)

"All" that He commanded them includes many things that the majority of the modern church is no longer teaching or doing.

These things have not "passed away." We just use that explanation to absolve the guilt of our somnolence. Yet, our marching orders are to teach, obey, and practice all He commanded His original disciples until the very end of the age, which obviously includes this current generation.

He has not changed His mind or revoked His original orders, and we need to carefully examine ourselves in the light of what He has commanded us from the beginning and what He has *counseled* us to respond to in the message to the seven churches.

What He commanded us to do and to teach from the beginning of the "Great Commission" until the end of the "Great Commission" on some future "last day" (1 Tishri) resurrection includes:

1. All of the appointed leadership assignments for the body of Christ, including apostles, prophets, evangelists, pastors and teachers;
2. All of the spiritual gifts;
3. Prophesying all of the truth, promises, and commands of the Lord;

4. Laying hands on the sick with the expectation of instantaneous healing;

5. Casting out demons;

6. Making disciples by leading them to faith and guiding them to maturity in Christ;

7. Hearing with spiritual ears and obeying the revealed truth and will of the Lord in all things.

What He will demand of us after our awakening includes:

1. Because we are spiritually "wretched" (afflicted with troubles we cannot overcome), "pitiable" (defeated) and "poor" (not manifesting an abundant faith life), we need to "buy" the gold of Christian character and practice refined in the "fire" of testing from Him;

2. Because we are "naked" (revealing the sinful man) we need to "buy" white garments of genuine righteousness (i.e. putting on Christ) to hide the sinful nakedness of the old man, nakedness that we should presume is not hidden by religious works;

3. Because we are spiritually "blind" (and, therefore, deceived by erroneous intellectual presumption and demonic deception) we need to "buy" eye salve from Him to anoint our eyes so we can "see" by revelation instead of depending on the "blindness" of intellect alone, and a dependence on Pharisaical religious "authorities" and "strongholds" of non-revelatory tradition opposed to the revelatory truth of God, to tell us what to believe and what to do apart from the guidance of the Holy Spirit, who is the voice of our true Teacher, the Lord Himself.

It is interesting to note that the message of the "wise virgins" to the "foolish virgins" who are running out of oil is to "buy" oil from the "vendors," metaphorically representing the Lord-appointed leadership assignments of apostle, prophet, evangelist, pastor and teacher, but not from those whose assignment of those appointments is from man and man's institutions without specific confirmation from the Lord.

We also notice that the Lord's discipline and correction is an expression of the Lord's love for the body of Christ.

As many as I love, I rebuke and chasten: be zealous therefore, and repent. Revelation 3:18 KJV

Zealousness, therefore, is not an increase in religious activity, or a greater expression of corporate praise. Zealousness is an eagerness to "hear" and repent or "hear" and obey the revelation of His will in all things, big and small, no matter what the cost, even if we have to abandon the doctrines or practices that we have built our reputations, our ministries, and our denominations around.

Examine the story of the rich young ruler again, but instead of wealth and possessions, imagine him as being a famous televangelist or denominational leader with a massive ministry built around some deceptive false doctrine(s) that tickle the ears of his many Laodicean followers.

What will he do when the Lord calls him to repent, saying, *"Abandon this false doctrine, apologize to those whom you have deceived, and teach the truth as you follow Me."*

What will WE do when He says:

Behold, I stand at the door and knock; if anyone hears My voice and opens the door, I will come in to him and will dine with him, and he with Me. Revelation 3:20 NASB

This is not, as has often been interpreted among Laodiceans, an evangelical call to the lost. This is a call to repentance of those Laodicean, Sardis, and Ephesian types of believers; those who believe they are spiritually rich, but are spiritually poor, those who blend truth with error and cannot distinguish the difference, resulting in the "nakedness" of our true condition being exposed to the world.

This is His invitation to those "wise virgins" who will awaken and begin to trim the wicks of their lamps, which is defined as cutting away false doctrine, false practice, and the sin that so easily besets us as we seek the truth from our only true authority, the Spirit of truth, who is the voice of the Lord and the interpreter of His written word.

This dining with Him, and Him with us, is genuine, full, Spirit empowered fellowship with Him as we obey His command to put away the old man and put on His righteousness through our obedience to the revelation of His will in our thoughts, words, and actions, zealously maintaining the intimacy of our fellowship with Him so that we can "hear" His voice and "see" His truth, promises, and commands with the eyes of our hearts.

In addition, this is His promise to those who will be zealous and repent, and, in true fellowship with Him, be fed the manna of God as we dine with Him:

To him...(the individual believer)...*that overcometh will I grant to sit with Me in My throne, even as I also overcame, and am set down with My Father in His throne. He that hath an ear, let him hear what the Spirit saith unto*...(ALL)... *the churches.* Revelation 3:21-22 KJV (inserts and emphasis are the author's)

A large number of people I know and have met in recent years report a longing in their spirits for the church (the entire body of Christ, not just their local fellowship or their specific denomination) to become all that it was intended to be, attaining to the full measure of Christ in the world in the unity of the faith.

This angst is from the Spirit, and we keep thinking that if we just start a new church and do it better than the last church we started, we will ultimately get there, but it is the Lord in response to our prayers who will awaken and revive His church for the great end time harvest of souls in the face of the worst Satan can do through his final manifestation of the beast kingdom.

Quoted from "World Aflame" by Billy Graham, pp. 79-80:

"Multitudes of Christians within the church are moving toward the point where they may reject the institution that we call the church. They are beginning to turn to more simplified forms of worship. They are hungry for a personal and vital experience with Jesus Christ. They want a heartwarming personal faith. Unless the church quickly recovers its authoritative Biblical message, we may witness the spectacle of millions of Christians going outside the institutional church to find spiritual food."

I try not to be moved by "movements" like the house church movement, but in a meeting with Tom Hall, pastor of Living Hope Church, and Dudley Hall of Christian Living Ministries, they took a group of pastors and elders through an exercise in which we identified the "essentials" for the church to function as a corporate group of any size. The group included leaders from evangelical fellowships that ranged from Southern Baptist to Pentecostal, but we were, surprisingly, in agreement where our primary conclusions were concerned. Some of these conclusions included:

1. A church building is <u>not</u> necessary;
2. A paid ministerial staff is <u>not</u> necessary;
3. Elder rule by corporate agreement in the Spirit is the preferred form of government;
4. Spirit led discipline by the same elder rule is necessary;
5. Exposure of the group to all the leadership and empowerment gifts of the Spirit is preferred;
6. Baptism and communion should be practiced;
7. The format for corporate worship, teaching, preaching, and various kinds of group ministry should not be overly formalized and should be responsive to the leading of the Spirit.

After our group came up with this list, Dudley told us that almost all of the groups with whom he had gone through this exercise came up with very similar lists, indicating that many leaders in the body of Christ are aware of the need for change, and that they are receiving this inner awareness of a need for change from the Spirit.

Yet, the group-think tradition of institutional denominationalism hinders the majority of Christian leaders and believers from making the changes that the Spirit is revealing as being necessary for the body of Christ on the verge of entering into the 4th seal beginning of *tribulation.*

Although many protestant churches, and even Catholic churches, are encouraging and organizing "home groups" and small group Bible studies for their churches, the control for what can or cannot take place in these home groups typically remains with the leadership of the parent church.

My wife and I are still engaged in corporate worship, the corporate edification of the saints, and both ministry and prayer in a large church setting, but at the same time we participate in small group Bible studies and small group ministry activities, because the time of our general, church-wide awakening has not yet come.

Many believers, discouraged and wounded by their experiences in traditional church organizations, are beginning to explore the house church option even before we are forced to choose this option if we want to remain faithful to Christ.

I believe that this is also the primary form of the "church" that will ultimately respond appropriately to the Lord's demands for repentance during "tribulation" as revealed in Revelation chapters 2 and 3.

Additionally, I believe that it is in this time, during which we will become progressively certain of the times in which we are living, and much less certain of the deceptions we have accepted in the past as being "truth," that the organic house church movement will experience a dramatic acceptance among believers.

Yet, it is my hope that more and more large group church organizations and denominations will begin to receive and respond to the Lord's unifying and empowering instructions for His body, because the time is short.

Very short.

10 – The Doctrine and Practice the Lord HATES

I have been advised by others, more concerned with acceptance and publishing success, that I need to leave this chapter, as well as the previous chapter, out of the book if I want it to be widely accepted by organized denominational Christianity.

Yet, truth that reveals and encourages change, not popularity and acceptance, is the task assigned to me by the Lord.

In this regard, of all the erroneous and deceptive doctrines and practices that the Lord will address in the awakened church, the doctrine and practice of the Nicolaitans is the only one He has told us He **HATES**. Yet, I know by experience that the exposure of this doctrine and practice that the Lord hates will be powerfully and angrily opposed by modern day Nicolaitans under the influence of that Satanic principality known by us as "the spirit of Jezebel."

Nor do I expect the organized body of Christ in all its denominational forms to repent of the Nicolaitan error until we are awakened and confronted by the Spirit of truth after the opening of the 4th seal and the beginning of what the Lord has identified as *"tribulation."*

Yet, we need to be aware of this one and only doctrine that the Lord has given us a double warning about so that the "wise" can begin addressing this doctrine and practice before the opening of the 4th seal.

Because this doctrine is promoted in the church by the enemy, we need to understand the nature of this antichrist spirit before addressing the Nicolaitan error.

The primary characteristic of the human Jezebel, after whom we have named this satanic prince, was that she usurped the legitimate authority of her husband, king Ahab, introducing the worship of Baal and Balaam into corporate Israel. At the same time she hated the true prophet of Israel, Elijah, who manifested the true authority of Jehovah God by calling down fire from heaven and then ordering the soldiers of Israel to kill the 450 prophets of Baal and the 400 prophets of Asherah who were unable to call down fire from heaven, though they had obviously been successful in doing so in the past through the power of Satan.

The Nicolaitan error introduced into the organized body of Christ in Paul's day, fully manifested in the organized body of Christ today, and specifically addressed by the Lord, will ultimately be overcome by the "wise virgins" after these have entered into tribulation, and by some of the "wise" prior to our awakening who will lead the way after our awakening.

Yet, much of organized Christianity is unknowingly engaged in the doctrine and practice of the Nicolaitans to some degree and these, believing that it is the will of God, are likely to resist any change, though the Lord **HATES** both the doctrine and the practice.

To the church at Ephesus: ***But this thou hast, that thou hatest the deeds*** ...(practice)...***of the Nicolaitanes, which I also hate.*** Revelation 2:6 KJV (insert and emphasis is the author's)

To the church at Pergamos: ***So hast thou also them that hold the <u>doctrine</u> of the Nicolaitanes, which thing I <u>hate</u>.*** <u>Revelation 2:15 KJV</u> (emphasis is the author's)

Traditionally this doctrine and practice the Lord hates has been examined and interpreted from two different approaches:

1. An identification of the specific practice of eating foods offered to idols, a practice associated with the worship of Balaam, and to what eating foods offered to idols means as a spiritual metaphor;

2. The meaning of the name as it relates to observable practices in the modern institutional church.

We also have to consider that this doctrine and practice is not mentioned or referred to by any of the other apostles or human authors of the New Testament.

Only John, imprisoned on the Isle of Patmos, was given this strong warning intended primarily for this present end time body of Christ immediately after our awakening and immediately before and during the testing of our faith in "tribulation."

Nor do we have any written consensus of opinion by the early church fathers, though many of these sought an answer, which is consistent with the fact that the Spirit of truth opens certain revelatory truths only at the time and to the people for whom they are specifically intended.

Thus, the Lord's revelation, given primarily for the instruction of the end time church, will identify the Nicolaitan doctrine and practice to those with "ears to hear" at the appropriate time.

It is obvious that we are not likely to be confronted about literally eating food offered to idols in the worship of Balaam, or for the promotion of fornication as a spiritual act of worship.

That leaves us with the conclusion that we desperately need the guidance of the Holy Spirit in regard to understanding the revelatory meaning of the word translated as "Nicolaitan," and the doctrines and practices that it represents.

We also need to acknowledge the importance of coming to a Spirit-revealed, Spirit-confirmed understanding, because this is the doctrine and practice that divides and emasculates the body of Christ, the doctrine and practice that drove the body of Christ into somnolence, and the doctrine and practice from which the Lord will **DEMAND** awakened end time believers to repent with serious consequences for those who do not repent and overcome.

Those then who ultimately repent of this false doctrine and false practice are the "wise," and those who refuse to repent of this false doctrine and false practice that the Lord **HATES** are the "foolish," the unrepentant who will someday hear Him say, "*I do not know you.*" (Matthew 25:12).

It is, therefore, worthy of considerable Spirit-led examination and both personal and corporate meditation.

What we notice in the message to the church at Ephesus, which we recognize as being applicable to the church of all ages, and specifically to the awakened end time church, is that this church was commended for their agreement with the Lord concerning His **hatred** of the practice (deeds) of the Nicolaitans.

What we notice in the message to the church at Pergamos, which we recognize as being applicable to the church of all ages, and specifically to the awakened end time church, is that this church was condemned for accommodating the doctrine of the Nicolaitans, a doctrine that the Lord **hates**, and the core doctrine that Satan, through the religious spirit of Jezebel, has used over the past two millennia to introduce massive volumes of false doctrine and practice into the church in his effort to divide and conquer by snuffing out our lamps (the source of our revelatory light).

In this regard, we need to be acutely aware that the Lord actually hates certain doctrines and practices in the corporate body of Christ, and because this specific doctrine and practice will obviously be present in the end time church at the time of our awakening, we need to sit up and take notice.

Yet, the vast majority of modern, western churches, including "our" church, and ourselves individually, dismiss this warning and demand for repentance by the Lord as historic and, therefore, irrelevant to the modern church even though the message to the seven churches was specifically intended for the end time church in which we are corporately and individually included.

What we will ultimately discover is that the doctrine and practice of the Nicolaitans dominates Catholic, Orthodox, Protestant, and non-denominational doctrine and practice to this very day.

Metaphorically, eating foods offered to idols can simply mean the introduction of doctrines and practices associated with Eastern mysticism or paganism as still is the practice amongst Roman Catholics in various third world countries where Christianity is combined with paganism in order to make Christianity palatable to the pagans. (i.e. eating food offered to idols is "leavened" bread, whereas God's food is unleavened manna from heaven)

It is also fully present with various "New Age" denominations, and fellowships, as well as the multitude of "Christian" cults who have compromised, and even abandoned, the truth of God.

But, more importantly, it also applies to the numerous doctrines and practices throughout Christianity today that are not in agreement with the truth and will of God, though these doctrines and practices are honored and believed by us to be traditions of faith and illuminated understanding.

Spiritual "fornication" (i.e. harlotry) is more easily identified as the introduction of doctrines and practices of demons into the body of Christ, which is spiritual harlotry by those who are covenanted to the Father in Christ.

In that regard, I am not aware of any denomination of Christianity completely free of this charge.

I do not even count myself as being free of this charge, though I continually ask the Lord to expose any falsehood that I may have accepted erroneously as "truth."

The name, "Nicolaitans" provides us with an understanding of the source of authority in the body of Christ that unknowingly allows and promotes the doctrines and practices of demons metaphorically identified as "eating foods offered to idols" and spiritual "fornication" (the act of harlotry, which is a metaphor for unfaithfulness in our covenant with the Father in Christ).

Nicolaitans (Strong's 3531, alliterated as *Nikolaïtēs*) has a literal translation of "destruction of the people" and/or "power over the people." *Nico-* is a form of nīko, "victory" in Greek, and *laos*, meaning people, or more specifically, the laity, and in the combined literal form should be understood to mean "conquerors of the laity" or "rulers over the laity."

Several of the early church fathers, including Irenaeus, Hippolytus, Epiphanius, and Theodoret mentioned this group, and stated that the deacon Nicolas, whose very name also means "power over the people," was the human author of both the heresy and the sect.

Yet, we can be certain that any doctrine and practice that is **hated** by the Lord was introduced, and is still being promoted, by Satan through Satan's deception of men.

Because of the metaphorical nature of the Revelation of Jesus Christ, applying initially to these two specific churches, but ultimately applying to the church at large after the awakening of the ten virgins (Matthew 25: 6), the reference to the Nicolaitans is applicable in some measure to the vast majority of the organized body of Christ prior to our awakening.

After our awakening the Lord will speak His commands of repentance, as recorded in Revelation 2 and 3, through His true prophets and shepherds, and the doctrine and practice of the Nicolaitans in all its forms will be at the top of the list.

The "foolish" virgins will resist the obvious challenge to the status quo, but the "wise" will repent during the storm. The "wise" will, then, be equipped by faith to overcome both the enemy and the storm, but the "foolish" will not.

At the Council of Nicaea in 325 AD, the emperor of Rome, Constantine, in agreement with certain deceived fathers of the church of that day, joined the church and the state of Rome in an unholy covenant.

The religious spirit ruling Babylon (in all its forms, historic, present, and future) is "Jezebel," the great high prince of false religion, and the principality ruling the world systems of Babylon, is "Mammon."

In the world money is power, and competitive political power ultimately results in war, dividing nation against nation, resulting in Christians being divided from other Christians through political loyalty. (Matthew 24:6-8)

Likewise, the spirit of "Jezebel" divides us further through spiritual deception as we are divided by differences of doctrine and practice, even denying that it is the will of God for us to be united in all ways with Him and with one another.

The organized, institutional church of that day was the Roman Catholic Church, and the Roman Catholic Church was seriously compromised through both worldliness and spiritual deception, ultimately leading to a breakout of the protestants who are now represented by thousands of denominations all of whom disagree in some way with the doctrines and practices of all other denominations.

This is the kingdom of God divided amongst ourselves through the influence of Satan dominated world systems and Satanically inspired divisions within the corporate body of Christ.

Yet, Jesus prayed that we would be one in unity with Him and with one another, and those of the early apostolic churches reflected this oneness (e.g. Acts 2:44-45; Acts 4:31-35).

They shared everything in common and had one common purse which was used to distribute wealth according to need, as opposed to according to greed and self-interest.

They were also unified in doctrine and practice, through the oversight of apostolic and prophetic leadership, with no tolerance for false doctrine or false practice.

The corrupting influence that came to full fruition as a result of the unholy joining of state and church through the Council of Nicaea was not the origin of Nicolaitan doctrine and practice, but it ultimately became the full-blown manifestation of Nicolaitan doctrine and practice.

As a metaphorical reference, the "teaching of the Nicolaitans" refers to a priestly domination of the people (laity).

After the Council of Nicaea the Roman Catholic Church believed and taught that its bishops were successors to the apostolic order of Jesus' first apostles, and the Bishop of Rome (later commonly referred to as the "Pope") was the head of the Bishops as the successor of Peter's role in the early church. The Pope was then presumed to be the ultimate authority concerning all doctrine and practice as indicated by his subtitle, "Vicar of Christ," the meaning of which is made clear in subsequent writings:

Pope Boniface VIII, Unam Sanctam, November 18, 1302:

"The pope, as the Vicar of Christ on earth, possesses the same full power of jurisdiction that Christ Himself possessed during His human life."

Vatican I, the Pope's recent 'Ecumenical Council',
"Official Proclamation" [Jan. 9, 1870]:
"We hold upon this earth the place of God Almighty....it came to pass in the secret design of God's providence that We were chosen to fill this Chair of St. Peter and to **take the place of** the Person of Christ Himself in the Church..."
(emphasis added by the author)

Response of Pope Pius IX to a Roman Catholic bishop's assertion that the pope's pronouncements could not be deemed infallible without the consent of the bishops as "witnesses of Tradition," meaning that the Pope was to be accountable to his peers (elders):

"**The pope** is not only the representative of Jesus Christ, but he **is Jesus Christ Himself**, hidden under the veil of the flesh. Does the pope speak? It is Jesus Christ who speaks. Does the pope accord a favour or pronounce an anathema? It is Jesus Christ who accords the favour or pronounces that anathema. So that when the pope speaks we have no business to examine." (emphasis is the author's) *End of quotes.*

This is the historic origin and escalation of both the doctrine and practice that has now impacted the vast majority of Christianity today.

Yet, our Lord and High Priest Himself addressed this heresy succinctly as recorded in Matthew 23:8-12 KJV (inserts and emphasis are the author's):

But be not ye called Rabbi: for one is your Master, even Christ; and all ye are brethren. And call no man your father... (absolute spiritual authority)...*upon the earth: for one is your Father, which is in heaven. Neither be ye called masters...* (rulers who lord it over others)...*for one is your Master, even Christ. But he that is greatest among you shall be your servant. And whosoever shall exalt himself shall be abased; and he that shall humble himself shall be exalted.*

This passage powerfully contradicts ANY assignment of absolute spiritual authority to men or their denominational organizations, and it clearly ascribes the sin of applying absolute authority to men or their denominational organizations for true doctrine and practice as being the doctrine and practice of the Nicolaitans.

Appointed and anointed leadership, yes. Absolute authority, no. This belongs only to the Father through our Lord.

In the years of the church prior to the Council of Nicaea the vast majority of those bodies of believers in various cities and countries were still led appropriately by apostles, prophets, evangelists, pastors and teachers who maintained the unity of faith and doctrine as they were led by the Spirit of truth.

Yet, history reveals the cancer-like growth of the Nicolaitan heresy from the time that our Lord identified it in His message to the seven churches (Revelation 2 and 3) all the way up to the time in which it will be addressed again as He commands His awakened church to repent of this error.

From 590A.D. to 1517A.D., the Roman Church dominated the western world, controlling religion, philosophy, morals, politics, art, and education. This was the dark ages for true Christianity and western society in general.

During this time, the vital doctrines of biblical Christianity almost disappeared, and with this neglect of true doctrine and practice came the passing of life and light manifested through the faith and worship of the one true God by the people.

The Roman Catholic Church was theologically and spiritually in bondage to the antichrist spirit of Jezebel, and, at the same time, it exercised political power through the most powerful nations in the world.

Jezebel and spiritual Babylon were thoroughly united with the authority of the Roman Catholic Church, and its Nicolaitan theology and practice led to many of the atrocious corruptions, heresies, and idolatries that the Lord "hates."

The Roman Catholic Church also seriously departed from the revelatory teaching of the written word of God and was engrossed in a massive amount of heretical, demonically inspired practices, including burning at the stake anyone other than clerics who possessed a copy of the scriptures in any language.

The obvious reason for this obscene heresy was to maintain absolute power and authority over the people.

Yet, we have passed this off as errors of the past, or as errors that are, or were, only applicable to the Roman Catholic Church, and we do not recognize that much of their false doctrine and practice has become an established tradition in most of organized, denominational, institutional Christianity in the western world.

The protestant reformation did ultimately break the yoke of this bondage to the absolute authority of the Pope, but the protestant reformation failed to expunge the priest-laity division that originated with the Nicolaitan movement and came to full fruition in the Roman Catholic Church.

This doctrine and practice of the Nicolaitans is the denomination-laity, priest-laity, pastor-laity, ordained minister-laity division that is common amongst the entirety of organized Christianity from Roman Catholic to supposed "non-denominational" and "charismatic" churches.

The body of Christ needs the organization and administrative leadership originally intended by God, but the organization and administration intended by God and manifested in the early church under apostolic leadership only exists at this present time in a minority of church bodies.

This absolute Nicolaitan authority, as opposed to the Spirit-guided and anointed "leadership" intended by God, is not, and cannot be demonstrated to be the will of God for the *ekklesia* of Christ.

The Lord tells us that He **HATES** both the doctrine and the practice, erroneously believed by most as being both "normal" and "correct," though it is entirely foreign to any New Testament scripture or apostolic church practice.

This is the doctrine and practice of the somnolent virgins of today divided into thousands of denominations, each of which claims that the authority for what they believe and practice comes from the written word of God, though what they believe differs from all others who also insist that what they believe and practice comes from the written word of God.

What our denominational division bears witness to is a massive disconnect from the Spirit of truth throughout the body of

Christ, not only to this specific truth, but to all areas of doctrine and practice.

Even the "wise virgins," as a whole, will not overcome the deeply imbedded traditions and "strongholds" of this doctrine and practice in its various forms and formats until the time of our God-ordained trouble and testing in the world.

Among protestant denominations the denominational organizations themselves have taken on rigid apostolic authority for the beliefs and practices of those who come under the denominational umbrella. Furthermore, each denomination differs in doctrine and practice from all others through a multitude of distinct doctrines and practices, demonstrating that they are obviously NOT ordained by the Lord to administer doctrine and practice to the laity with apostolic authority.

Now I beseech you, brethren, by the name of our Lord Jesus Christ, that ye all speak the <u>same</u> <u>thing</u>, and that there be <u>no</u> <u>divisions</u> among you; but that ye be <u>perfectly joined</u> <u>together</u> in the same mind and in the same judgment. 1 Corinthians 1:10 KJV (Emphasis is the author's. See also Romans 16:17; 1 Corinthians 3:3; 1 Corinthians 11:18)

In "non-denominational" churches the doctrine and practice of the Nicolaitans is expressed more often as a pastor-laity division. And in charismatic churches an apostle/prophet/pastor–laity division.

In this regard I am not denying the God-given authority and leadership of the fivefold ministry as both administrative and spiritual bond-servants of the Lord, and the fact is that the body of Christ in large part is stuck with the present organized, denominational authority until the time of our awakening and testing.

Yet, there is still a God-ordained order imposed by the Lord on His *ekklesia* through those apostles, prophets, evangelists, pastors and teachers (fathers of our faith) that He has appointed to LEAD (not "rule" in the absolute sense) the body of Christ.

But our understanding of denominational authority and the office of "pastor" through what we refer to as the God-appointed fivefold ministry of apostles, prophets, evangelists, pastors, and teachers has frequently been corrupted to mean "ruler" over what we believe and practice in the absolute unquestioning sense.

Thus, assigning absolute authority to both pastors and denominational organizations over what those in their congregations believe and practice is an obvious contradiction to the Lord's own words recorded in Matthew 23:8-12, previously quoted.

This "leading" has frequently been corrupted throughout the institutional church through the false, and frequently corrupt, authority presumed by the Pope down to pastors who are no longer "leading," but "ruling" without the authority of the Lord, as they expect and demand members of their congregations to obey them, as though whatever they teach and command is coming directly from the Lord, when, in fact, it frequently is not.

It is not against the will of God for a church or denomination to publish what they believe and practice, but screening out those believers who are not in perfect accord with a specific set of doctrines and practices, or demanding a signed confession of agreement or covenant by members of the local fellowship is a practice inherent in the Nicolaitan error.

Be AWARE. Any such covenant attaching conditions and requirements that subjugate and supersede our covenant with the Father in Christ are an abomination on a par with the covenants freemasonry demands.

Requiring members of a church body to sign a covenant, or oath of agreement, is to attach specific limitations and requirements on the covenant between God the Father and God the Son.

This written covenant or letter of agreement and spoken oath of agreement, though not intention of those who practice it, is literally a denial of the command spoken to us by the Lord.

Again, you have heard that it was said to the men of old, 'You shall not make false vows, but you shall fulfill your vows to the Lord [as a religious duty].' But I say to you, do not make an oath at all, either by heaven, for it is the throne of God; or by the earth, for it is the footstool of His feet; or by Jerusalem, for it is the city of the Great King. Nor shall you make an oath by your head, for you are not able to make a single hair white or black. But let your statement be, 'Yes, yes' or 'No, no' [a firm yes or no]; anything more than that comes from the evil one. Matthew 5:33-37 Amplified

Anything other than that comes from the evil one.

Our authority for what we believe and practice is the Lord Himself as His truth, promises, and commands are conveyed to us through the Holy Spirit, our Counselor, the Spirit of truth.

No organizational entity or individual of the body of Christ should usurp that authority through a written or spoken covenant in which the believer-member of an organized church body agrees to obey whatever the denomination or the specific church body believes and practices.

Support...YES. Lead...YES. Demand absolute control and compliance with an organized body of believers who may or may not be teaching and practicing the perfect will of God in Christ...NO.

There are those in the house church movement, and particularly the persecuted underground house church, such as those in Communist China, various Muslim dominated countries, Africa, India, and elsewhere, who are manifesting doctrine and practice more closely related to the early church model as described by Paul in 1 Corinthians 12:4-12 KJV: (inserts and emphasis are the author's)

Now there are diversities of gifts, but the same Spirit. And there are differences of <u>*administrations,*</u> *...*(administrative <u>servants</u> of the Lord - apostles, prophets, evangelists, pastors and teachers)*...but the same Lord. And there are diversities of* <u>*operations,*</u>*...*(Spirit empowered manifestations)*...but it is the same God which worketh* <u>*all*</u> *in* <u>*all.*</u> *But the* <u>*manifestation*</u> *of the Spirit is given to* <u>*every*</u> <u>*man*</u>*...*(not just some "special" believers)*...to profit withal* *...*(to profit the corporate body with which each believer is associated)*.... For to one is given by the Spirit the word of wisdom; to another the word of knowledge by the same Spirit; To another...*(unique)*... faith by the same Spirit; to another the gifts of healing by the same Spirit; To another the working of miracles; to another prophecy; to another discerning of spirits; to another divers kinds of tongues; to another the interpretation of tongues: But all these worketh that one and the selfsame Spirit, dividing to* <u>*every*</u> <u>*man*</u> *severally as* <u>*he*</u> *...*(The Holy Spirit)*...will. For as the body is one, and hath many members, and all the members of that one body, being many, are one body: so also is Christ...*(demonstrating that our denominational division and our obedience to ungodly denominational, or specific organized church body sub-covenants, is not of God, much less the absolute authority of various leadership positions within the organized church).

The absolute unity of the entire body of Christ under the headship of our Lord, Jesus Christ, as expressed in   1 Corinthians 12:4-12 is seldom found in the world-wide *ekklesia* of Christ today. What we see, instead, is a divided and emasculated *ekklesia* with many "heads," opposed to other "heads," and a multitude of conflicting doctrines and practices.

What we also see is an absence of this believer to believer ("every man") administration of the gifts of the Spirit in most congregations, because it is suppressed and controlled by the designated leadership of the congregation and the denomination as though the "laity" is merely a receiver of the professional leadership's authority and "ministry."

At the same time, Jezebel has introduced false gifts, false practices, and false doctrine throughout the body of Christ over a relatively long period of time in order to emphasize the lies and to mask the truth and intent of our Lord, which divides the sheep from one another and the sheep from the Shepherd Himself.

What is not in view in 1 Corinthians 12:4-12 is the seminary trained, ordained pastor-priest being either the unique, singular source or the unique, singular controller of this believer-to-believer ministry under the direct authority of Christ. What is also not in view is the absence of either "administrations" (leadership of apostles and prophets who are presumed in our time of somnolence to have "passed away") or "operations" (manifested gifts of the Spirit), though a majority of the church today presume erroneously that both the administrative gifts and the manifestation gifts of the Spirit are no longer applicable to the church. (i.e. This is the belief that all we have left of the administrative gifts are evangelists, pastors, and teachers, and all we have left of the manifestation gifts are wisdom gifts.)

Yet, they have not passed away. They have merely been suppressed in the church in which the Nicolaitan error has become the accepted norm just as Satan has schemed from the beginning through the Roman Catholic Church, which spiritual virus is now fully manifested in and through denominational Christianity.

Satan hates those believers who expose and oppose the Nicolaitan error in their local church organizations, and he frequently uses men and women in positions of authority in the local church or denomination to denounce those believers who expose the Nicolaitan doctrine and practice, even calling those in obedience to Lord in spirit and truth as being "cursed" by God.

Yet, those who are "in Christ" by grace through faith cannot be "cursed" by the God who redeemed them from the curse through their faith in Christ.

Judged and disciplined by the Father, yes. But not cursed.

In the 1 Corinthians passage quoted above we see that each believer is gifted in some specific way to minister both to the lost and to other believers, and that it is the Lord who orchestrates His believer to the lost and believer to believer ministry, whether through "administrations" or "operations."

How is it then, brethren? When ye come together... (as a church assembl...*everyone of you hath a psalm, hath...*(the God-given understanding of)...*a doctrine, hath a tongue, hath a revelation, hath an interpretation. Let all things be done unto edifying. If any man speak in an unknown tongue, let it be by two, or at the most by three, and that by course; and let one interpret. But if there be no interpreter, let him keep silence in the church;...*(assembly of believers)...*and let him speak to himself, and to God. Let the prophets speak two or three, and let the others judge...* (examine and agree or disagree, bearing witness in agreement or in disagreement as they are guided and confirmed the Spirit)... *If any thing be revealed to another that sitteth by, let the first hold his peace...* (as directed by the Spirit, and not by his own wil.... *For ye may all prophesy...*(express the *rhema* truth of God)...*one by one, that all may learn, and all may be comforted. And the spirits of the prophets...* (those who have a revelatory understanding of the will and truth of God as it is being applied to the circumstance)...*are subject to the prophets. For God is not the author of confusion,...*(and division)...*but of peace, as in all churches of the saints.* 1 Corinthians 14:26-33 KJV: (inserts and emphasis are the author's)

What this passage describes (active Spirit-directed, Spirit-empowered believer to believer ministry and believer to the lost ministry willed by God for the body of Christ) does not typically fit large corporate gatherings of the church (organized priest-laity division) today, and yet it does not condemn large corporate gatherings for the purpose of worshipping God with songs of praise or receiving the teaching of a specific apostle, prophet,

191

evangelist, pastor, or teacher. Or receiving various manifested ministries.

However, it does indicate that the primary *ekklesia* is a relatively small group in which "each one" can and should participate under the guidance of the Holy Spirit and authority of the Lord.

At the same time, most organized churches want to completely control and limit the doctrine and practice of all small group assemblies, i.e. Sunday school classes and home groups, though it is only in small group gatherings that Paul's instructions in 1 Corinthians 14:26-33 will normally manifest.

In many of these home groups the groups are required by the leadership to study the pastor's message from the previous Sunday, and any unique study or ministry is strongly frowned upon.

Why? Because anything else is not controlled by denominational or church authority, which, in turn, inhibits the possibility of anything like Paul's instruction in 1 Corinthians 14:26-33 from happening.

Yet, in my experience over the years, many believers yearn for what Paul has described as the intent of God in Christ for the church.

The fear of "administrators," whether referring to the denominational association assuming, without the Lord's authority, the apostolic role, or referring to pastor-priests as the sole source of doctrinal truth and practice by the "laity," is that what they believe and practice is the absolute, immutable, revelatory truth of God, and all who disagree with them hold to an apostate view and practice.

In many cases, any disagreement, or even any discussion, with denominational or pastoral authorities in this regard is condemned and punished, and those who challenge absolute denominational or pastoral authority are branded as having a "rebellious, divisive spirit."

Hebrews 13:7 is frequently quoted as demonstrating that pastor-priests have absolute spiritual authority over believers in the same way authority is always manifested in cults.

Remember them which have the <u>rule</u>...(Strong's primarily signifies "to lead;" then, "to consider;" translated as "accounting" in Hebrews 11:26, RV (AV, "esteeming"; 2 Peter 3:15, "account")...*over you, who have spoken unto you the word of God: whose faith follow, <u>considering</u> <u>the</u> <u>end</u> <u>of</u> <u>their</u> <u>conversation.</u>* Hebrews 13:7 KJV (inserts and emphasis are the author's)

The rule or authority here is the "word of God," as revealed by the Spirit of truth to the one leading, not controlling positional authority or the whimsical, self-important will or inaccurately spoken word by the leader(s) in reference.

What follows immediately afterward in this passage is that we are to follow their manifestation of faith, not their mere word and will, as we consider the result of this same word in their lives.

A better translation of "*...consider the end of their conversation*" would be "consider and judge the authority of the word they have spoken on the basis of their lives (i.e. what they say and do, and whether or not what they say and do bears genuine kingdom of God fruit).

In Hebrews 13:7 quoted above, it is emphasized that the word being spoken is for the believer's benefit, and that the one speaking a word authoritatively is not moved in any way by personal ambition or soulish motives, but is speaking because he/she is under the authority, anointing, and compulsion of the Lord. This is further demonstrated in Hebrews 13:17 KJV:

Obey them that have the <u>rule</u> over you, and submit yourselves: for they watch...(unselfishly)...*for your souls, as they that must give account, that they may do it with joy, and not with grief: for that is unprofitable for you.*

The Strong's (G2233) definition for what is interpreted as "rule" in this passage is defined as:

I.to lead
    A. to go before
    2. to be a leader…

The *rhema* word of God received, believed, and obeyed by believers is the secondary result of those leaders who are empowered to teach the truth, promises, and commands of the Lord to whomever, whenever, and however the Spirit instructs.

The primary reception and obedience to the *rhema* word of God, though, is still through the personal Spirit-led, Spirit-given truth promises and commands of the Lord.

If "leaders" are truly under the authority of God in what, when, how, and to whom they bring the word of God for instruction or reproof, and then those to whom it is given reject that word, it grieves the Spirit.

But if the one who brings the word of God for instruction or reproof is offended and angered by those who have rejected his/her authority, this is proof of the presence of a Jezebellian spirit of religious pride and control, and the Spirit is grieved by the one who is offended, rather than by the supposed "offender."

The visible proof of our continuing domination by this Nicolaitan error of presuming God-ordained spiritual authority where none is given, is our division into countless thousands of denominations concerning the truth and will of God.

We are not all submitting to the same authority. If we were, we would be united in doctrine and practice under the headship of our Lord, Jesus Christ.

In reality we have replaced our fear and respect of God with the fear and respect of man by surrendering the authority for what we believe and do to our denominations (established traditions of doctrine and practice) and to our pastor-priests, without discernment on our part in regard to whether or not our pastor-priests are truly submitted to the Lord in their ministry.

Like the Pope's excommunication of Catholics who do not agree with Roman Catholic doctrine and practice, modern protestants practice "excommunication" in a more subtle way.

Most "disobedient" believers are simply "invited" to leave the specific fellowship or denomination with which they find themselves in disagreement. Others are literally denounced as being "cursed" by God for their rebellion against local denominational or pastoral authorities.

We should easily recognize this threat of being cursed by God as being strongly suggestive of both Roman Catholicism (excommunication) and of cultism. But the LIE is disguised under the deceptive doctrine that any disagreement with and disobedience to pastoral or denominational authorities (whether appointed by God or merely appointed by men) is rebellion against God. Therefore, the believer is removed from the spiritual "covering" of the individual pastor, leader, or denomination through disagreement or disobedience.

The belief that this applies to any disagreement or disobedience is often compared to the incident in the church of Corinth in which a man was guilty of committing adultery with his mother-in-law.

But what we see in that event is that the church was given a prophetic word from Paul to remove the man from the congregation so that Satan's assault would lead to the man's repentance.

Then he was restored to fellowship both with the Lord and with the congregation.

That is not the intent in most church groups when a believer considered to be in opposition to the congregational leadership is asked to leave the congregation because of "disobedience" or disagreement with church doctrine and practice.

And it is supposedly this pastoral "covering" that keeps the "errant" believer from being "cursed," though the believer who is in Christ will not be "cursed" by the One who delivered him from the curse.

Disciplined, yes, if appropriate and from the Lord, but not "cursed."

It is Jesus who became a curse for our sakes, that those who believe would no longer be cursed by their fallen state of being. (Galatians 3:13,14)

Who, then, is our "covering," the denominational organization, the local church pastor, or Jesus Christ?

There is a protective influence, blessing, and spiritual oversight that comes from anointed leaders who are manifesting the truth, promises, and commands of the Lord correctly and effectively.

But this appropriate and biblical protection is only taking place effectively when the anointed leader is speaking, teaching, and leading in complete submission to the Lord.

> *Remember those who led you, who spoke the...(rhema)... word of God to you; and considering the result of their conduct,...*(manifesting the presence of Christ)...*imitate their faith.* Hebrews 13:7 NASB (inserts and emphasis are the author's)

This truth does not take place appropriately when any such leader is motivated by personal power, control, selfish ambition, or false doctrine and false practice.

In these instances, it is the leaders who have removed themselves from both the complete truth of God and the specific authority of God in Christ, and those believers who blindly follow without spiritual discernment are weakened spiritually as a result.

My personal understanding from experience and from guidance by the Spirit is this: If any leader in the body of Christ is not thoroughly submitted to Christ, he or she is not likely to be reachable, teachable or accountable to those over whom they presume authority.

What they exhibit instead, when disobeyed, is the ungodly anger, unforgiveness, and spiritual vengeance empowered by the spirit of Jezebel.

My advice, then, based on experience, is to flee the influence of any church leader, or church organization that demands absolute obedience, and exhibits anger and unforgiveness toward anyone resists it.

Yet, at the same time, we should respond to those who lead us as the Spirit confirms the truth, promises, and commands of the Lord appropriately through them.

In the example of Paul's word to the church at Corinth in which he instructed them not to continue in fellowship with a specific fornicator-adulterer, but to turn him over to Satan by removing him from fellowship and prayer, his instructions were in perfect alignment with the Lord. (1 Corinthians 5)

But note that his instructions for the leaders of that fellowship who believed that Paul's instructions were directly from the Lord Himself, resulted in the restoration of the adulterer, and, according to Paul, the salvation of his soul.

In that case the result itself demonstrates the appropriate leadership of Paul, and the appropriate response of the leaders and the fellowship in the church at Corinth.

What happens in most churches today results in church wounds resulting in bitter unforgiveness on both sides rather than repentance and healing.

In this regard I am in no way denying that the Lord places us under the anointed leadership of apostles, prophets, evangelists, pastors and teachers so that we receive impartations of their anointing, their leadership, and their teaching as though it is from the Lord itself.

Though we might miss the blessing intended for us, and even experience judgment by the Lord if we remove ourselves from receiving the impartations of His truth, promises and commands, through their anointed leadership, and teaching, we will not be cursed by God as long as we remain in Christ.

Yet, there will be both natural and spiritual consequences directed by the enemy, and allowed by God, if we disobey the word and will of God communicated to us by those who shepherd us appropriately through their own submission to the Spirit-revealed truth, promises, and commands of the Lord.

Any teaching otherwise is evidence of the influence of the religious spirit of Jezebel who was Elijah's greatest enemy.

What concerns me most is the false positional authority of those Nicolaitan pastor-priests who lord it over the flock for the purpose of personal control, so that none dare challenge their doctrine, practice, or absolute authority in all things.

In regard to challenging or confronting leadership in the church even apostles and prophets are not beyond reproach or instruction, much less pastors, but I believe we need to follow the instructions of the Lord as recorded in <u>Matthew 18:15-17 Amplified</u> (inserts and emphasis are the author's):

"If your brother sins,...(through personal behavior, false teaching, or abuse of any kind)...*go and show him his fault in private; if he listens and pays attention to you, you have won back your brother. But if he does not listen, take along with you one or two others, so that every word may be confirmed by the testimony of two or three witnesses. If he pays no attention to them [refusing to listen and obey],...*(in denial of the truth)... *tell it to the church; and if he refuses to listen even to the church, let him be to you as a Gentile (unbeliever) and a tax collector.*

This instruction applies both to the apostle-prophet-evangelist-pastor-teachers who are dealing with a concern they have for a believer under their ministry, or for the believer or believers who have a concern about the teaching and leadership of an apostle-prophet-evangelist-pastor-teacher.

If the leader lacks patient humility and a willingness to receive and respond to appropriate, Spirit-led teaching or correction by those he shepherds, this is a sign that the leader himself or herself is not under the authority of the Lord.

If this attitude is ultimately demonstrated to be a permanent condition in the leader it is time for the believer to remove himself/herself from the fellowship, but without bitterness and unforgiveness.

In the Southern Baptist church where I served as a teacher in the earliest years of my walk with the Lord a significant number of people in that fellowship, having heard my testimony, approached me for help regarding various demonic manifestations and afflictions, including night terrors, ghosts, voices, schizophrenia, the influence of homosexual spirits, and numerous other demonic influences and assaults.

When the pastor began to hear reports about my ministry to these afflicted believers in his congregation, he did not approach me directly to find out what was taking place. Instead, he taught the congregation that anyone who is born-again cannot be afflicted by demons, and that those who were experiencing such controls and manifestations were merely "lost" and in need of a genuine conversion.

Instead of initiating a meeting with the pastor to discuss the issue I took the easy way out by not confronting him with the truth in a one on one situation where he might have received the truth, and this was a mistake on my part.

At the same time, when the pastor preached against the ministry of deliverance, none of those who had been freed from demonic controls and afflictions came forward, either to me or to the pastor, to bear witness to the truth.

These were, instead, inhibited by the fear of man instilled through Nicolaitan doctrine and practice, and they remained quiet as my wife and I left that fellowship peacefully without confronting the issue.

In retrospect I should have approached the pastor when the first church members requested the ministry of deliverance. Then I might have had the opportunity to lead the pastor into faith for that ministry without breaking fellowship with him.

But, as a new believer, the Lord was merciful to me, and three years later I encountered my former pastor in a Bible bookstore as he approached me with two books about spiritual warfare in his hand.

"Jim," he said enthusiastically, "this spiritual warfare is real. Can you recommend a good book?"

Later, I heard from one of my closest friends in the Lord, John Todd, who was present with that pastor two years after my wife and I left the fellowship, as our former pastor delivered someone from demonic controls.

Thus, our pain in feeling that we had to leave that fellowship ultimately resulted in that pastor coming to the truth and being equipped with faith for deliverance ministry though deliverance ministry is not taught or practiced in most Southern Baptist churches.

John the Baptist was identified by Jesus as being the greatest of the prophets and as having the spirit of Elijah.

The "spirit of Elijah" anointing turns the hearts of the fathers of the faith back to the children of the faith, and the hearts of the children and disobedient of the faith back to God in order to prepare a generation for the coming of the Lord. (Matthew 11:14)

This same anointing is in the body of Christ today to prepare a generation for the return of the Lord, and it is this anointing that will expose Jezebel and all those who hold to the doctrine and practice of the Nicolaitans.

It is also this spirit of Elijah anointing that will be powerfully opposed and rejected by those operating under the Nicolaitan influence, which will be the primary manifestation of the conflict between future "wise" and "foolish" virgins, literally leading to the persecution of the "wise."

The juggernaut of the modern church drawing on centuries of increasingly erroneous tradition is not likely to change, but while we wait and prepare for the awakening of the end time church entire, the onus is on each one to discern and respond to the absolute, immutable, revelatory truth of God in this regard.

But Jesus called them unto Him, and said, Ye know that the princes of the Gentiles exercise dominion over them, and they that are great exercise authority upon them. But it shall not be so among you: but whosoever will be great among you, let him be your minister; And whosoever will be chief among you, let him be your servant: Even as the Son of man came not to be ministered unto, but to minister, and to give His life a ransom for many. Matthew 20:25-28 KJV

I recently discovered the elder-led doctrine of a church whose Senior Pastor was taught and mentored by me while he was in college.

I have deliberately withheld his name and the name of the church for their privacy and protection, but it is the clearest statement I have yet seen concerning God-ordained and appointed leadership in the body of Christ.

Quoted from the website:

Leadership in the church is not authority as the world understands it. Jesus Christ modeled what a true godly leader is when he washed His disciples' feet with His own clothes, and when He died on the cross in our place. The historical examples set by our Lord and the Apostles stands against the way the world sees leadership and authority. In Matthew 23, Christ compares the way religious leaders in His time behaved with the way the church would live:

"Everything they do is done for men to see: They make their phylacteries wide and the tassels on their garments long; they love the place of honor at banquets and the most important seats in the synagogues; they love to be greeted in the marketplaces and to have men call them 'Rabbi.' "But you are not to be called 'Rabbi,' for you have only one Master and you are all brothers."

Alexander Strauch, author of Biblical Eldership, describes the early church as a brotherhood, not a hierarchy. "In complete obedience to Christ's teaching on humility and brotherhood, the first Christians and their leaders resisted special titles, sacred clothes, chief seats, and lordly terminology to describe their community leaders. They also chose an appropriate leadership structure for their local congregations–leadership by a council of elders. The first Christians found within their biblical heritage a structure of government that was compatible with their new family and theological beliefs." (blank) Church is likewise set apart from the common practices of denominations and worldly authority. While our foundational documents do assign the titles of Senior Pastor, Elder, and Deacon to its leaders these positions are defined in the biblical tradition, not the tradition of modern churches. Church leaders are servants, appointed by Christ (Ephesians 4) to promote order and biblically sound teaching in the church. They are called to be "first among equals," to enable the church for every good thing God has called us to do. *End of quote.*

This brief statement of faith is an accurate representation of the truth that the Lord will demand His awakened church to respond to after we enter into *"**tribulation**."*

For now, denominational leaders and believers simply need to be aware that the authority for what we believe and practice is the AUTHOR of truth, the FATHER, who has delegated that authority to the SON.

Usurping that authority by asserting personal authority in any form other than the specific authority received directly from the Lord is, then, a dangerous practice, and a practice that the Lord **HATES**.

11– False Prophets and Lying Shepherds

Those who will be primarily responsible for leading the "foolish virgins" astray during the 4th, 5th, and 6th seals of "*tribulation,*" so that many who were included in the body of Christ will ultimately be included in the "Synagogue of Satan" and become persecutors of those with whom they were once united by faith, are identified in scripture as "false prophets" and "lying shepherds."

However, those who might currently be identified as "false prophets" and "lying shepherds," not knowing that they are false prophets and lying shepherds, will be given an opportunity to repent immediately following the awakening of the body of Christ that takes place after the opening of the 4th seal.

For now, it is important just to recognize what the Spirit of truth is warning us about concerning the false prophets and lying shepherds already amongst us, as these are prophesied to increase dramatically during that specific time immediately in front of this current generation of believers.

For years I have heard the call to prayer for the nation of America in numerous churches as being a response to the promise of 2 Chronicles 7:14 KJV:

If my people, which are called by my name, shall humble themselves, and pray, and seek my face, and turn from their wicked ways; then will I hear from heaven, and will forgive their sin, and will heal their land.

The initial promise given to national, ethnic Israel as those who temporarily held the title-deed to the promises of God included the natural healing of geopolitical Israel. But what we have missed in this original promise to national, ethnic Israel is that the promise is now applicable only to spiritual Israel, the covenant nation of God in Christ, and the promise is the healing of the spiritual nation of God, not the healing of America, Germany, England or any other geopolitical entity. (Romans 9:6-8, 30-33; Galatians 6:13-16)

Of great interest to me is God's preface or condition to this promise in which He states that He has withheld the natural rain, allowed the natural locusts to devour the land, and sent natural pestilence among His people because of their sin.

The original application was for national, ethnic Israel, and the drought, locusts, and pestilences were natural events. Yet, the ultimate prophetic application is for the deceived, divided, and somnolent nation of God today, the true church of Jesus Christ.

This current application reveals:

1. That God is withholding the spiritual "rain" of His Spirit that was initially manifested in fullness in the early church from those in the body of Christ today who are in unbelief;

2. That He is allowing the demonic "locusts" to devour the nation of God in various ways through our acceptance of the doctrines of demons as though they are the absolute immutable, revelatory truth of God, and;

3. That He has sent spiritual "pestilence" among us because of our sin, all for the specific purpose of correcting us and bringing us to repentance.

It is "My people," the true church of Jesus Christ, who must turn from their "wicked," pharisaical spirit of Jezebel and flesh influenced unbelief and disobedient ways in order for the nation of God to be healed as will ultimately be the experience of the "wise virgins".

This turning of the true church away from our "wicked," unbelieving, spiritually adulterous ways is taking place in various believers and fellowships of believers today, but a general faith response to 2 Chronicles 7:14 during a time of intense trouble in the world will be led by the prophets and shepherds of spiritual Israel, the true "fathers" of our faith after our awakening.

These true prophets and shepherds will lead the "wise" of the emerging Philadelphian church through the 4th, 5th, and 6th seals of Revelation to their ultimate destiny. But the false prophets and lying shepherds who will not turn from their wicked ways and will not repent of their sin, and their lies, will lead the "foolish" into apostasy and into participation in both the Harlot church and, ultimately, the metaphorical "synagogue of Satan."

This will result in the great falling away (apostasy) of the "foolish virgins," which according to the prophecy of Zechariah 13:8-9 KJV, will be **two thirds** of the body of Christ at that time:

And it shall come to pass, that in all the land, saith the Lord, two parts therein shall be cut off and die; but the third shall be left therein. And I will bring the third part through the fire,...(of tribulation)... *and will refine them as silver is refined, and will try them as gold is tried: they shall call on My name, and I will hear them: I will say, It is My people: and they shall say, The Lord is my God.*

This part of Zechariah's prophecy is preceded by his declaration as recorded in Zechariah 13:1 that the prophecy specifically relates to the end time body of Christ, not to national, ethnic Israel at the time this prophecy was given to Zechariah.

In that day...(when the prophecy will be fulfilled)...*a fountain will be opened for the house of David and for the inhabitants of Jerusalem, for sin and for uncleaness.* Zechariah 13:1 KJV

The "fountain" is Jesus Christ, and the house of David from that time forward are those who are in Christ by grace through faith.

It is, therefore, the end time body of Christ to whom this prophecy belongs, from the initial fulfillment of Pentecost forward, though the very ones who will experience the judgment of this prophecy are in total denial that it will happen.

Yet, this prophecy will be fulfilled to the "wise" one third during the 4th, 5th, and 6th seals of "tribulation."

Many years ago, my wife and I were in Key West watching the sunset as we strolled the harbor front. Out on the distant horizon was a storm front with heavy, dark clouds and a constant array of lightning flashes, but the storm was so distant that we could not hear the rolling thunder associated with the lightning flashes.

As we strolled hand in hand, we watched two ships filled with tourists leave the harbor for their respective sunset cruises. The larger of the two ships was diesel powered and the other was a sailboat. The first ship under its own power went south, the second, under wind power went north. Both captains, with their crews and passengers, were certain that the distant storm would not blow in until the cruises were finished and all were safely ashore.

But as the first gusts of offshore wind hit us, I remember thinking, "They're not going to make it."

That event is etched in my memory, and the Spirit made the prophetic application by causing me to "see" the ship under its own power as the professing church driven by religion, and the boat under sail, a ship carrying half as many passengers, as the believing church empowered by the Spirit. Yet, both captains and all their passengers presumed erroneously that the storm would not reach them until the pleasant sunset cruise was completed.

Later, both captains and all their passengers were shocked when the full force of the storm with driving winds, blinding rain, and the heavens filled with lightning flashes and deafening thunder hit them.

My wife and I watched the debacle under a store front awning as both ships scurried back to the harbor with their drenched and frightened passengers hoping to make it safely ashore.

The most important observation the Spirit caused me to make concerning this event is that the captains of these two ships, responsible for the safety and welfare of their passengers, should have had better judgment. Neither one knew the truth of their situation, though the truth was available to them, and it is likely that both made the decision on the basis of not wanting to lose the tourist dollars that a cancelled cruise would have cost (i.e. unwillingness to interrupt the status quo).

The prophetic applications are obvious, and I will begin this testimony with the final passage of Jeremiah's prophecy concerning false prophets and lying shepherds in the latter days, which has been identified in scripture as the entire post-resurrection of Christ era.

In scripture "former" refers to the pre-Christ Old Testament and "latter" refers to the post-resurrection of Christ New Testament. Therefore, this prophecy is clearly for the church, because it is the church that is now "the Israel of God" in the latter days.

<u>Jeremiah 23:20 KJV</u> (inserts and emphasis are the author's):

> ***The anger of the Lord shall not return, until He have executed, and till He have performed the thoughts of His heart: in the latter days***...(Christian era)...***ye shall consider it perfectly***....(understand the revelatory application and experience it as a reality).

As Paul reminded us, all of the things that happened to national, ethnic Israel were written down for our instruction upon whom the fulfillment of the ages has come in these "latter days" (1 Corinthians 10:11). "Latter days," then, includes the entire church age, but the emphasis of this prophecy is on the church during the end time of the latter days, which has already begun and is quickly escalating to a finale.

A significant portion of the regenerated believers in Jesus Christ today accept the current condition of the divided and emasculated church (the drought-stricken, locust infested, pestilence ridden church) as being "normal," because we judge normality on the basis of our own experience or on the basis of recent church history.

Yet, as Watchman Nee, the preeminent founder of the underground house church movement in China, wrote in his excellent book, "The Normal Christian Life," <u>normal</u> for the church is the standard established by God in Christ (i.e. functioning as originally designed), not by our experience.

Paul described this standard in Ephesians 4:13 as being "...***oneness in the faith and in the full and accurate knowledge of the Son***...(resulting in)...***the completeness of personality which is nothing less than the standard height of Christ's own perfection***..." (insert is the author's)

Because the sin conscious church cannot imagine the standard revealed by Paul as being "normal," or even achievable, we make excuses for our current status and for the obvious presence of huge amounts of deception and error being preached and taught by unknowing false prophets and lying shepherds, many of whom are consumed by the Nicolaitan doctrines and practices that the Lord hates.

And though we emotively resist acknowledging the truth, this may also include those beloved shepherds who have ministered the word of truth to us in many ways, but have wounded us spiritually by teaching error authoritatively in other ways so that we know the truth in some things, but believe lies in others without any apparent ability to distinguish the difference between the two (i.e. the Laodicean error).

This is like the two ship captains at Key West, who had safely carried their passengers on previous sunset cruises but exposed their passengers to extreme danger when the storm that we all sense in our spirits out there on the horizon, struck much sooner than they expected.

We are, therefore, the "drowsy" virgins of the parable of the ten virgins who, because the Lord tarried, ultimately fell asleep.

Spiritual somnolence, though, is not what the Lord has defined as "normal" for His church, even if spiritual somnolence and division is the only "normality" the majority of this generation has ever known.

False prophets and lying shepherds in the church of Jesus Christ today, consumed with spiritual pride and intellectual arrogance, and shielded by fortresses of denominational and doctrinal strongholds of tradition, exactly like the Pharisees of Israel at the time of the Lord's first advent, are not likely to recognize or receive this word of warning as being applicable to them.

However, the warning is intended by the Lord to stir the hearts of the remnant of spiritual Israel who clearly hear the voice of the Lord in these trying and confusing times.

In regard to the powerful antichrist traditions in the church, a younger man I have been closely associated with in ministry, Greg VanScoy, had a dream from the Lord identifying this antichrist, Jezebellian power of deception and error in the church as a giant

209

black beetle with huge pincers and an impenetrable exoskeleton.

The dream came to him immediately prior to a confrontation Greg later had with the pastor of the local fellowship he was serving in at the time.

In the dream, Greg, armed only with a knife (small sword representing truth), was in danger of being killed (spiritually) by this "beast" until he managed to roll the beast over and thrust his knife into the unprotected belly.

Instantly the true nature of the beast was exposed as the beast was transformed into the image of an unwashed man with long, unkempt hair wearing dirty ragged clothes.

As Greg gave me the details of his dream, the Spirit caused me to understand that the man in the dream was a manifestation of the deceived, divided, and defeated spiritual body of Christ (like a ragged, homeless man) that had been held captive inside the beast representing the strongholds of non-revelatory denominational tradition.

But the ragged, homeless man, representing the "drowsy" virgins, was freed when Greg thrust his small sword (of truth) in the beast's unprotected underbelly.

By the Spirit, the truth WILL be spoken into the hearts of those who have "ears to hear" what the Spirit is saying to the church through both Zechariah's prophecy and Jeremiah's prophecy, so that "wise virgins" will ultimately disengage from the false prophets and lying shepherds through whom the father of lies has deceived, divided, and emasculated the church for two millennia.

These, then, will "hear" with spiritual ears and "see" with the eyes of their hearts what the Lord is revealing to them so that they are enabled to respond by faith.

Some who have been identified by the Lord as "false prophets" and "lying shepherds" will repent, and walk the narrow way of the absolute, immutable, revelatory truth of God in Christ, regardless of personal sacrifice.

But, sadly, many will not.

Mine heart within me is broken because of the prophets; all my bones shake; I am like a drunken man, and like a man whom wine hath overcome, because of the LORD, and because of the words of His holiness. Jeremiah 23:9 KJV

Jeremiah reeled in heartbreak at the stinging condemnation of false prophets and lying shepherds in the Israel of his own day. And like Jeremiah we are shocked, dismayed, and broken when the corrective word of the Lord comes to us, whether individually, requiring our repentance, or corporately, warning us of His judgment against false prophets and lying shepherds in the church; a warning that applies specifically to the lying shepherds and false prophets of these "latter days," (Jeremiah 2:23:20) who unknowingly expose the sheep to danger.

And, as it was in the days of Jeremiah, the lying shepherds and false prophets who do not "hear" and respond to the correction of the Lord will be judged.

Their failure to hear and respond to the Lord's word of correction after our awakening will cause them to be plunged into darkness during the time of testing that will come upon us much sooner than any of us expect.

Even as I write this, my heart and my hands tremble because of this judgment. At the same time, I am aware that we have been experiencing the influence of false prophets and lying shepherds for a long, long time.

For the land...(the kingdom nation of spiritual Israel)... *is full of adulterers;* ...(those in covenant with God who participate in the cup of demons, which are the doctrines of demons and false practices introduced into the church)...; *because of swearing*... (unknowingly participating in the covenant cup of demons)... *the land* ...(the kingdom nation of spiritual Israel)... *mourneth;* ...(not understanding why the power and glory of the Lord is not being manifested in fullness among us)...*and the pleasant places of the wilderness* ...(the uncompromised pastures where the unleavened bread and hidden manna intended for the sheep is found)...*are dried up*...(and the nation of God that dwells there is starving)....

Their... (adulterous)...*course is evil*,... (referring to the false prophets and lying shepherds and those sheep who follow them)... *and their force*... (spiritual authority)... *is not right.*

"For both prophet* and priest** are profane; yea, in my house...(the church)...*have I found their wickedness,"* saith the LORD. (*Those who claim status as prophets but teach falsehood; **those who have been assigned responsibility for shepherding but have become "wicked servants" who unknowingly beat, manipulate, and starve the sheep by feeding them the leavened bread of deception and error).

"Wherefore their way...(the way of the false prophets, lying shepherds and all those foolish sheep that follow them)... *shall be unto them like slippery ways in the darkness:* ...(devoid of revelatory light)...*They shall be driven on, and fall therein:*...(away from faith in Christ)... *for I will bring* ...(the)...*evil*...(of apostasy)... *upon them, even the year of their visitation,"*...(upon these whose lies have resulted in the apostasy of the sheep)...*saith the LORD.*

And I have seen folly in the prophets of Samaria; ...(the false prophets who claim to be of spiritual Israel but are not)...*they prophesied by Baal*...(Satan masquerading as an angel of light)... *and led my people Israel* ...(the Israel of God, the *ekklesia* of Christ)...*astray.*

I have seen also in the prophets of Jerusalem...(the prophets of spiritual Israel, the church)...*an horrible thing:* ...(even worse in the eyes of God than what is being committed by the false prophets outside the true body of Christ)...*they commit adultery,*...(only those who are in a covenant relationship with God can commit spiritual adultery, and they do this by participating in the cup of demons, which are the doctrines and practices that demons teach)... *and walk*... (unknowingly)... *in lies; they strengthen also the hands of evildoers, that none*...(of the sheep)...*doth return from his wickedness; they are all of them* ...(the false prophets and the sheep that follow them)... *like unto*

me as Sodom, and the inhabitants thereof as Gomorrah."
…(subject to judgment)…

Therefore thus saith the Lord of hosts concerning the prophets; Behold, I will feed them with wormwood,…(I will give them over to the lies and deceits of Satan)…*and make them drink the water of gall:*… (the water of deception that produces death instead of the life-giving water of God's revelatory word)…*for from the prophets of Jerusalem*… (spiritual Israel, the church)…*profaneness hath gone forth into all the land"*….(into the entire nation of God in Christ, the church)…

Thus saith the Lord of hosts, Hearken not unto the words of the prophets that prophesy unto you: they make you vain:…(hopes…the hope of escaping the testing of our faith in tribulation)…*they speak a*…(non-revelatory)…*vision of their own heart,*…(filled with the deceits of the father of lies)…*and not out of the mouth of the Lord.*

They say still unto them that despise me,…(and My *rhema* word)…*The Lord hath said, Ye shall have peace;* …(by escaping the "trouble" through a pre-tribulation "rapture")…*and they say unto every one that walketh after the imagination of his own heart, No evil shall come upon you."*…(and say, "You cannot reject your salvation by rejecting your faith through the hardness of your stubborn and rebellious heart.")…

"For who…(among the false prophets and lying shepherds)…*hath stood in the counsel of the Lord, and hath perceived and heard his word?*…(with the eyes of their hearts and with spiritual ears)…*Who*…(among them)… *hath marked*…(sincerely regarded)… *his word, and heard it?*…(as they believe and obey).

Behold, a whirlwind of the Lord…(the time of testing and judgment)…*is gone forth in fury, even a grievous whirlwind: it shall fall*…(suddenly and without warning)… *grievously upon the head of the wicked. The anger of the Lord shall not return, until he have executed, and till he have performed the thoughts of his heart: in the <u>latter days</u> ye shall consider it perfectly*….(and experience it as a reality)…" <u>Jeremiah 23:10-20 KJV</u> (inserts and emphasis are the author's)

Up to this point many of those reading Jeremiah's prophecy presume hopefully that this prophecy only applies to pre-Christ Israel. Then Jeremiah 23:20 slaps us in the face.

"Latter days" includes the entire church age, but the obvious inference is on the final part of the latter days, *"tribulation,"* beginning with the opening of the 4th seal, which is the specific end time event on our immediate horizon.

The Jeremiah 23 prophecy then takes place after the awakening of the true church as the initiatory event of the 4th seal, during which time the church, having already been scattered into thousands of denominations by false prophets and lying shepherds, will experience even greater persecution and intense demonically-empowered deceptions by false prophets and lying shepherds than we have already experienced.

But, at the same time, the Lord will raise up the true fathers of our faith, the anointed apostles, prophets, evangelists, pastors, and teachers, as He exposes the lies and reveals His truth, promises, and commands to the "wise" who will be the one-third minority of the body of Christ.

We should be generally aware, in the light of the Lord's warning (Matthew 24:11), that false prophets will multiply along with true prophets as the former and latter rains are fully restored to spiritual Israel after our awakening. However, apart from recognizing various cult leaders as "false prophets," the church today presumes that all who seemingly prophesy as the mouthpiece of God are prophets of God. Subsequently, in awe of their ministry, we receive their prophecies without discernment, receiving both truth and lies without the ability to distinguish one from the other. This is the subtlety of the father of lies, and the reason for the Lord's primary warning to end time believers: *"Do not be deceived."*

214

It is not, therefore, the Jim Jones and David Koresh's of the professing church who will deceive the "foolish" virgins. It is those who have received the Holy Spirit by grace through faith; those who have ministered the word of truth in many ways, who unknowingly through pharisaical intellectualism, spiritual pride, and undetected demonic entanglements, receive the deadly lie of the Jezebellian antichrist spirit and falsely proclaim it as the very word of the Lord, who will deceive and lead the "foolish" into apostasy.

In this regard, I am only able to repeat what Jeremiah has already said, *"My heart is broken within me...,"* because of the revelation of the Lord concerning false prophets and lying shepherds in the last days whose antichrist lies will lead two thirds of the body of Christ into condemnation.

12– Apostasy of the "Foolish Virgins"

The dispensational (pre-tribulation "rapture") presumption is that the message to the seven churches in Revelation 2 and 3 relates specifically to those churches in existence in what is now the nation of Turkey and to no others. However, in the Lord's message to the seven churches, the Philadelphian church, the church of brotherly love, is the only church to receive the promise that they will be kept from (harm by) the hour (appointed time) of temptation that will come on the whole world, indicating that the message is exclusively for those who qualify as being end time "Philadelphian" believers in the final 3.5 years identified as *"great tribulation."*

Because thou hast kept the word of my patience...(endurance and perseverance)... *I also will keep thee from*...(being tested and harmed by)... *the __hour__*...(appointed time)...*of temptation,*...(testing)... *which shall come upon all the world, to try them that dwell upon the earth.* Revelation 3:10 KJV (insert and emphasis is the author's)

That "hour" (appointed time) of testing that will come upon the whole world is the 7th seal of *"great tribulation,"* but not the 4th, 5th, and 6th seals of *"tribulation."*

Why would these original Philadelphian believers be the exclusive recipients of that promise if the *"hour of temptation, which shall come upon all the world,"* did not happen in their lifetimes and does not, therefore, apply to them?

What this promise demonstrates is that the message, though applicable in some ways to the original seven churches in Turkey, is prophetically applicable to those seven types of churches and types of believers at the time of our testing, which begins with the opening of the 4th seal to begin that rather lengthy period of time known as *"tribulation."* (4th-6th seal events)

The content of the rest of the message in the Revelation of Jesus Christ reveals that the "hour," or appointed time of temptation being referenced here includes all of the events of the 7th seal after the antichrist "man of sin" has declared himself to be both "God" and "Messiah" in the third temple.

This is the same "hour" (appointed time) of 3.5 years or 42 prophetic months that the 7th and final form of the beast kingdom is given to rule and reign as recorded in Revelation 17:12 (i.e. *"great tribulation"*).

The obvious prophetic context of the Lord's promise to the Philadelphian church, is that it is only applicable to believers who have overcome (persevered in) *"tribulation"* during the 4th, 5th, and 6th seals of Revelation.

The *"temptation"* they will not have to face during the specific 3.5 years of 7th seal *"great tribulation,"* before the return of the Lord, is to obey the edict of the 7th and final "head"/"mountain" world-ruling empire of *"Babylon the great,"* whose capital will be Jerusalem, by worshipping, obeying, and taking the covenant "mark" of the beast kingdom under the rule of the antichrist *"man of sin"* who has claimed himself to be "God" and "Messiah."

It is this temptation that will try and test all the rest of mankind at that time, but not the "wise" who are identified as Philadelphian believers.

The promise for the end time Philadelphian church/believers who have overcome the 4th, 5th, and 6th seal time of "tribulation" is that they will not experience the 7th seal trial or "*hour*…(God appointed time)… *of temptation*" like the rest of mankind, even though they will still be present in the world, which has been a great mystery, and the source of a great deal of false doctrine up until now.

It is obvious that the entire body of Christ from the first Pentecost forward has escaped this specific "*hour of temptation*" up to this point. However, the promise of Revelation 3:7-10 applies only to those who will qualify as conforming to the Philadelphian identity at that specific time, believers who have remained faithful and steadfast during extreme deception and persecution by some future "*synagogue of Satan*" during the 4th, 5th, and 6th seal events.

In this regard I need to remind readers that we are currently in the 3rd seal of "*the beginning of birth pains*," and we are expecting the opening of the 4th seal at some point in our immediate future to begin a rather lengthy time identified as "*tribulation*."

At the same time, dispensationalists and other Jewish supremacy, dual covenant theologians, already fully engaged in the deceptions of the spirit of antichrist, make the claim that this promise, made only to a Philadelphian church that has undergone persecution by the metaphorical "*synagogue of Satan*" immediately prior to the opening of the 7th seal, now belongs to the "universal church" who have not met the conditions of this promise.

It is the dispensational, pre-tribulation "rapture" view that the Lord will be coming back for a defeated, worldly, lukewarm church, the church that Lord threatens to spew out of his mouth, unless they repent, the church that has blended truth with error without the ability to distinguish one from the other, the church from which there will be a massive apostasy of "foolish virgins" too heart-rending to imagine. And the reason the Lord is coming back to carry this "lukewarm," church back to His Father's house in glory is His promise to the Philadelphian church, the church that will persevere and overcome during the 4th, 5th, and 6th seal events, as they exemplify His truth, His unity, His glory, and His love under extreme persecution.

The dispensational explanation for this illogical argument is that the literal Philadelphian church no longer exists, and that this promise is now to a non-existent church and is, therefore, a promise to the "universal church."

Are not, then, the other six churches and individual identities included in the "universal church"?

Yet, the promise was to a literal church, meeting very specific requirements at the time of John's revelation, and it was given to them and no other church existing at the time because of their extreme faithfulness in a time of persecution by the Jewish synagogue from which they had defected.

We must, then, recognize that this is a conditional promise based on each believer's uncompromising faithfulness during the lengthy 4th, 5th, and 6th seal events of *"tribulation"* that precede the opening of the 7th seal of *"great tribulation."*

Therefore, the ultimate application of this promise is for those believers included in the Philadelphian identity during the time in which the 7th seal is ultimately opened.

Not even the church at Smyrna, for whom the Lord had no criticisms, received this promise. It follows, then, that if the promise did not apply to any of the other six literal churches at the time, it would not apply to any of the six other "types" of church or "types" of believers present at the 7th seal beginning of the *"hour of trial that will come upon the whole world"* (the same "hour" or appointed time during which those who are included in the Philadelphian identity will be "kept" from being harmed).

Nor would it apply to the "universal church" that primarily exhibits the characteristics of the Laodicean, Sardis, and Ephesian churches.

The fact that there were more than seven churches in existence at the time of this prophetic utterance by the Lord indicates that the weight of the message, though it did apply specifically to those seven literal churches at that time, was made primarily and prophetically to seven characteristic "types" of believers throughout the ages.

The promise, then, is to the individual's identity with the Philadelphian prototype.

The Laodicean church and believer, as well as the other church identities and believers, by contrast, are in deep trouble. They have no such promise.

Likewise, the promise that those who qualify as Philadelphian believers immediately prior to the opening of the 7th seal will be "kept" from the temptation (of strong delusion) that will test the whole world, does not include a promise that they will escape the 4th, 5th, and 6th seal events of *"tribulation"* by removal in a secret (undisclosed in scripture) "rapture" event.

It is, in fact, their perseverance in the 4th, 5th, and 6th seal events of tribulation that qualifies them for the promise of being "kept" (protected and preserved) during the 7th seal "hour" (appointed time) of *"great tribulation."*

Because you have <u>kept</u> the word of My perseverance, …(during the persecutions of the 4th, 5th, and 6th seals of "tribulation")…***I also will <u>keep</u> you from the hour of testing, that hour which is about to come upon the whole world, to test those who dwell on the earth.*** <u>Revelation 3:10 NASB</u> (inserts are the author's)

Both "kept" and "keep" in this passage are the Greek word "tereo," the same word used in *"keep My commands."*
  I. to attend to carefully, take care of
    A. to guard
    B. metaph. to keep, one in the state in which he is
    C. to observe
    D. to reserve: to undergo something
This has absolutely nothing to do with removal from the trouble but indicates protection and preservation during the trouble.

For that first Philadelphian church, the "synagogue of Satan" that persecuted them was merely the synagogue from which the Philadelphian believers had defected. That synagogue, like all other synagogues from the resurrection of Jesus Christ forward, have had Satan as their "father" (John 8:42-44).

I am aware that the above statement will be regarded as "anti-Semitic" by those Jewish supremacists who emotively deny the truth in scripture. Yet, I have the same affinity that other true Christians have for the ethnic brothers and sisters of Jesus of Nazareth, and for the state of Israel.

At the same time, I am not deceived concerning the current status of Judaism or ethnic Jews who are not in Christ by faith.

We want to believe, as dispensationalists and all dual covenant theologians do, that religious Jews are "God's people in waiting" and that they worship the same "Father" that we worship. Yet, the reality revealed in scripture by the Spirit of truth is that Judaism, in complete denial that the Father has already sent the Son in the flesh to redeem all Israel, is desolate (without hope).

Who is a liar but he that denieth that Jesus is the Christ? He is antichrist, that denieth… (both)… *the Father and the Son.* 1 John 2:22 KJV (insert is the author's)

Note that John tells us the denial of Jesus of Nazareth as Christ, the Messiah, is a denial of both the Father and the Son, and that Judaism, the legitimate worship of the Father up until the death and resurrection of the Son, is now devoid of legitimacy and is instead an expression of the spirit of antichrist.

And we have seen and do testify that the Father sent the Son to be the Saviour of the world. 1 John 4:14 KJV

*And every spirit that confesseth not that Jesus Christ is come in the flesh is **not** of God: and this is that **spirit** of **antichrist**.* 1 John 4:3 KJV (emphasis is the author's)

What many messianic congregations, Jews and Gentiles who practice Christianity by observing the Sabbath and the appointed times feasts, as well as other practices within Judaism itself, are frequently guilty of teaching, is the emotive belief that modern Israel and the Jewish people as a whole will ultimately receive Christ at His second coming.

This is partially true, as previously stated, but only applicable to those Jew and Gentile "*survivors*" at the post-resurrection return of Christ on the 10 Tishri, great and terrible "day of the Lord."

These will be those "survivors" who have not taken the covenant mark of the beast kingdom or persecuted the spiritual body of Christ during the 4th, 5th, 6th and 7th seal events. (Joel 2:32)

What Zionist believers today miss is the fact that modern Judaism, denying that the covenant of grace has been fulfilled to Jesus of Nazareth, and through Him to all those Jews and Gentiles who have come to faith, is now fully engaged with the spirit of antichrist.

How, then, do we legitimize Judaism as being a sister faith or ethnic Jews as "God's people in waiting"?

It is the fundamentalist Jews of Israel, currently represented by the Temple Mount and Land of Israel Faithful Movement, who in complete, but unknowing, antichrist denial of both the Father and the Son, will rebuild the temple and begin temple worship and sacrifices again in obedience to their "father," Satan.

This will ultimately result in the "revealing" of the antichrist "man of sin" who will call down fire from heaven and declare himself to be both "God" and "Messiah" from the *secret chambers* of the third temple. (Matthew 24:26)

It is this specific event that will result in the opening of the 7th seal to begin the time identified as "*great tribulation*" during which Jerusalem and Israel will be identified by God as "*Babylon the great*" and as the "*habitation of devils*." (Revelation 14:8; 16:19; 17:5)

It is, therefore, these end time religious Jews about whom the Lord prophesied:

I am come in my Father's name, and ye receive me not: if another shall come in his own name, him ye will receive.
John 5:43 KJV

Those Jews and Gentiles who receive the antichrist "man of sin" as "God" and "Messiah"...(i.e. by taking the covenant mark of the beast kingdom)...will be the final form of the synagogue of Satan. However, the identification of the original end time form of the "synagogue of Satan," referenced in Revelation 3:9 as "those who say they are Jews but are not," is even more sinister and disturbing to us than the abovementioned final form.

This earlier "synagogue of Satan" identified by the Lord as being *"those who say they are Jews but are not"* has nothing whatsoever to do with their ethnicity. The instructions of Jesus Christ given to Paul reveal that one is not a "Jew" as far as the covenant is concerned if one is racially a Jew and circumcised only in the flesh.

Instead, one is only a "Jew" as far as the covenant is concerned if one is circumcised in the heart.

For he is not a Jew,...(as far as the covenant is concerned)...*which is one outwardly; neither is that circumcision, which is outward in the flesh: But he is a Jew, which is one inwardly; and circumcision is that of the heart, in the spirit, and not in the letter; whose praise is not of men, but of God.* Romans 2:28-29 KJV

The synagogue of Satan that persecuted the original Philadelphian church were ethnic Jews claiming covenant status with God that they no longer had, and the *"synagogue of Satan"* that will persecute the end time church during the 4th, 5th, and 6th seal events will be those who say they are "spiritual Jews" (i.e. Christians) but are not. These are those who claim to have faith in Jesus Christ but are following another "god."

These are the apostate foolish virgins who, during that time identified by the Lord as *"tribulation"* (4th, 5th, and 6th seals), fail

223

to repent as directed by the Lord and begin to follow the demonically empowered false prophets and lying shepherds of the Harlot and her daughters.

Likewise, our identification of this end time "Harlot" and her "daughters" (also metaphorically identified as those who say they are spiritual Jews but are not) is easy. One is a spiritual "harlot" only when one is or has been in a covenant relationship with God, and then commits spiritual harlotry by giving heed to and obeying or worshipping another god.

The example specifically given to us in scripture were God's covenant people, Israel, from Moses forward, who after having received and ratified the Law were frequently rebuked by the prophets of God for their "harlotry" as they compromised their worship of the Father through the syncretic worship of other gods.

The end time "Harlot" and the end time *"synagogue of Satan"* that will persecute Philadelphian believers are both metaphors for the apostate church, having taken the covenant mark of the beast kingdom and claiming the covenant name of Christ, but "worshipping" (obeying) a false "Messiah."

Thus these presume to be Christ followers, but they are not experiencing either His presence or His power, *having a form of* ...(pretended)...*godliness, but denying the*...(source of)...*power thereof*...(2 Timothy 3:5 KJV)

It is the age old spirit of Jezebel, the religious Luciferian prince answering only to Satan himself, who will empower these so-called "prophets" of the end time "Harlot" church, a.k.a. "the synagogue of Satan," which is the ultimate identity of the "foolish virgins" who will persecute those wise virgins who have remained faithful to Christ.

The reformers of the sixteenth century, having broken away from the Roman Catholic Church, identified the "Harlot" of Revelation as the apostate Roman Catholic Church of their own day, and if I had been alive at that time, I would likely have reached that same conclusion.

And these were heavily persecuted by the Roman Catholic Church (i.e. "foolish" Christians persecuting "wise" Christians).

Yet, from God's point of view the end time "Harlot" can only be applied to a form of that which He has covenanted to Himself through His Son that has become unfaithful and apostate. Therefore, THE end time "Harlot" of the 4th, 5th, and 6th seal events will be an apostate form of Christianity that includes apostate believers from the entire gamut of "Christian" denominations, including "non-denominational" denominations.

Therefore, the Harlot and her daughters are identified with the foolish virgins of the awakened church who refuse to repent as commanded in Revelation 2 and 3, and ultimately reject their faith in Jesus Christ through extreme deception by "false prophets" and "lying shepherds."

For such men are false apostles [spurious, counterfeits], deceitful workmen, masquerading as apostles (special messengers) of Christ (the Messiah). And it is no wonder, for Satan himself masquerades as an angel of light; So it is not surprising if his servants…(men, not demons)…*also masquerade as ministers of righteousness. [But] their end will correspond with their deeds.* 2 Corinthians 11:13-15 Amplified (insert is the author's)

At the same time, we need to recognize that those who are currently engaged in unknowing harlotry are not the "Harlot" of prophetic note. That identification belongs to the entirety of Christian believers who will become apostate during *"tribulation,"* which will not take place until after the awakening of the entire church identified in the parable of the ten virgins at the groomsman's announcement, *Behold! The bridegroom is coming.*

It is after that awakening, which is on our immediate horizon at the time this book is being written, that the "wise virgins" of the true church will begin to come out of those corrupt aspects of the organized institutional church in all its forms and denominations in response to the Lord's instructions in Revelation 2 and 3.

Conversely, the "foolish" will continue to identify with the unrepentant aspects of the organized institutional church in denial of the Lord's primary end time warning, ***"Do not be deceived"*** (Do not be led astray from the truth).

This division will be totally unlike the current denominational division of the body of Christ. This will be a division between two separate but united bodies. The "wise" will be united by the Spirit in the absolute, immutable, revelatory (*rhema*) truth of God, and the "foolish" who have become apostate will be united against the "wise" in the "***strong delusion***" that overcomes all those who do not love the truth that the Father has already sent the Son to redeem "all Israel." (i.e. Christian Zionism fully expressed through Dispensationalism)

There is, then, no identifiable denomination of organized institutional Christianity, including those claiming to be "non-denominational," who will not ultimately include participants in the "Harlot and her daughters" among their ranks.

The current denial by many that "born again" believers can become apostate (reject the faith that they once had in Christ) is addressed succinctly in Luke 17:26-28 KJV:

> ***Then shall ye begin to say, We have eaten***…(received the Word)…***and drunk***…(the communion cup)…***in thy presence, and thou hast taught in our streets.***…(we attended church and participated in its activities)
>
> ***But he***…(the Lord)…***shall say,*** …(on some future day)…***I tell you, I know you not whence ye are; depart from me, all ye workers of iniquity.***
>
> ***There shall be weeping and gnashing of teeth, when ye shall see Abraham, and Isaac, and Jacob, and all the prophets, in the kingdom of God, and you yourselves thrust out***….(indicating that they were once included IN the kingdom of God in Christ, but have rejected their faith).

This "Harlot," also identified as "***the synagogue of Satan***," is made up of those "foolish virgins," apostate former believers who say they are spiritual Jews but are not, those who are unknowingly influenced and empowered by Satan as they increasingly persecute the "wise virgins" of the true church during the 4th, 5th, and 6th seal events as recorded in the revelation of Jesus Christ and elsewhere.

And these whose fate is described in 2 Peter 2:21-22 are led by the false prophets and lying shepherds of the end time harlot: *For if, after they have escaped the defilements of the world by the* ...(experiential, relationship)... *knowledge of the Lord and Savior Jesus Christ, they are again entangled in them and are overcome, the last state has become worse for them than the first. For it would be better for them not to have known the way of righteousness, than having known it, to turn away from the holy commandment handed on to them.*

Hence, it is the wise virgins of the end time Philadelphian church persecuted by this worldwide *"synagogue of Satan"* to whom the promise of Revelation 3:10 will belong.

Original Synagogue of Satan	Synagogue of Satan during 4th, 5th, & 6th seals	Final form of the Synagogue of Satan
Jewish synagogue in Philadelphia	Apostate Christianity ("foolish virgins"), a.k.a. the "Harlot"	Religious Jews and apostate "Christians" who receive the antichrist as "Messiah"
Persecuted Christians of Jewish descent in Philadelphia	Persecute the Philadelphian type of believers (both Jew and Gentile) worldwide	Persecute the multitude saved by the Lord through the end time Philadelphian church, a.k.a. the 144,000

Because thou hast kept the word of my patience, ...(the "Word" that comes to, and is obeyed by, the "wise" during persecution by the Harlot a.k.a. the synagogue of Satan)...*I also will keep thee from*...(being harmed by)...*the hour*...(appointed time of 3.5 years)...*of temptation,*...(great temptation)...*which shall come upon all the world, to try*...(test)... *them that dwell upon the earth.* Revelation 3:10 KJV (insert is the author's)

Though we shake our heads in denial, it is totally evident that the "foolish virgins" of apostate Christianity, having become participants in the end time "Harlot," are those who will betray and persecute the "wise virgins" of the true body of Christ during *"tribulation."* (Matthew 24:9,10)

At the same time those "wise virgins" who repent, endure, and persevere during persecution and deception by this apostate "synagogue of Satan" will ultimately receive the promise given to the Philadelphian church.

This entire end time scenario was prophesied synoptically by the Lord in Matthew 24:9-14 Amplified (inserts and emphasis are the author's):

"Then...(during the 4th-6th seals)...*they will hand you* ...(My awakened ones)...*over to [endure] tribulation, and will put you to death, and you will be hated by all nations because of My name. At that time many*...(of My people)...*will be offended and repelled [by their association with Me] and will fall away*...(become apostate, i.e. the foolish virgins)... *[from the One whom they should trust] and will betray one another [handing over*...(remnant "wise")... *believers to their persecutors] and will hate one another. Many false prophets will appear*...(from among the foolish who have fallen away)...*and mislead many. Because lawlessness*...(of the spirit)...*is increased, the*...(*agape*)...*love of most*...(majority of My)...*people will grow cold. But the one who endures and bears up [under suffering] to the end will be saved*...(i.e. the "wise virgins" who have become the metaphorical 144,000 of the "Israel of God" who are ultimately sealed and redeemed as "firstfruits unto God and the Lamb," but not removed from the earth)....Revelation 7:1-8 Amplified (inserts are the author's)

Note that agape love is the love that originates from God and is expressed by faith through born again believers. It is this love growing cold in believers because of tribulation that is the symptom that precedes apostasy.

What is also noted in this passage is that those who fall away from faith during that time will become subject to demonic control, and it is these "foolish" former believers who will persecute the true body of Christ during the 4th, 5th, and 6th seals of "tribulation."

In my years of being involved in freedom ministry I have become aware that the spirit of rejection, originating in most cases from some form of either true or perceived rejection by their earthly fathers, results in the angry rejection and unforgiveness of others by the one who was seemingly or literally rejected by his/her earthly father.

This spirit of rejection is one of the most difficult freedom issues to deal with. The reason it is difficult to deal with is that the chronic unforgiveness by those who have been rejected separates the believer from the voice of the Holy Spirit leading to restoration.

This, then, will be the primary condition of the "foolish" during the extreme troubles of tribulation, angered by their perceived rejection by the Father, because of the "trouble," as well as the lies of those whom they trusted to lead them (Revelation 7:1-8) who will, in turn, reject the Father and the Son in their anger-filled unbelief, unbelief that was initiated by their false belief in a pre-tribulation escape from the trouble itself.

Then these, empowered by demons masquerading as angels of light, will wreak unrelenting, rejection inspired revenge on those who remain faithful to the Father and to the Son.

Then it is at the end of the 6th seal that a powerful false prophet in Jerusalem will display false signs and wonders as he prophesies the coming "Messiah."

At that time the "man of sin," a Jew whose lineage can be traced back to David and to the tribe of Judah, will call down fire from heaven and declare himself to be both "Messiah" and "God" in the secret chambers of the Third Temple rebuilt by the Temple Mount and Land of Israel Faithful Movement.

At that very moment the 7th seal will be opened, and the "hour" (appointed time) of trial (3.5 years/42 months/1260 days of "great tribulation") will come upon the whole world.

Of interest concerning the opening of the 7th seal immediately after the antichrist "man of sin" declares himself to be "Messiah" is God's unique response, a response that will be seen by the entire world.

And the angel taketh the censer; and he filled it with the …(spiritual)…fire of the altar…and cast it upon the earth: And there followed thunders and vices, and lightnings, and an earthquake. And the seven angels that had the seven trumpets prepared themselves to sound. <u>Revelation 8:5 KJV</u>

The antichrist "man of sin" will, of course, use this event demonstrating the judgment of God to convince mankind that he is both "God" and "Messiah," and the frightened masses will swarm to the courts of justice that he sets up all around the world to receive the covenant "mark" of the beast kingdom, which they will falsely believe to be the manifested kingdom of God.

The "trial," or test, of course, is whether or not men will accept the covenant seal of the beast kingdom, which is the famed, and greatly mis-identified "mark" of the beast.

All mankind will be under extreme deception and fear as those who refuse to receive the covenant mark of the beast kingdom are not only denied access to food, goods, and services in the marketplace (Mammon), but they are also persecuted unto death if they refuse the covenant mark of the beast kingdom in denial that the "man of sin" is the "Messiah."

Immediately after this dramatic opening of the 7th seal, on some future Pentecost, the metaphorical 144,000, a.k.a. Philadelphian believers, a.k.a. "wise virgins," will receive the covenant seal of the Lord as *"firstfruits*...(of the wheat harvest)...*unto God and the Lamb.*"

Yet, these will NOT be removed from the earth, and they will not be hurt at all by the manifestations of God's judgment as described in Revelation 8:5.

And...(during the 7th seal of "great tribulation")... *this good news of the kingdom [the Gospel] will be preached throughout the whole world*...(by the metaphorical 144,000 sealed and redeemed wise virgins of the end time Philadelphian church)... *as a testimony to all the nations,*...(i.e. the "multitude," who are an uncountable number from every nation, tribe, and tongue)... *and then will come the end*...(at the 7th trumpet of the 7th seal on 1 Tishri, the Feast of Trumpets a.k.a. the "last day" resurrection of both living and deceased saints of all time.) Matthew 24:9-12 Amplified (inserts are the author's)

13 – The 144,000

At the end of the "tribulation" events of the 4th through the 6th seals, including the initial dominance of the 4th horseman and the increasing world-wide persecution of the church, we are introduced to an event that takes place immediately before the 7th and final seal is opened, initiating the final 3.5 years of "great tribulation."

After this…(at the end of the 6th seal events and immediately after the opening of the 7th seal)… ***I saw four angels standing at the four corners of the earth, holding back the four winds of the earth, so that no wind would blow on the earth or on the sea or on any tree. And I saw another angel ascending from the rising of the sun, having the seal of the living God; and he cried out with a loud voice to the four angels to whom it was granted to harm the earth and the sea, saying, "Do not harm the earth or the sea or the trees until we have sealed the <u>bond-servants</u> of our God on their foreheads."***
And I heard the number of those who were sealed, one hundred and forty-four thousand sealed from every tribe of the sons of Israel. <u>Revelation 7:1-4 NASB</u> (emphasis and insert are the author's)

So, who is this mysterious group sealed with the seal of the living God prior to the seven trumpets of *"great tribulation"* and the last day resurrection of the saints of all time?

Are they 12,000 literal Jewish male virgins from each of the twelve literal tribes? If so, what is their purpose, and how did they suddenly appear on the scene without any identifiable relationship to the events taking place prior to their appearance?

The dispensational, Zionist, dual covenant position is that these are 144,000 literal Jewish male virgins from twelve literal tribes, ignoring the Spirit's metaphorical use of numbers, types and shadows throughout scripture, and, particularly, in the book of Revelation. (i.e. "Israel" in the covenant intent of the Father has now become *one new man*, "spiritual Israel' the *Israel of God*, which is the body of Christ).

The literal interpretation appeals to Zionists, because the appearance of the 144,000 seems to support their doctrinal position of Jewish supremacy in the covenant intent of the Father, which is Satan's greatest, faith-killing deception related to the end time generation of the body of Christ.

Dispensationalists and most Jewish supremacy, dual covenant theologians also presume that the woman clothed with the sun is national, ethnic Israel during tribulation after the antichrist "man of sin" has been revealed and the Jews flee into the Jordanian wilderness in 747 jumbo jets. (Really...this is the belief of some).

Some even believe that the two witnesses who appear suddenly on the streets of Jerusalem are the ones sent by God to select and anoint the 144,000 for evangelizing every nation, tribe, and tongue during the final 3.5 years of the beast kingdom's reign over the world while the failed church rests in heaven and watches Israel, as they take our place in the commission given to us until *"the end of the age."*

Yet, the Lord, our Teacher, identifies the *"end of the age"* as the resurrection of all the saints, living and dead, and in Matthew 24:19-20 He tells us that our commission remains intact until the *"end of the age."*

Thus, to remove the body of Christ before the end of the age and replace them with national, ethnic Israel would be a LIE, and our Lord, Jesus Christ, does not lie.

Furthermore, the two witnesses do not appear in Jerusalem until the 2nd Woe of the 7th seal, after the 144,000 are sealed. And they appear in sackcloth and ashes like prophets of old declaring God's judgment on the antichrist "man of sin," and on "Babylon the great," where the antichrist "man of sin" and the "false prophet" demand the entire world to "worship" (obey) the 7th and final "head"/"mountain" empire of the beast kingdom, **Babylon the great**, whose capital is now Jerusalem, by receiving the covenant "mark" of the beast kingdom in imitation of the covenant sealing that the metaphorical 144,000 have received prior to this 7th seal event.

These two witnesses, therefore, cannot be the proselytizers of the 144,000.

The first and most important thing we should note is that the 144,000 are identified as experienced, overcoming "***bond-servants***" of the Lord, meaning that these "virgins," innocent before God because they are in Christ, however many there are literally, whether Jew or Gentile, did not just suddenly appear on the scene.

As proven "bond-servants" these have been serving the Lord in the world during the 4th, 5th, and 6th seal events of "***tribulation***" prior to their sealing.

There will be Jewish believers amongst them, but "bond-servants" does not indicate Jewish only believers.

Thus, these are born-again believers, both Jews and Gentiles united as "***one new man***" in Christ. These are also experienced, steadfast, battle-hardened, Philadelphian overcomers a.k.a. the "wise virgins" in the war between the beast kingdom and the kingdom of God in Christ during the 4th, 5th, and 6th seal time of extreme persecution and deception.

Likewise, we need to consider whether this interpretation reflects what we know as truth concerning God's covenant intent in Christ.

> *Behold, the days are coming, says the Lord, when I will make a __new__ __covenant__ with the...(spiritual)... __house of Israel__ and with the...(spiritual)... __house of Judah,__ Not according to the covenant which I made with their fathers in the day when I took them by the hand to bring them out of the land of Egypt, My covenant which they __broke__, although I __was__...(past tense)...their Husband, says the Lord.* (i.e. the "new covenant" is different from the covenant "broken" by Israel)
> *But this shall be the covenant that I will make with the house of Israel; After those days, saith the Lord, I will put my law in their inward parts, and write it in their hearts; and will be their God, and they shall be my people.* Jeremiah 31:31-33 KJV
(emphasis and inserts are the author's)

This prophecy was fulfilled on the day of Pentecost when the kingdom of God fell with power upon the remnant of Israel, the 120 upper room believers, incorporating those believers into born again, spiritual Israel, the "*Israel of God*" in Christ, as the Law was written on their hearts (spirit-soul connection) through the indwelling presence of the Holy Spirit.

It is clear, then, that the "*house of Israel*" and the "*house of Judah*" has been applied through Jeremiah to the church. And it is clear that both the "*house of Israel*" and the "*house of Judah*", consisting of both Jews and Gentiles as "*one new man*" in Christ, is the body of Christ.

1. The old covenant with the house of Israel and the house of Judah is broken. It no longer exists, and the Father is no longer in a covenant relationship with national, ethnic Israel;

235

2. A new everlasting covenant is now established in the blood of Jesus Christ, THE seed of Abraham for whom it was always intended;

3. The "*house of Israel*" and the "*house of Judah,*" as well as the promise "*I will be their God, and they will be My people,*" now applies to the *ekklesia* of Christ, spiritual, born again Israel, made up of Jews and Gentiles as "*one new man*" in Christ identified as the *Israel of God*, and it will continue to apply without interruption throughout all eternity just as the Father originally intended.

Knowing this, what possible purpose does it serve for God to suddenly, without any apparent connection to previous events, or any apparent connection to the eternal covenant established "in" Christ, to select 12,000 literal Jewish males from each of twelve literal tribes to act as His evangelical emissaries in the final 3.5 years of "*great tribulation*" in place of the church who have been given His commission to the end of the age? (i.e. the last day resurrection of the saints of all time)

To believe that these are literal Jewish male virgins without guile from each of the twelve tribes is literally a denial of God's covenant intent in and through the body of Christ to the end of the age, which is the last day resurrection of the saints of all time from Adam forward on the 1 Tishri, "last day" 7th trumpet fulfillment of the feast of trumpets.

Remember what is revealed in God's very specific calendar of redemption. The Father's intent for the crucifixion and resurrection of Jesus of Nazareth is demonstrated in the initial fulfillment of Pentecost as Jew and Gentile were united as "*one new man*" in Christ (a.k.a. spiritual Israel, the "*Israel of God*" in Christ. (Ephesians 2:15; Galatians 6:16).

This is a forever thing in terms of God's covenant intent, and there is not demonstrated in this prophetic calendar or anywhere else in scripture any possibility that God will covenant separately with national, ethnic Israel again in some separate way from the one and only redemptive covenant written in the blood of Jesus Christ.

Also keep in mind that the Revelation of Jesus Christ was given to John in partially sealed metaphorical and parabolic language for the church, not for national, ethnic Israel apart from the church. Those, then, who propose a strict literalist approach to the interpretation of this book, and to all prophetic scripture, will only be able to "see" what the deceived intellect can perceive apart from the revelatory light of the Spirit of truth, who was given to "guide" us into all truth, including the truth about "things to come" (John 16:13).

One glaring error promoted by literalists, who have ignored even the obvious intellectual truth, is their claim that the Revelation of Jesus Christ only applies to the church through Chapter 3. This deception was introduced deliberately by the anti-Reformation Roman Catholic Church in order to escape the Reformation Movement's identification of the Pope as the "Antichrist" and the Roman Catholic Church as the "Harlot."

Examine these obvious facts:

1. Revelation 1:1 announces that the Revelation of Jesus Christ was given to His bondservant, John, an apostle of the church;

2. It was given to be written down and sent to the churches;

3. It was to be written down and included in the New Testament of the Bible to be read and heeded by the church;

4. Then, in the final chapter, the Lord makes certain that He has made Himself clear, and He tells us that the revelation

given to John is FOR the <u>churches</u>, not for national, ethnic Israel.

I, Jesus, have sent mine angel to testify unto you these things in…(and for)…*the* <u>***churches***</u>*.* <u>Revelation 22:16a KJV</u> (insert is the author's)

Because the Revelation of Jesus Christ was given to the church, in the church, and for the church, we must presume it is for OUR instruction. Why would we presume that the Father will suddenly end our evangelical commission under the headship of Christ (making Christ Himself a liar) to suddenly re-insert and re-appoint national, ethnic Israel to this covenant cause?

And this at a time in which Jerusalem has become the world capital of "***Babylon the great***"? (Revelation 14:8)

Are we in such fear of "things to come" that we are willing to accept the abject failure and replacement of the church in God's covenant intent in order to take comfort in our flesh with the thought that we will, at least, not experience the "hour" of trial that will come upon the whole world?

What is revealed in the message given to John "***in the churches***," concerning the 144,000 and the woman clothed with the sun, is the most significant and amazing prophetic event of the entire end time, but it has nothing at all to do with national, ethnic Israel in the final days of the age except for Jerusalem's identification with "***Babylon the great***" after the "man of sin" declares himself to be both "God" and "Messiah" in the rebuilt temple.

Instead, the Spirit-revealed truth concerning the prophetic future of the church in the end time is so characteristic of the Father's purpose and intent in Christ that only a plethora of powerful, emotive deceptions could prevent us from "seeing" it, and only a fresh anointing of the Spirit of truth can reveal it and confirm it to the HEROIC Joshua generation of Christian believers for whom it is intended.

As demonstrated in a previous chapter, the prophetic end time events are patterned in Old Testament events, and the primary interpretational key is found in the "appointed times" and feasts of the Lord given to Israel. These appointed times of annual Sabbaths and feasts are a literal blueprint and time chart for the unfolding of the seven primary prophetic events related to the redemption of fallen mankind in Christ, from the crucifixion of Jesus Christ to our eternal home in the New Jerusalem on the New Earth renovated by spiritual fire.

This is, therefore, now, our calendar, the calendar for spiritual Israel, and those events of redemption not yet fulfilled by Jesus Christ, will be fulfilled by Him for what the Father has identified as *"the Israel of God,"* and not in any separate way to national, ethnic Israel.

Thus, any prophetic interpretation of the redemptive events in scripture that do not fit within this God-given calendar are false, and the revelatory truth must come forth from and conform to this calendar as revealed by the Spirit of truth.

What this prophecy concerning the 144,000 metaphorically represents is the perfection of spiritual Israel, the Israel of God in Christ, albeit, the literal number of this group could be in the millions.

That each is from one of the twelve tribes is also metaphorical and a spiritual assignment by God rather than a natural designation.

What we have seen throughout scripture is that 12 is the number for the kingdom of God in the earth (12 tribes of Israel, 12 apostles of the initial body of Christ).

12 x 12 = 144. Thus, 144,000 represents the perfection of Jew and Gentile as *"one new man"* in Christ who represent the kingdom of God in the earth at that time.

These are those Jews and Gentiles who are counted as being the surviving **"bond-servants"** of the Lord at the end of the 6th seal events of *"tribulation."*

As tried and tested, overcoming "bond-servants" of the Lord how and why would these be separated again, so that only the

Jewish believers are chosen to evangelize every nation, tribe, and tongue, yet, evangelize both Jews and Gentiles who themselves become "*one new man*" in Christ?

There is an interpretive key here. The "key" is that if there is an apparent contradiction in scripture, the contradiction only exists because we have not arrived at the *rhema* truth of what we are reading.

If we are to interpret these as being literal Jewish male virgins from each of the literal twelve tribes of Israel God is demonstrated to be a respecter of persons, and the selection of this group is based on merit as some presumptively imagine. But God is not a respecter of persons or nationality (Acts 10:34, Romans 2:11). Thus, this metaphorical group will not be a select group of Jewish "top performers."

"*I most certainly understand now that God is not one to show partiality,*...(or favoritism toward ethnic Jews)... *but in every nation the man who fears Him and does what is right is welcome to Him.*" Acts 10:34,35 NASB (insert and emphasis is the author's)

Yet, there is a selection process, and the Lord defines that process in His prophetic parable of another group of "virgins," innocent of sin because they are in Christ. These are also identified as spiritual Israel, the *Israel of God* in Christ. This group metaphorically identified as ten virgins makes up the entire corporate body of Christ consisting of both Jews and Gentiles at a specific point in time.

The selection process, though, is not by God's sovereign election of 144,000 top performers, but by the response to God by an unidentified number of believers during the 4th, 5th, and 6th seal events of "*tribulation*."

It is, therefore, the entirety of those "wise virgins" (a.k.a. "*bond-servants*") who persevere, endure, and overcome the extreme testing of their faith during the 4th, 5th, and 6th seal events of tribulation who ultimately become the metaphorical 144,000, while those who fall away from faith during the same time, are the "foolish" virgins who will ultimately be identified with the Harlot.

What we also need to notice about the sealing of the 144,000 (representative of the perfection of the kingdom of God in the earth) is that they are sealed for protection IN the final three and a half years of *"great tribulation,"* not removal FROM *"great tribulation."*

This has HUGE implications.

We also notice that the sealing of the 144,000 takes place at the end of the time that the "wise virgins" are separated from the "foolish virgins," with the sealing of the 144,000 corresponding to the "wise virgins," who have trimmed their wicks in response to the repentance demanded in Revelation 2 and 3 and maintained oil in their lamps throughout the testing of their faith in the 4th, 5th, and 6th seal events of "tribulation."

At the same time, we notice that the great apostasy corresponds with the "foolish virgins" running out of oil, who did not repent in the manner demanded by the Lord in Revelation 2 and 3.

Thus, the 144,000 includes all of the "wise virgins" of the end time Philadelphian identity still alive at the end of the 6th seal. These are those *bondservants* who have responded to the Lord's demands for repentance and His encouragement to endure (remain faithful) during the hardships, trials, and persecution of the 4th, 5th and 6th seals.

We also see that the 144,000 are fully redeemed as the *"first fruits*...(of the wheat harvest)...*unto God and the Lamb"* before the last day resurrection. (Revelation 14:4)

We have read this before, but because we believed that this mysterious group had something to do with national, ethnic Israel during tribulation, we ignored the implication as it relates to the church.

Immediately after all four horsemen appear (the first four seals of Revelation 6), the first three of which are already on the scene and are dominated by the black horsemen at the time of this writing, we are given the Lord's prophecy concerning an event that takes place after the fourth horseman becomes dominant. This is also after the death of 25% of the world's population by war, famine, and disease toward the end of the 5th seal of "tribulation."

And I beheld when he had opened the <u>sixth seal,</u> and, lo, there was a great earthquake; and the sun became black as a sackcloth of hair, and the moon became as blood; <u>Revelation 6:12 KJV</u> (emphasis is the author's)

Keep in mind that the 4th through the 6th seals are identified by the Lord as "*tribulation*," and the 7th seal as "*great tribulation*," (Matthew 24). So, this earthquake takes place during the 6th seal events, and takes place prior to the antichrist man of sin calliing down fire and declaring himself to be "Messiah" on some future 1 Tishri feast of trumpets.

The opening of the 7th seal is described in Matthew 24:29 as being after (at the end of) the "tribulation," i.e. at the end of the 6th seal events of "tribulation": *But <u>immediately after the tribulation</u> of those days*…(and immediately after the "man of sin" claims messiahship on some future feast of atonement)…*the sun will be darkened, and the moon will not give its light, and the stars will fall from the sky, and the powers of the heavens will be shaken.* <u>Matthew 24:29 NASB</u> (emphasis is the author's)

Then in Luke 21 we discover that this event also takes place immediately after the redemption of the saints who are still alive at that time, meaning that the living body of Christ (as we are now) is still in the earth at the end of the events of the 6th seal.

And there shall be signs in the sun, and in the moon, and in the stars; and upon the earth distress of nations, with perplexity; the sea and the waves roaring; Men's hearts failing them for fear, and for looking after those things which <u>are coming</u>…(after the signs in the heavens and the distress of nations)…*on the earth:*

for the powers of heaven shall be shaken. Luke 21:25-26 KJV
(insert and emphasis are the author's)

And when these things...(all of the prior events described in
Luke 21, Matthew 24:9, and Revelation 6:12)... *begin to come to
pass, then look up, and lift up your heads; for your redemption
draweth nigh.* Luke 21:28 KJV (insert and emphasis are the
author's)

Luke 21:28 has been mistakenly interpreted to describe events
immediately prior to the "last day" resurrection of the saints of all
time. It does, in fact, describe a redemption, but it does not
describe the "last day" resurrection of the saints of all time.
What it describes is a *"firstfruits"* redemption of all the saints
still alive and still in the faith at the end of the 6th seal.

In Revelation 7:1-4 we see that the 144,000 are the ones who
are sealed during the brief interim immediately prior to the opening
of the 7th seal after being told that their redemption is "near"
toward the end of the 6th seal events. The indication, then, is that
the entire surviving, overcoming bond-servants of the body of
Christ at the end of the 6th seal events (i.e. *"tribulation"*) are
expecting the completion of their redemption, and they are
expecting it immediately prior to the opening of the 7th seal
identified as the final 3.5 years of *"great tribulation."*
This, then, is NOT the "last day" resurrection of the saints of
all time from Adam forward. It is the complete redemption of all
the living saints present in the earth 3.5 years prior to the "last day"
resurrection of all the saints of all time on some future Feast of
Trumpets (1 Tishri).

So, the body of Christ is present **in the earth** all the way
through the 6th seal, which concludes a time described by the Lord
as *"tribulation."* And it is near the end of this rather lengthy time,
prior to the 7th seal events, identified as the specific three and a
half years of *"great tribulation,"* that the entire body of Christ still

alive in the earth at that time is looking forward to the immediate completion of their redemption.

But, at the same time, the completion of their redemption is not a resurrection. These who are alive in the earth, are not only "sealed" for protection against harm during the 7th seal events (the fulfillment of the promise to "Philadelphian" believers who have endured and persevered during the 4th, 5th, and 6th seals of "tribulation") but these are also a fully redeemed body still present in the earth **during** the 7th seal.

Pause, and **think of that.**

This company of the metaphorical 144,000, representing the perfection of spiritual Israel, are those who will bring in the multitude from every nation, tribe, and tongue during the six trumpet judgments of the 7th seal in their fully redeemed spiritual bodies, like the Lord's own body when He came back to them after His resurrection.

This event also corresponds with the ultimate fulfillment of Pentecost, God's appointed time for the redemption of the firstfruits of the "wheat" harvest.

Jesus was the firstfruits of all mankind represented by a barley sheaf without leaven (symbolic of sin). These are firstfruits of the wheat harvest (with leaven) a.k.a. the harvest of the wise virgins, a.k.a. "bond-servants" of the Lord who have endured, persevered, and overcome during the 4th, 5th, and 6th seals of tribulation

These are they which were not defiled with women; for they are virgins. These are they which follow the Lamb whithersoever he goeth. These were redeemed from among men, being the firstftuits...(of the wheat harvest)...*unto God and to the Lamb.* Revelation 14:4 KJV (emphasis is the author's)

This event concerning the metaphorical 144,000, a.k.a. the tried and tested Philadelphian identity, is prophetically foreshadowed by the three Hebrew children walking around in the fire with the Lord after having refused to worship the golden idol representing the king of Babylon as "God."

During the 5th trumpet judgment of the 7th seal we see that there is a class of living mankind who have received the seal of protection upon their foreheads prior to the "last day" resurrection of the living and dead saints of all time.

And it was commanded them…(the "locust" demons)…that they should not hurt the grass of the earth, neither any green thing, neither any tree; but only those men which have not the seal of God in their foreheads. Revelation 9:4 KJV (insert and emphasis is the author's)

Only one group is identified as having the seal of God in their foreheads, and these are the metaphorical 144,000 who were sealed prior to this 5th trumpet judgment of the 7th seal event recorded in Revelation 9:4.

The event reported in Revelation 9:4 above takes place during the 5th trumpet judgment of the 7th seal, positively identifying those who experienced the complete fulfillment of their redemption and are still present through the 5th trumpet judgment of the 7th seal.

This is ultimately followed by the 7th trumpet of the 7th seal, which corresponds with the "last day" resurrection of the saints of all time on 1 Tishri, a.k.a. the Feast of Trumpets.

This "last day" resurrection on 1 Tishri will include the dead saints of all time along with those who are still living among the multitude from every nation, tribe, and tongue who were brought to faith during the 7th seal ministry of the 144,000.

It will also include the metaphorical 144,000 who experienced the completion of their redemption but remained in the earth in their "sealed" and fully redeemed bodies until the "last day" resurrection, meaning that these will not taste death prior to their resurrection.

Then the last day resurrection of all the saints, living and dead, from Adam forward, is followed nine days later on 10 Tishri, a.k.a. the Feast of Atonement, by the return of the Lord with ALL of His saints on the *"**great and terrible day of the Lord**"* to destroy His enemies and establish the millennial kingdom in the earth.

So, we see that the 144,000 were not sealed until the Pentecost immediately prior to the opening of the 7th seal.

So these were present in their natural bodies during the 6th seal, which includes the intense persecution of the church and the shaking of all that can be shaken, including an earthquake off the Richter scale, the sun turning to darkness, and the moon turning to blood (i.e. "signs in the heavens" - Isaiah 13; Ezekiel 32:7; Joel 2; Matthew 24:29).

Therefore, the 144,000 are present as natural, but "born again," believers during the final events of *"tribulation"* (Matthew 24:9-14), and present but fully redeemed on the Pentecost immediately after the opening of the 7th seal. Then these are in their sealed bodies during the 1st and 2nd Woes of *"great tribulation"* (Matthew 24:15-31)

Another group specifically identified as the Philadelphian church, the church that has endured and persevered under extreme persecution, is promised that they will be "kept" (protected) by God <u>during</u> the *"**hour** ...(appointed time)...**of trial that will come upon the whole world.**"* That "hour" or "appointed time" is the final 3.5 years of 7th seal of *"great tribulation"* that the "whole world" will experience.

Most notably, "kept" in this instance does not indicate removal as previously demonstrated by the Strong's G5083 interpretation of the word translated as "kept," meaning "protected" and "preserved."

The 144,000 are, then, those faithful Philadelphian believers who have endured and persevered in the spiritual battles that take place during the 4th through the 6th seals of *"tribulation*," which includes the Gog-Magog war, famine, disease, anarchy, the rise of the final "little horn" beast kingdom, to power, a world government, and the worldwide persecution of the church.

This worldwide persecution by the beast kingdom, also includes specific persecution by the apostate "foolish virgins" who

246

have become the "synagogue of Satan," a.k.a. those who say they are "Christian" but are instead the apostate "foolish virgins," empowered by Satan and included in the "Harlot" (those who were once in covenant with God, but have become unfaithful and have lost their covenant standing with God)...*Then they will deliver you*...(Christian believers)...*to tribulation and will kill you, and you will be hated by all nations because of My name. At that time many*...(of My people)...*will fall away*...(from faith in Me)...*and betray one another and hate one another. Many false prophets will arise and mislead many*...(into apostasy)...*Because* ...(spiritual)...*lawlessness is increased most people's*...(*agapeo*)... *love will grow cold. But the one who endures to the end*...(of the 6th seal)...*he will be saved. ...*(and at the opening of the 7th seal)...*This gospel of the kingdom shall be preached in the whole world*...(by the 144,000)...*as a testimony to all the nations, and then the end will come....*(at the "last day" resurrection of all the saints from Adam forward on 1 Tishri, the Feast of Trumpets) Matthew 24:9-14 NASB (inserts are the author's)

Those who persevere during this same time of escalating "tribulation" are the "wise virgins" of the true *ekklesia* of Christ. These have endured and overcome during the 4th-6th seal events, and it is these who will be sealed immediately prior to the antichrist "man of sin" being revealed when as calls down fire from heaven in the viewing presence of the entire world and declares himself to be "Messiah" and "God" in the "*secret chambers*" (Matthew 24:26) of the Third Temple in Jerusalem.

We do not see the 144,000 again until we see them in Revelation Chapter 14, which is a heavenly scene that gives details not given in Chapter 7 or Chapter 9.

And I looked, and, lo, a Lamb stood on the mount Sion, and with him an hundred forty and four thousand, having his Father's name written in their foreheads. And I heard a voice from heaven, as the voice of many waters, and as the voice of a great thunder: and I heard the voice of harpers harping with their harps: And they sung as it were a new song before the throne, and before the four beasts, and the elders: and no man could learn that song but the hundred and forty and four thousand, which were redeemed from the earth.

These are they which were not defiled with women; for they are virgins...(innocent before God because they are in Christ)...*These are they which follow the Lamb whithersoever he goeth*...(after they have been sealed).... *These were redeemed from among men, being the firstfruits*...(of the wheat harvest)...*unto God and to the Lamb. And in their mouth was found no guile: for they are without fault before the throne of God.* Revelation 14:1-5 KJV (inserts and emphasis are the author's)

To follow the Lamb "*whithersoever he goeth*" is indicative that these are perfectly united with the word and will of the Lord as demonstrated in Paul's prophetic passage:

"...*until we*...(born again believers)...*all attain to the unity of the faith, and of the*...(exact)...*knowledge of the Son of God, to a mature man, to the measure of the stature which belongs to the fullness of Christ.*" Ephesians 4:13 NASB (insert is the author's)

Revelation, like the prophetic aspects of the book of Daniel and much of the Old Testament, is given to us in metaphorical language with types and shadows for the express purpose of "sealing" (not revealing) the specific truth of those passages except as the Father allows the Spirit of truth to reveal it for His purposes (Daniel 12:9-10).

Literalist speculations, then, made prior to the specific revelation of the Spirit of truth are not only likely to be erroneous, but these also become "strongholds" of error assaulted against the true knowledge of God (2 Corinthians 10:3-5).

Note the following:

1. The "seal" (described in Chapter 7 as giving them an identification for protection, and identity as those whose covenant redemption is complete) is the name of the Father written spiritually upon their foreheads (i.e. spiritually visible);

2. They have been "redeemed" as a *"firstfruits unto God and the Lamb."* Their spiritual "virginity" and sinless perfection, then, is the result of their completed redemption, just as it will be for all the saints, living and dead who are resurrected on the last day, 3.5 years after the sealing of the 144,000. It, therefore, has nothing to do with their natural virginity, whether men or women, at the time of the sealing;

3. This "firstfruits" harvest of the "wheat" crop on some future Pentecost definitely identifies these as "Christian" believers who are "harvested" (fully redeemed) prior to the "last day" 1 Tishri resurrection of all the saints of all time;

4. This firstfruits company, the metaphorical 144,000, remain in the earth during the 7th seal, the 3.5 years of *"great tribulation,"* while the resurrection on the last day, 3.5 years after the sealing of the 144,000, causes the entire bride of Christ from Adam forward, living and dead, including the 144,000 company, to meet Christ in the spiritual realm.

While we were still under the Zionist, dispensational delusion that these were 144,000 literal jewish male virgins we did not understand the enormous importance of this event for the body of Christ.

This sealing of the 144,000 is identified specifically as the fulfillment of the "firstfruits" offering of the wheat harvest "unto

God and the Lamb," which is the ultimate fulfillment of Pentecost. Hence, we understand this offering demonstrates that this event cannot be anything other than a firstfruits redemption of the body of Christ (the two wheat loaves, signifying both Jews and Gentiles as "wheat") waved over the altar on Pentecost.

This is clearly understood as meaning that it will include the entire body of Christ still alive in the faith immediately prior to the opening of the 7th seal. Thus, the number 144,000 representing the perfection of spiritual Israel is metaphorical rather than literal.

The Holy Spirit seals all born again, regenerated believers in Jesus Christ, but our sealing at the moment of saving faith is different from this sealing upon the foreheads of the 144,000 for the completion of their redemption.

Notice that an angel is carrying the seal, which is one obvious difference between this seal and the sealing of the Holy Spirit for the purpose of regeneration.

If we compare the passages that describe our "sealing" by the Holy Spirit at the moment of saving faith with this "sealing" in the foreheads of the 144,000 we will clearly note the difference.

> ***Who hath also sealed us, and given the earnest***...(down payment)...***of the Spirit in our hearts.***
> 2 Corinthians 1:22 KJV (emphasis is the author's)

This passage uses the preposition transliterated from the Greek as (Strong's G1722 - *en*), meaning "in," and notice that the sealing takes place in the heart (spirit-soul connection).

Whereas the sealing of the metaphorical 144,000 is upon their foreheads. (Strong's G1909 - *epi*)

> ***And I saw another angel ascending from the east, having the seal of the living God: and he cried with a loud voice to the four angels, to whom it was given to hurt the earth and the sea, saying, Hurt not the earth, neither the sea, nor the trees, till we have sealed the servants***...(bond-servants)...***of our God in their foreheads.*** Revelation 7:2,3 KJV (emphasis is the author's)

What is evident here is that the sealing in our hearts, our unique spirit-soul connection, joins us to Christ and to one another through the presence of the Spirit. But 2 Corinthians 1:22 reveals that this baptism of the Spirit is an *"earnest,"* indicating that is not the completion of the covenant promise of redemption but a down payment ultimately leading to the transfer of title as long as certain conditions are met.

Initial sealing of our hearts	Subsequent sealing in our foreheads
A deposit or conditional guarantee of final and complete redemption	The completion of our redemption

The sealing upon our foreheads, though, is the completion of what began with the baptism of the Spirit. "Forehead" also metaphorically represents a prominent position, like the phylacteries of religious Jews on their foreheads. But the "seal" itself is spiritual.

6th seal	7th seal
The final events of *"tribulation"* take place	The final 3.5 years of *"great tribulation"* begin: including 7 trumpet judgments and the 1st and 2nd Woes
The entire surviving body of Christ, the "wise" Philadelphian believers, are told that their redemption is *"near."* These are then sealed on the Pentecost immediately prior to the opening of the 7th seal. (Revelation 7:3)	The body of Christ, spiritual Israel, metaphorically represented as 144,000 Jewish male virgins, is sealed (redemption completed) but still in the earth in their "sealed" bodies as they bring in the multitude from every nation, tribe, and tongue. (Luke 21:38)

This is also seen in Ezekiel's vision during the Babylonian captivity concerning a future judgment against the inhabitants of Jerusalem (symbolic of the institutional church) because of idolatry, with emphasis on the idolatry of the priests, and the corresponding protection of the faithful who are repentant concerning the idolatries of the church. (i.e. the "wise virgins")

It would be impossible for me to relate how important this understanding is for those who are reading this book. But I trust that the Spirit of truth will reveal it to the "wise."

We should also note that there is no event in the entire history of Israel from Ezekiel forward that lines up with this prophecy. Yet, we are certain, that the prophecies of Ezekiel intended for the end time body of Christ WILL take place.

And the LORD said unto him, Go through the midst of the city, through the midst of Jerusalem....(which we should receive as a type of the church)..., *and set a* __mark__ *upon the* __foreheads__ *of the men that sigh and that cry*...(in an attitude of repentance)... *for all the abominations that be done in the midst*...(of the church)... *thereof*...(which is the response of the "wise virgins" to the message of the Lord recorded in Revelation 2 and 3).

And to the others...(those "foolish virgins" who are unrepentant concerning the same abominations)... *he said in mine hearing, Go ye after him through the city* ...(spiritual Jerusalem)..., *and smite*...(kill)...*: let not your eye spare, neither have ye pity: Slay utterly old and young, both maids, and little children, and women: but come not near any man upon whom is the mark; and* __BEGIN__...(this act of judgment)... __AT MY SANCTUARY__. Ezekiel 9:4-6 KJV (inserts and emphasis are the author's)

This is a shocking judgment that does not compare with any previous event in Jerusalem or Israel. (i.e. Ezekiel's prophecy was not fulfilled to national, ethnic Israel, and is yet to be fulfilled)

It is, however, in complete denial of the traditions and teachings of some denominations. But it is confirmed, as previously demonstrated, in Matthew 24 and 25 in the Lord's own words, in response to His disciples when they questioned Him about the time of His return.

It should be of particular interest to us that the judgment of God is to begin at His sanctuary, which is the *ekklesia,* the spiritual body of Christ.

This is also obviously the subject of the parable of the ten virgins. It is the ten virgins who are awakened from their spiritual somnolence by some universally recognizable event, presented metaphorically in the parable as the groomsman's (Holy Spirit) announcement: ***"Behold! The bridegroom is coming."***

All ten virgins wake up and begin to trim their wicks (their response of repentance to the Lord's letter to the churches) by cutting away the false doctrines, false practices, and the "doctrines of demons" that have been introduced into the church, which is idolatry, idolatry that has been introduced by ***"the cunning and cleverness of unscrupulous men,"*** identified as otherwise "good" (in the eyes of men) men and women under the unknowing demonic influence of Satan for the purpose of dividing and emasculating the church (Ephesians 4:14).

The "wise" virgins respond in repentance during a time of great difficulty and persecution. The "foolish" virgins fail the testing of their faith and not only become apostate, but become deceived, demonically empowered persecutors of the wise.

As one who has been engaged in freedom ministry for many years, primarily ministering to "born again" believers, I am completely aware that Satan is able to powerfully control and manifest his will through born again believers in Jesus Christ through various demonically induced and empowered "strongholds," which hinder the influence of the Holy Spirit in that believer's life, and, like spiritual cancer, can lead to the ultimate rejection of the believer's faith in Jesus Christ.

What is demonstrated in the parable of the ten virgins, and in Matthew 24 and 25, is an escalation of this satanic corruption of believers resulting in extreme and violent persecution of the "wise" by the "foolish" who may remain in the organized church, but will demonstrate the hatred of the Lord's beloved faithful "virgins" by Satan.

If we examine the early history of the Roman Catholic church "excommunicating" believers, and even burning them at the stake for having a copy of the scriptures we can imagine, then, what this final persecution of the "wise" by the "foolish" might entail.

It is of interest, too, that there is an opposite marking upon the forehead noticeable in both the Old Testament and the New Testament. Leprosy upon the forehead was a physical sign of spiritual uncleanness, and in Revelation we see that the whore of Babylon, the apostate church (to which the "foolish virgins" are ultimately covenanted), as well as apostate Judaism, is marked in the forehead with her name,

"MYSTERY, BABYLON THE GREAT, THE MOTHER OF HARLOTS AND ABOMINATIONS OF THE EARTH." (Revelation 17:5)

The "whore" or "harlot" (spiritually unfaithful) of Babylon is both an institution and a spiritual body of mankind under the direct empowerment and control of Satan through the antichrist "man of sin," and the inference here is not of a flashing neon sign but a spiritually discernible identification of that body in all of its forms.

Likewise, those who submit to the antichrist "man of sin" are *marked* with a seal in the forehead, and this seal, identifying them as being covenanted to spiritual Babylon, *Babylon the great*," the *"mother of harlots*," is a permanent spiritual seal. They cannot change their minds and experience faith in Christ once they have taken this mark. This seal is, therefore, not just a means of submitting to the one world system of economics and government. It is a spiritual covenant action in which the ones receiving the spiritual, covenant mark of the beast kingdom confess allegiance to the "head-mountain" kingdom of Israel and the antichrist "man of sin" after he declares himself to be both "God" and "Messiah" returned to the earth to rule the world with an iron rod.

But these "foolish" ones ultimately learn that the one they trusted is not the Lord, Jesus Christ, but the ruler of **Babylon the great**, Satan, who is fully manifested through the antichrist "man of sin."

Nor is the "mark" of the beast kingdom something that is administered in some secret way, like a microchip being inserted under the skin.

This covenant "mark" will be eagerly sought by mankind all over earth as they declare their faith in the antichrist "man of sin" as "Messiah" and king, pledging their unswerving loyalty and obedience to all his edicts.

Therefore, we see the stark contrast between the "wise virgins" receiving the seal of God in their foreheads, and the "foolish virgins" receiving the seal (mark) of the beast in their foreheads as the ultimate fulfillment of Ezekiel 9:4-6 and Revelation 17:5 above.

And it is these "foolish" ones who will tragically someday hear the Lord say, "*I do not know you.*," though He did know them at one time. (Matthew 25:11-13)

Therefore, the 144,000, who are sealed as "*firstfruits unto God and the Lamb,*" are a group of living men and women who are sealed in the forehead, indicating the completion of their redemption, but not removed from the world.

Thus, this group is not merely protected during the trumpet judgments of the seventh seal, they are a completely redeemed group with the protective seal of God on their foreheads, but still interactive with the rest of the inhabitants of the world during the first 6 trumpet judgments of the 7th seal, which take place in the final three and a half years of "*great tribulation.*"

While we were still under the dispensational delusion that this event and this group were unrelated to the church, it had no impact on us. Now, we are stunned by this amazing prophecy.

We must also presume that Satan is aware of this prophecy and that he has been planning and scheming for two millennia to conceal this prophetic truth and prevent it from happening. The grievous truth is that he will be successful in preventing the "foolish virgins" from being included in the metaphorical 144,000, but he will not be able to stop the "wise virgins" of the end time overcoming "Philadelphian" identity.

Paul told us that the things that happened to the Israelites were written down for the instruction of those upon whom the fulfillment of the ages has come, and we find two unusual events in Daniel that foreshadow the truth concerning both the "wise virgins" and the 144,000.

Daniel's refusal to comply with King Darius's edict that none in his kingdom pray to any god or human being other than himself, caused Daniel to be thrown into the lion's den.

Strangely it was King Darius who prophesied that God would preserve Daniel, and God supernaturally inhibited the lions (representative of demonic forces) from killing Daniel.

This then is a forerunner event representing the future individual "virgin's" obedience to the revelation of God's will at a time when the beast kingdom will be openly persecuting Christians.

Similarly, and subsequently the Hebrew children were thrown into the fiery furnace for refusing to worship the golden idol that Nebuchadnezzar, king of Babylon set up as his "god" (i.e. a Satanic idol). This is a forerunner of the "wise virgins" who have refused to conform to the world systems (*kosmos*) dominated by the beast kingdom, and have proven that they have the faith-filled mind of Christ during their steadfast pursuit of God's truth, promises, and commands during extreme pressure to conform to the final beast kingdom identity.

Thus, the 144,000 are sealed and redeemed to protect them from the wrath of the beast. And the presence of the Lord with the Hebrew children is specifically representative of the Lord's presence in and with the metaphorical 144,000 during the three and a half years of 7th seal *great tribulation*" as previously demonstrated in the true, revelatory understanding of Daniel 9:24-27, and as prophesied by Paul. (Ephesians 4:11-17) as these bring in the multitude from the nations in the face of the worst Satan can do through his beast kingdom.

We also note that the Hebrew children in Daniel's day emerged from the fire without even the smell of smoke on their clothing, indicating that they were not impacted in any way by the fiery furnace though the fire was so hot that the guards who threw them into the fire were destroyed by it, picturing the fate of those who are servants of the beast kingdom during great tribulation.

Earlier the claim was made that all the major events of God's redemptive plan in Christ fit perfectly into the prophetic blueprint of God's appointed times, Sabbaths and feasts.

It is worthwhile, now that we have explored the greater picture, to review this mysterious firstfruits redemption of Christian believers found in the pattern of the appointed times and feasts given to Israel to demonstrate and confirm God's perfect timing for all seven primary events related to the redemption of fallen mankind in Christ.

The Jews were instructed in the Torah to observe the appointed times for the redemption of the remnant of fallen mankind in Christ with special emphasis on three "solemn assemblies," also known as Sabbaths and high holy days. The three times of the year were Passover (which includes the Feast of Unleavened Bread and the Feast of Firstfruits), Pentecost, and Tabernacles or Booths (which includes the Feast of Trumpets and the Feast of Atonement).

In Israel fall is the seedtime, and spring and early summer is the harvest. Thus, on the Hebrew calendar the first three spring feasts take place in the month of Nisan. These first three appointed times or feasts all occur in succession beginning on 14 Nisan, and all three have been fulfilled by Jesus Christ.

The Feast of <u>Passover</u> on 14 Nisan was fulfilled when Jesus was crucified on the day of Passover, and His fulfillment of Passover took place at the very same hour that the *pesach* lambs were being slaughtered all over Israel for the Passover meal that evening.

The Feast of <u>Unleavened Bread</u> was fulfilled by the sinless life of Jesus Christ.

Then on 16 Nisan, <u>Firstfruits</u> (barley sheaf containing no leaven) was fulfilled by His resurrection on the third day after His crucifixion, as Jesus became the firstfruits of the entire harvest (1 Corinthians 15:20), which is an amazing confirmation of how the Holy Spirit provided Israel with the exact pattern and timing of the most important prophetic event in all history. Yet, all but a few Israelites failed to recognize this time of their visitation.

Those events were foreshadowed by the historic events related to God's rescue of Israel (the inheritors of God's covenant promise to Abraham at that time) as Israel came out of bondage in Egypt (a type of the world under Satan's beast kingdom influence). Then these foreshadowing historic events were memorialized in the appointed times and feasts given to the Israelites afterwards, events that would ultimately be fulfilled as prophetic Messianic events in the future.

Yet the ultimate fulfillment of Passover, Unleavened Bread, and Firstfruits went unrecognized by the Pharisees, the intellectual giants of Israel, just as the future prophecy concerning the 144,000 has gone undetected by the intellectual giants of spiritual Israel, the church, blinded by the strongholds of Dispensationalism, Christian Zionism, Preterism, Historicism, and a number of other "isms."

It is also interesting to note that Caiaphas, the high priest, waved the firstfruits grain offering of a barley sheaf in the temple on 16 Nisan (Firstfruits), not knowing that Jesus, the Messiah, was resurrected at that very time. Yet, Caiaphas must have been a little rattled by the massive earthquake and the solar eclipse that had taken place on14 Nisan immediately prior to the twilight start of 15 Nisan.

It must also have disturbed him to find that the heavy curtain separating the holy place in the temple from the holy of holies had been torn from top to bottom as if slashed by a giant sword.

From <u>Passover</u> on 14 Nisan is the counting of Omer (49 days) to the <u>Feast of Weeks</u>, celebrated beginning the fiftieth day ("Pentecost"). Thus, Passover (fulfilled by the Lord's crucifixion) is linked directly to the Feast of Weeks (wheat harvest) which begins on Pentecost.

You shall observe the Feast of Weeks, the <u>firstfruits</u> of the <u>wheat</u> harvest, and the Feast of Ingathering… (Feast of Tabernacles)…*at the year's end.* <u>Exodus 34:22 Amplified</u> (emphasis and insert are the author's)

Firstfruits on 16 Nisan is a celebration of the **barley harvest** with the wave offering of the barley sheaf without leaven in the holy of holies as Jesus of Nazareth literally manifested the firstfruits harvest of the only "seed" of Abraham who was able to fulfill all the Law and the prophets.

The Feast of Weeks (Pentecost) was observed after the Israelites settled in the Promised Land. On this day, no work was permitted. The people gathered at the Tabernacle to thank God for the entire harvest, marking the time when the firstfruits of the **wheat harvest** were gathered and offered to the Lord in the form of two wheat loaves containing leaven representing Jew and Gentile as "*one new man*" in Christ, though Israel was ignorant of the true meaning until after the resurrection of Jesus Christ.

It also commemorated the giving of the Law at Mount Sinai, and subsequently the Law being written on the hearts of Christian believers on the day of Pentecost when the spiritual body of Christ in the earth was birthed as the kingdom of God fell with power on the upper room believers a.k.a. the remnant of Israel.

The firstfruits of the wheat harvest was presented by the high priest as an elevated or wave offering of two wheat loaves containing leaven.

Note the difference. The firstfruits wave offering of the barley sheaf, representing Jesus Christ as the "firstfruits" of the entire harvest on 16 Nisan contained no leaven (sin). Conversely, the "firstfruits" offering of the two wheat loaves on Pentecost (6 Sivan) during the Feast of Weeks, specifically contained leaven (sin), indicating the firstfruits harvest of sinful but redeemed mankind, including both Jew and Gentile as "*one new man*" in Christ (the two loaves).

Following the death, burial, and resurrection of Jesus Christ, the disciples were commanded to tarry at Jerusalem until the Spirit came (Acts 1:4), and they knew exactly how long they would have to wait. The disciples waited as they were commanded, and on Pentecost (Feast of Weeks), 6 Sivan, the Holy Spirit descended on the remnant 120 Jewish believers just as it had always been prophesied through God's calendar of the appointed times and feasts. This Passover event was the fulfillment of the coming of the "kingdom of God" with power. (Mark 9:1)

This is demonstrated to be an initiation event for the coming of the kingdom of God to spiritual Israel, the "Israel of God," in Christ, but not the complete "kingdom of God" fulfillment.

Before Jesus was crucified, He told His followers that the kingdom of God was "near," not meaning in the sense of His presence, but meaning that the kingdom of God would soon be manifested in and through the body of believers from Pentecost forward, all the way to the last day resurrection of the saints of all time on some future 1 Tishri feast of trumpets.

What Daniel 2:44 reveals is that this was the specific time planned by God from before the foundations of the world, for the kingdom of God to be present in the world in the form of the *ekklesia* of Christ (the church), and this form of the kingdom of God: 1) would not be destroyed; 2) would not be left to another people (i.e. returned to national, ethnic Israel); 3) would break all these other kingdoms (i.e. the beast kingdoms) in pieces; and 4) would stand forever.

And in the days of these kings... (ending with the Roman Empire)...*shall the God of heaven set up a kingdom, which shall never be destroyed: and the kingdom shall not be left to other people, but it shall break in pieces and consume all these kingdoms, and it shall stand for ever.* Daniel 2:44 KJV (insert is the author's)

This truth does not leave room for the possibility that God will somehow select 12,000 Jewish male virgins from each of the twelve tribes of national, ethnic Israel to represent the kingdom of God in the final 3.5 years of *"great tribulation"* before the last day resurrection.

However, because we have presumed that the Feast of Weeks was completely fulfilled spiritually by the coming of the Holy Spirit on Pentecost, uniting Jews and Gentiles as *"one new man"* into one new spiritual body, we have not imagined that this was an initiatory event followed by the ultimate event, the "firstfruits" of the wheat harvest, which is the sealing and complete redemption of the metaphorical 144,000.

The initial coming of the Holy Spirit was <u>not</u> the ultimate fulfillment of a "firstfruits" offering of the wheat harvest, because the upper room believers were NOT "harvested" at that time.

They were sealed by the Holy Spirit in their hearts (soul-spirit connection), but they were not, yet, sealed in their foreheads, indicating the ultimate fulfillment of their redemption, which for all the redeemed of mankind from Adam forward, other than the 144,000, takes place on the last day resurrection on some future 1 Tishri Feast of Trumpets.

The Lord's fulfillment of the wave offering of the barley sheaf on 16 Nisan as the firstfruits of the entire harvest was the literal fulfillment of the Feast of Firstfruits, but at this present time none, from Adam forward, other than Jesus of Nazareth, have been "harvested" (i.e. received the completion of their redemption that takes place for all but the metaphorical 144,000 on the "last day" resurrection as the fulfillment of the Feast of Trumpets).

There is a multitude from Adam forward in the heavenly presence, but even these await the ultimate event of redemption on the feast of trumpets a.k.a. the "last day" resurrection of the saints of all time.

Thus, the literal fulfillment of the wave offering of the two **wheat** loaves on Pentecost as *"firstfruits unto God and the Lamb"* has not yet taken place. (Revelation 14:4) But it will take place on some future Pentecost 3.5 years before the resurrection of the saints on some future 1 Tishri Feast of Trumpets.

To my knowledge, there were no Gentiles present in the upper room for the initial fulfillment of Pentecost, because it was not until later that the disciples even acknowledged that Gentiles were included in the spiritual body of Christ. Therefore, even the possibility that the coming of the Holy Spirit to the upper room believers was the complete fulfillment of the wave offering of the two wheat loaves, as the firstfruits of the wheat harvest, does not exist.

Likewise, most have not recognized that regeneration is not the fulfillment of redemption. It is the initiation of what will ultimately be redeemed (harvested) at the resurrection on the last day.

Though the dead in Christ await the "last day" resurrection in heaven in their spiritual bodies and cannot, therefore, reject their faith, their redemption will not be complete until the last day resurrection of all the saints from Adam forward on some future 1 Tishri, Feast of Trumpets at the same time that those who are still alive in Christ will be resurrected.

The Feast of Weeks (Pentecost) is also a celebration of the giving of the Law on Mount Sinai, and the coming of the Holy Spirit is the fulfillment of that event on Mount Sinai with the New Covenant fulfillment being the Law written in our hearts by the presence of the indwelling Spirit.

The coming of the Holy Spirit was a promise or guarantee of a future redemptive harvest, but it was not the harvest itself.

And not only the creation, but we ourselves too, who have and enjoy the firstfruits of the [Holy] Spirit [a foretaste of the blissful things to come] groan inwardly as we wait for the redemption of our bodies [from sensuality and the grave, which will reveal] our adoption (our manifestation as God's sons). Romans 8:23 Amplified (emphasis is the author's)

Receiving the Holy Spirit at the moment of saving faith is the sealing of our hearts as a deposit or title-deed to the sealing in our foreheads upon the completion of our redemption, which is the "harvest."

The coming of the Holy Spirit on that first Pentecost was, therefore, an initiatory event, not a harvest event. The resurrection of all the saints, living and dead, on the last day is the "harvest."

Therefore, a "firstfruits" offering of the entire harvest has already taken place on 16 Nisan two millennia ago when Jesus was resurrected as the firstfruits of the entire harvest, but the "firstfruits" offering of the "wheat" harvest containing both Jew and Gentile as *"one new man"* in Christ, must take place before the wheat harvest can be completed (i.e. before the last day resurrection).

The foreshadowing of Pentecost	The initial fulfillment of Pentecost	The ultimate fulfillment of Pentecost
The Law is received in the wilderness by national, ethnic Israel	The Law is written in the hearts of spiritual Israel, the *Israel of God* which we know as the *ekklesia* of Christ	The firstfruits of the wheat harvest, including Jews and Gentiles, are fully redeemed but not removed from the earth.

263

This is an amazing kingdom mystery, impossible to deny, yet many who are reading this will presume that there is some way to explain this mystery away.

In this regard, I have learned that all the mysteries in scripture are a Holy Spirit signpost indicating the presence of a significant revelation of "*hidden manna*" that we will only receive at the time in which it is intended to be revealed, and to the people for whom it was intended (i.e. this current generation).

Review the order demonstrated in the appointed times of the feast days:

1. Feast of Passover (14 Nisan) – originally pictured in the first Passover in Egypt - fulfilled by the crucifixion of Jesus Christ, our "Passover";

2. Feast of Unleavened Bread – fulfilled by the sinless perfection of Jesus of Nazareth;

3. Feast of Firstfruits (16 Nisan) – memorialized by the wave offering of the barley sheaf (without leaven); literally fulfilled by the resurrection of Jesus of Nazareth, the "firstfruits" of the entire harvest (Colossians 1:18, Corinthians 15:20);

4. Feast of Weeks – Pentecost (6 Sivan) a.k.a. Feast of Harvest – foreshadowed by the giving of the Law on Mt. Sinai; partially fulfilled by the coming of the indwelling Holy Spirit, writing the Law of God upon our hearts; yet to be ultimately fulfilled by a literal "firstfruits" offering of the <u>wheat</u> <u>harvest</u> (the wave offering of two wheat loaves representing Jews and Gentiles as "*one new man*" in Christ, i.e. the 144,000, unto God and the Lamb;

5. Feast of Trumpets – (1 Tishri) to be fulfilled at the final trump of God (the 7th trumpet of the 7th seal), the one and only "last day" resurrection of all the saints from Adam forward;

6. Feast of Atonement – (10 Tishri) to be fulfilled and witnessed by the entirety of the elect remnant of mankind as the saints of all time return to the earth with the Lord on the great and terrible day of the Lord nine days after the feast of trumpets;

7. Feast of Tabernacles – (15-22 Tishri) to be initiated when the Lord Jesus Christ establishes His millennial Davidic kingdom, and ultimately fulfilled when the earth is renovated by fire, and the New Jerusalem comes to the renewed earth as we tabernacle with Him for all eternity.

As born again, regenerated believers in Christ we have the Holy Spirit's presence with us as a "firstfruits" promise of the experience to come, received as a "sealing" of our spirits (hearts) by the Holy Spirit. (Ephesians 1:14)

Thus, the sealing of the Holy Spirit experienced as the baptism of the Spirit when we are baptized into the spiritual body of Christ is not the final inheritance and completion of our redemption as adopted sons of God, but a promise or title-deed guaranteeing that final inheritance and the completion of our redemption as long as we remain in Christ by faith until death.

Jesus of Nazareth is the *firstfruits* of that final inheritance, but we and those who are dead in Christ, from Adam forward, are yet to receive the completion of our redemption.

But the fact is that Christ (the Messiah) has been raised from the dead, and He became the firstfruits of those who have fallen asleep [in death].

But each in his own rank and turn: Christ (the Messiah) [is] the firstfruits, then those who are Christ's [own will be

265

resurrected] at His coming. 1 Corinthians 15:20, 23 Amplified (emphasis is the author's)

"***His coming***" is represented in three events:

1) He is perfectly united and spiritually present in the earth through the 144,000 (whose literal numbers may be in the millions) sealed and redeemed believers during the events of the 7th seal, as He fulfills the prophecy of Daniel 9:24-27 through them;

2) At the end of the 7th seal events on 1 Tishri, the Feast of Trumpets, the Lord appears in the "sky" (spiritual realm) to receive the saints of all time, living and dead, from Adam forward, which is the "last day" resurrection;

3) On 10 Tishri, the Feast of Atonement, also known as the "***great and terrible day of the Lord,***" the Lord returns to the earth with His saints of all time to establish His millennial kingdom in the earth.

The 144,000 will have been redeemed as a "***firstfruits unto God and the Lamb***" prior to the last day resurrection, and that event will take place on some future 6 Sivan. This is not the "promise" of redemption but the actual fulfillment of redemption.

The 144,000 are not yet sealed in the foreheads through the opening of the first six seals, which means that they are present during the ultimate ride of the four horsemen/beasts. Therefore, these metaphorical 144,000 will have been tested by "tribulation" prior to their sealing, but we do not know why some of the "wise virgins" are allowed to be martyred prior to this time while others ultimately become the metaphorical 144,000.

When the Lamb broke open the fifth seal,...(the middle event of "tribulation")... ***I saw at the foot of the altar the souls of those***

whose lives had been sacrificed for [adhering to] the Word of God and for the testimony they had borne.

They cried in a loud voice, O [Sovereign] Lord, holy and true, how long now before You will sit in judgment and avenge our blood upon those who dwell on the earth?

Then they were each given a long and flowing and festive white robe and told to rest and wait patiently a little while longer, until the number should be complete of their fellow servants and their brethren who were to be killed as they themselves had been. Revelation 6:9-11 Amplified

Yet, these "wise virgins" who are martyred during "tribulation," are honored by God as being faithful bondservants unto God and the Lamb, and theirs will be the martyrs' crown.

The seals are opened progressively, and it is not until immediately before the opening of the seventh seal, which will be the beginning of the three and a half years of *"great tribulation"* when the antichrist "man of sin" is "revealed," that the metaphorical 144,000 are sealed for protection and redeemed as firstfruits of the wheat harvest unto God and the Lamb.

So, the metaphorical 144,000, whose actual numbers are not revealed, are present in the earth as bondservants in Christ during the 4th, 5th, and 6th seals of "tribulation." But immediately after the opening of the 7th seal of "great tribulation," these surviving bondservants of the Lord are sealed and fully redeemed, but not removed from the earth.

Scripture reveals that it has always been God's purpose to reveal His love and express His victory over Satan through an elect remnant of mankind in Christ, and not only to reveal it, but to rub it in the enemy's face like a fourth quarter, last minute, game winning touchdown.

This is perfectly demonstrated by Paul in Ephesians 3:9-10.

And to make all men see what is the fellowship of the mystery, which from the beginning of the world hath been hid in God, who created all things by Jesus Christ: (Col. 1:15-20) To

267

the intent that <u>now</u>…(through the body of Christ)…***unto the
principalities and powers in heavenly places***…(Satan and his
minions)… ***might be known by the <u>church</u>***…(NOT through
national, ethnic Israel, but through the "Israel of God")…***the
manifold wisdom of God, According to the eternal purpose which
he purposed in Christ Jesus our Lord: In whom we have
boldness and access with confidence by the faith of him.***
<u>Ephesians 3:9-10 KJV</u> (inserts and emphasis are the author's)

Tertullian, AD 160-220, a church father still living under the
apostolic tradition, also penned this purpose of God succinctly,
though he was unaware of the astonishing way it would be carried
out in the final three and a half years of the age:

*"By allowing a permission for the operation of [Satan's]
designs, God acted consistently with the purpose of His own
goodness. He deferred the devil's destruction for the very same
reason that He postponed the restitution of man. For He afforded
room for a conflict, wherein man might crush his enemy with the
same freedom of his will as had made him succumb to Satan…
[And it enables man] to worthily recover his salvation by a victory.
In this way, also, the devil receives a more bitter punishment, by
being vanquished by him whom he had previously injured. By these
means, God is discovered to be so much the more good."*

Thus, the purpose of the firstfruits sealing and redemption of
the metaphorical 144,000, who represent and minister the fullness
of Christ in the final three and half years of "***great tribulation***," is
to manifest God's eternal purpose for the "Israel of God" in Christ
in the face of the enemy's own fully manifested presence in the
earth.

This will be the great, HEROIC, end time Joshua generation
fulfillment of the great commission given to the body of Christ
until the ***end of the age***. Thus, those who are included in the
144,000 company as the ***firstfruits unto God and the Lamb*** will
experience the most glorious and celebrated event of the entire

268

church age, other than the life, death, and resurrection of Jesus Christ Himself, though this is an event that the vast majority of the church is not, yet, expecting, and Satan has been desperately trying to prevent.

Immediately after the sealing of the 144,000 we notice an emerging "multitude" or a "vast host" of uncountable numbers from every nation, tribe, and tongue. These appear later in heaven before the throne of God, and they are identified as the saints who have come *from* the tribulation, indicating the 3.5 years of 7th seal "great tribulation.".

And they have overcome (conquered) him by means of the blood of the Lamb and by the utterance of their testimony, …(about who they are in Christ)…*for they did not love and cling to life even when faced with death [holding their lives cheap till they had to die for their witnessing].* Revelation 12:11 Amplified (insert is the author's)

He…(the antichrist "man of sin")…*was further permitted to wage war on God's holy people (the saints) and to overcome them. And power was given him to extend his authority over every tribe and people and tongue and nation…* Revelation 13:7 Amplified (insert is the author's)

Here we see a paradox. We see that the antichrist beast kingdom is permitted to wage war on God's holy people, the saints who have been sealed in their hearts with the pledge of their future redemption during the 7th seal *great tribulation*, but have not yet experienced the completion of their redemption.

So, who is it that is preaching the gospel of Jesus Christ with great anointing and power to this uncountable number of tribulation saints from every nation, tribe, and tongue without themselves being hurt or martyred by the antichrist "man of sin" who is now possessed by Satan himself?

269

It is the metaphorical 144,000 who have been sealed for protection and redeemed as *firstfruits unto God and the Lamb* immediately before the 7th seal events described by Revelation 12:11 and Revelation 13:7 who then minister the truth of the gospel to the multitudes from every nation, tribe, and tongue in the midst of the beast kingdom's reign and power over these same people.

As demonstrated previously, this cannot be the two witnesses (Enoch and Elijah) who appear only in Jerusalem, the capital of Babylon the great. These two appear in sackcloth and ashes, as they proclaim judgment on Babylon the great before they are killed three days before they are resurrected on 1 Tishri, the Feast of Trumpets.

If this was the only revelation we had concerning the glorious future of the "wise virgins" of the end time body of Christ, it should be enough to light a fire in the heart of anyone who receives it. Albeit, there is MORE as we examine another mysterious group, the woman clothed with the sun, the ultimate form of which Dispensationalists and Zionists have erroneously identified as being national, ethnic Israel.

Among the prophecies related to the 144,000 are the promise to the Philadelphian church of protection during "great tribulation," the "wise virgins," the 144,000, the woman clothed with the sun, the fulfillment of Daniel 9:24-27 and Paul's little known prophecy expressed through Ephesians 4:11-16, and the Bozrah sheepfold (Micah 2:12-13).

There are also a multitude of types and shadows related to this astonishing end time group such as the Hebrew children thrown into the fiery furnace for refusing to worship Nebuchadnezzar as "god." These are IN the furnace, but they cannot be harmed by the fire, and they are in the full presence of the LORD though they are still in the world.

We also have Zephaniah's prophecy concerning the "remnant of Israel," the metaphorical 144,000 in the "fire" of "great tribulation" after their sealing and redemption as "firstfruits unto God and the Lamb," of whom we are told in Revelation 14:5 that they have no guile in their mouths, which is also spoken of the 144,000 in Revelation 14:5.

"The <u>remnant</u> of Israel shall not do iniquity, nor speak lies; neither shall a deceitful tongue be found in their mouth: for they shall feed and lie down, and none shall make them afraid." Zephaniah 3:13 KJV (emphasis is the author's)

The obvious truth in Zephaniah's prophecy is that the body of Christ in its present condition does not and cannot conform to the prophecy, but the metaphorical 144,000 firstfruits offering unto God and the Lamb, will conform to this prophecy.

And, finally, we have Isaiah's glorious prophecy, the prophecy with which I opened this testimony concerning the 144,000 company who will bring in the final harvest from every nation, tribe, and tongue in the face of the worst Satan can do through his beast kingdom, Isaiah 60:1-2 NASB:

Arise, shine; for your light has come,
And the glory of the LORD has risen upon you.
For behold, darkness will cover the earth
And deep darkness the peoples;
But the LORD will rise upon you
And His glory will appear upon you.

14 – The Woman Clothed With the Sun

Note: the spiritual body of mankind empowered by Satan is referred to as a woman, the "Harlot," which includes apostate Israel and the apostate church.

The spiritual body of mankind in Christ is also referred to as a woman, the "bride."

Here is the mind which has...(revelatory)...*wisdom. The seven heads*...(beast kingdom authorities)... *are seven mountains*...(kingdoms)...*on which the woman*...(the Harlot)... *sits, and they are seven kings*...(rulers of the mountain kingdoms)...*; five have fallen, one is, the other has not yet come; and when he comes, he must remain a little while*...(the 3,5 years of the 7th seal). Revelation 17:9,10 NASB (inserts are the author's)

The Kingdom of God and the Beast Kingdom overview at the time the revelation is given to John:

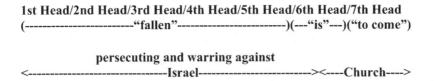

1st Head/2nd Head/3rd Head/4th Head/5th Head/6th Head/7th Head
(-----------------------"fallen"------------------------)(---"is"---)("to come")

persecuting and warring against
<-----------------------------Israel------------------------><----Church---->

These "head" kingdoms in order are: Egypt, Assyria, Babylon, Greece, Persia (all of which are "fallen" at the time of the prophecy is given). Rome is the 6th "head" at the time the prophecy is given, persecuting both Israel and the new body of Christ.

The 7th "head," yet to come, is the "mountain" empire that "was" Israel as a free theocratic nation, "is not" at the time the prophecy was given, and, yet, "is" from 1948 forward. And it is this head/kingdom under the authority of its "king" and "Maschiac" that will persecute the body of Christ during the 7th seal events.

I saw one of his...(the beast's)...*heads as if it had been slain,*...(the destruction of the temple and diaspora of the Jews in 70AD by the prince of Rome, Titus)...*and his fatal wound was healed*....(in 1948 when Israel became a nation again)...*And the whole earth was amazed and followed after the beast;*...(after he manifests through the antichrist "man of sin" in the third temple that will be rebuilt in our immediate future)...*they worshiped the dragon*...(Satan)...*because he gave his authority to the beast; and they worshiped the beast, saying, "Who is like the beast, and who is able to wage war with him?" There was given to him a mouth*...(the antichrist "man of sin")... *speaking arrogant words and blasphemies, and authority to act for forty-two months was given to him*....(the 3.5 years of the 7th seal)...*And he opened his mouth in blasphemies against God, to blaspheme His name and His tabernacle, that is, those who dwell in heaven.*

Israel is the "head" mountain-kingdom that rejected their Messiah when He came to them and was judged by God through the destruction of the temple and the scattering of the Jews into the nations in 70AD by Titus the prince of Rome.

This was the deadly wound to the "head" by the "sword" (war).

Then the deadly wound to the "head," Israel, was healed in 1948, and Christians unilaterally celebrated this as a demonstration of God's mercy.

But this 7th "head" mountain kingdom will ultimately be exalted against the kingdom of God in Christ under the authority of the antichrist "man of sin" after he calls down fire from heaven in the third temple and declares himself to be "Messiah" and "God."

Essential to our understanding of Revelation 12:

Daniel 2:44 / Ephesians 2:14-16 – the kingdom of God is now wholly represented by the body of Christ, including both Jews and Gentiles, who are now "one new man" in Him.

Immediately before Revelation 12: *The second woe*...(of the 7th seal)...*is past; and, behold, the third woe cometh quickly*. Rev. 11:14 KJV

It is during the 2nd woe that the two witnesses prophesy judgment of the beast kingdom in the streets of Jerusalem.

Then comes the third woe, the final woe of judgment.

Revelation 12 NASB:

A great sign appeared in heaven: a woman clothed with the sun,...(the light of divine glory)...*with the moon under her feet,*...(the light of the reflected glory of the saints)... *and on her head a crown of twelve stars;*...(initially Israel, ultimately the "wise virgins" of the body of Christ)...*and she was with child; and she cried out, being in labor and in pain to give birth....*(to the Messiah).

Then another sign appeared in heaven: and behold, a great red dragon having seven heads...(beast kingdom nations having political authority over Israel as previously demonstrated in Revelation 11)...*and ten horns,*...(sources of political power related to the 7th and final "head")...*and on his heads were seven diadems*....(the seven kingdoms beginning with Egypt, and ending with Rome, who progressively had authority over Israel)...*And his tail swept away a third of the stars of heaven*...the angelic host under Lucifer's authority – Revelation 8:12)...*and threw them to the earth*....(the original rebellion of Lucifer)...*And the dragon stood before the woman*...(literally Mary, but the revelatory intent identifies the "woman" as Israel)...*who was about to give birth, so that when she gave birth he might devour her child*....(the activity of Herod). Revelation 12:1-4 NASB

The KEY to understanding the identity of the woman in this passage is God's covenant relationship with her.

The "woman," as national, ethnic Israel, gave birth to the man-child, Jesus of Nazareth. But at His resurrection national, ethnic Israel was no longer in a direct covenant relationship with the Father.

From that point forward the woman is identified as spiritual, born again Israel, the bride of Christ.

The "woman" who is protected in the wilderness is also identified by the fact that the "rest of her children" are the tribulation saints. The tribulation saints are Christian believers from every nation, tribe, and tongue, brought to faith by the metaphorical 144,000, the perfection of the "wise virgins" who have overcome all the strategies of Satan during the 4th, 5th, and 6th seals of "tribulation."

Thus the "woman" protected in the wilderness includes all those born-again believers still alive at the end of the 6th seal of "tribulation."

But because of the spiritually corrupt Zionist influence throughout the body of Christ the presumption most Bible scholars make concerning the woman clothed with the sun in Revelation 12 is that she is identified as a singular entity from first to last. This is based on the observation that she obviously represents national, ethnic Israel at the beginning of this passage, therefore she must represent national, ethnic Israel throughout the entirety of the passage.

Yet, the woman's offspring provides us with the clear evidence that she is national, ethnic Israel in the beginning, but ultimately becomes spiritual, born again Israel, the Israel of God in Christ in the final passages.

We see this as the woman, initially representing national, ethnic Israel, gives birth to the man-child, Jesus of Nazareth, and from Pentecost forward her "children" are identified as born-again believers, Jew and Gentile as *"one new man"* in Jesus Christ.

Thus the ultimate identity of the woman is spiritual, born again Israel, including both Jews and Gentiles as one new man identified as the *Israel of God* in Christ, and we cannot ignore the fact that this progressive change of identity took place when the man-child of the woman was resurrected and the Holy Spirit fell on the remnant of Israel forty-nine days later to establish the *ekklesia* of Christ as the sole presence of the kingdom of God in the earth.

And she gave birth to a son, a male child, who is to rule all the nations with a rod of iron; and her child was caught up to God...(the resurrection of Jesus of Nazareth)...*and to His throne. Then*...(at the opening of the 7th seal)...*the woman*...(who is no longer national, ethnic Israel, but is now the "Israel of God" in Christ)...*fled into the wilderness*...(a spiritual refuge not corrupted in any way by the natural world or Satan)...*where she had a place prepared by God, so that there she would be nourished*...("kept" or protected as in the promise to the Philadelphian overcomers)...*for one thousand two hundred and sixty days....*(The 1260 days, 42 months, or 3.5 years of 7th seal "great tribulation." The same time that the Philadelphian church is "kept" from harm, and the 144,000 are sealed and redeemed, but still in the world, identifying all of these as the body of Christ).

And there was war in heaven, Michael and his angels waging war with the dragon....(This is not the initial war in which Satan and the angels under his command were condemned. This is a second event)...*The dragon and his angels waged war, and they were not strong enough, and there was no longer a place found for them in heaven. And the great dragon was thrown down, the serpent of old who is called the devil and Satan, who deceives the whole world; he was thrown down to the earth, and his angels were thrown down with him.*

Being "thrown down" in this instance means Satan no longer has access to God as "the accuser," as he literally possesses the body of the antichrist "man of sin." Likewise, the fallen angels with him will no longer be invisible to the human eye. They will take on the form of mankind, and, possibly, the form of supposed alien life forms during the final 3.5 years.

Then I heard a loud voice in heaven, saying,
"Now the salvation, and the power, and the kingdom of our God and the authority of His Christ have come, for the accuser of our brethren has been thrown down, he who accuses them before our God day and night. And they...(the multitude brought to faith by the 144,000)...*overcame him because of the blood of the Lamb and because of the word of their testimony, and they did not love their life even when faced with death. For this reason, rejoice, O heavens and you who dwell in them. Woe to the earth and the sea, because the devil has come down to you,*...(as he possesses the antichrist "man of sin")...*having great wrath, knowing that he has only a short time. "*...(the final 3.5 years of "great tribulation").
And when the dragon saw that he was thrown down to the earth, he persecuted the woman...(now the body of Christ, the "bride")...*who gave birth to the male child. But the two wings of the great eagle*...(the Holy Spirit)...*were given to the woman,*...(spiritual Israel immediately after the opening of the 7th seal)...*so that she could fly into the wilderness to her place,*

where she was nourished...("kept" as in the promise to the Philadelphian type of believer, the "wise virgins")... *for a time and times and half a time,*...(the 3.5 years of the 7th seal)...*from* ...(being harmed or hindered in any way by)...*the presence of the serpent. And the serpent poured water like a river*...(of deception)... *out of his mouth after the woman, so that he might cause her to be swept away with the flood*....(of deception)...*But the earth*...(representing the supernatural wilderness of protection)... *helped the woman, and the earth opened its mouth and drank up the river*...(of deception)... *which the dragon poured out of his mouth. So the dragon was enraged with the woman,*...(the 144,000)...*and went off to make war with the rest of her children,*...(the tribulation saints, the multitude who came to faith through the witness and ministry of the 144,000 of spiritual Israel)...*who keep the commandments of God and hold to the testimony of Jesus.*

The key to the identity of the woman is her relationship with God and her children. The woman (Israel) is God's wife at the time that Jesus of Nazareth is born. In verse 5 she gives birth to a man-child, Jesus of Nazareth. This identifies the woman at this point as national, ethnic Israel, the temporary title-deed holders to the covenant promises of God.

But as has been clearly demonstrated, God's covenant promise to Abraham was ultimately inherited by Jesus of Nazareth, the only ethnic Jew to fulfill all the requirements of the Law and the prophets, and, therefore, the sole "seed" of Abraham to inherit the covenant promises.

At the death and resurrection of Jesus Christ, He was the only "offspring" of national, ethnic Israel in covenant with God. All of the old testament saints from Adam forward to the thief on the cross were not included until after the resurrection of Jesus Christ as they waited in paradise for His resurrection to be complete. And from the resurrection of Jesus Christ forward, only those Gentiles and Jews who are in Christ by faith through the baptism of the Spirit are included as joint heirs in the everlasting covenant with

God as adopted sons and daughters in Christ. These Jews and Gentiles as *"one new man,"* make up the *"Israel of God,"* and are the final identity of the woman clothed with the sun, who is now the "virgin bride."

And there came unto me one of the seven angels which had the seven vials full of the seven last plagues, and talked with me, saying, Come hither, I will shew thee the <u>bride</u>, the Lamb's wife. Revelation 21:9 KJV

Thus, the woman is demonstrated to be that body of mankind in covenant with God. At the birth of Christ that woman was Israel, but on Pentecost after His resurrection, the "woman" became the "bride" of Christ; those who are in covenant with the Father because of their spiritual incorporation in Christ.

A "wife" has a direct covenant relationship with her husband, and judgment was based on the faithfulness of both corporate Israel and individual Israelites. This was the covenant of Law that Israel ratified in the desert, the covenant that only one "seed" of Abraham was able to fully uphold.

As the promised "bride" of Christ, the *ekklesia* of Christ has an indirect covenant with the Father, because she is in Christ spiritually, just as Eve was originally in Adam spiritually.

Thus, when Adam fell, Eve fell. However, Jesus cannot fail, and as long as we remain in Him by faith we are joint heirs to the covenant promises of the Father.

Those national, ethnic Jews, who were not spiritually incorporated in Christ on the Pentecost after His resurrection, ceased to be identified with the woman at that same time.

Still, there is another point of separation at the opening of the 7th seal. The "latter times" woman (the church, spiritual Israel) is given the two wings of the *"great eagle."*...(the Holy Spirit)...to escape from the wrath of Satan immediately after he is cast down from the heavenlies, which is also the point at which Satan possesses the antichrist "man of sin," and the false prophet confirms him to be "God" (the Messiah) returned to earth to rule the world with an iron rod, requiring all men and women everywhere to worship him and take the covenant "mark" (seal) of the beast kingdom upon their foreheads.

This opening of the 7th seal by the Lord begins the "*appointed time*" of "*great tribulation*" lasting 1260 days or 3.5 years.

The fall of Satan at this time is not the original fall of Satan and his hierarchy, but the result of a second war in the heavenlies in which Satan and his horde are cast down to earth. They still have the same powers and abilities that were given them in the beginning, but from this point forward they are confined to operate only on earth.

Moreover, the protection of the woman in the "wilderness" (a place not corrupted by the world) corresponds exactly with the sealing of protection and the "firstfruits" redemption of the 144,000, which leads us to conclude that the woman clothed with the sun, the 144,000, and the end time Philadelphian church receiving the promise of protection during the 7th seal of "*great tribulation*," are all one and the same.

In addition to the promise of protection in the "wilderness" (a place of supernatural nourishment and protection) examine the Lord's promise to the Philadelphian overcomers:

Him that <u>overcometh</u> will I make a pillar in the temple of my God, and he shall go no more out: and I will write upon him the name of my God, and the name of the city of my God, which is new Jerusalem, which cometh down out of heaven from my God: and I will write upon him my new name. Revelation 3:12 KJV (emphasis is the author's)

These will ultimately have the following names (identification) spiritually written upon them:
1. The name of the Father;
2. The name of the city of God;
3. The new (complete) name of Jesus Christ, our Lord.

This specific promise was made to the Philadelphian overcomers, ultimately identified as the metaphorical 144,000 and to no others that I can identify until the resurrection on the "last day,"1 Tishri, at the end of the three and a half years.

The New Jerusalem will ultimately be inhabited by all the saints from Adam forward, but it is those identified as "Philadelphian" believers, who remain steadfast in the faith and overcome all the assaults of the enemy, even the assault of the "foolish virgins" who are ultimately identified with the demonically empowered end time "Harlot" a.k.a. "Synagogue of Satan" during the 4th, 5th, and 6th seals of "tribulation," who will first receive this promise.

The identity of the 144,000 is relatively simple once we acknowledge that there are no future covenant promises of God for the redemption of national, ethnic Israel after the resurrection of Jesus Christ. All covenant references, covenant activities, and covenant promises are related to "spiritual Israel," the *Israel of God*" in Christ.

That is not to say that God has no interest in national Israel. It still is the land promised to THE "seed" of Abraham, it is the land and the people of His natural origin, and it is the land where Jesus as King of Kings and Lord of Lords will set up His millennial kingdom inhabited by spiritual Israel consisting of both Jews and Gentiles as *"one new man"* in Him.

Notably, it is Jesus Christ and those who are joint heirs in Him to whom the land will belong at the return of Christ in glory, not to the national, ethnic Jews now occupying a small portion of the Promised Land at this time...unless they have been grafted back into the olive tree, Jesus Christ. Therefore, these 144,000 cannot be 144,000 literal Jewish male virgins without sin.

Although the 144,000 are referred to as "virgins" who have not defiled themselves with women, their redemption from among "men" is not gender specific; their metaphorical identification as "virgins" is neither gender specific nor indicative of their experience in the world. When Paul used the same terminology in his letter to the church at Corinth, he said that he wanted to present

281

them as a chaste "virgin" to the Lord. In this he was speaking metaphorically in reference to their spiritual chastity and virginity, their innocence before God, because they were in Christ, not their natural virginity.

As *"bond-servants of God"* these must be experienced, overcoming Christian believers, because after the resurrection of Jesus Christ there are no "bond-servants" of God apart from the spiritual body of Christ.

The number, 144,000, being comprised of the perfect number of 12,000 from each tribe is also metaphorical, indicating the spiritual completion of the kingdom of God in Christ, but the literal number of the metaphorical 144,000 may be in the millions.

When the 144,000 (however many they represent) are "sealed" in or upon the forehead they are redeemed as "firstfruits" to God and the Lamb in fulfillment of the Feast of Weeks firstfruits offering of the wheat harvest.

The 144,000, as the firstfruits of the "wheat" harvest unto God and the Lamb, also represent the Philadelphian identity at the end of the 4th, 5th, and 6th seals of "tribulation," having received the seal of protection and redemption upon their foreheads, who are no longer tested and tried. These living men and women are fully redeemed and perfectly united with Christ in spirit, soul, and body while still in the earth, thus demonstrating the fulfilled prophecy of Ephesians 4:11-16.

"...until we all attain to the unity of the faith, and of the knowledge of the Son of God, to a mature man, to the measure of the stature which belongs to the fullness of Christ." Ephesians 4:13 NASB

This is also represented in the Old Testament as the Bozrah sheepfold deliverance prophesied by the prophet Micah (Micah 2:12-13) and typified in the Old Testament by the three Hebrew children cast into the fiery furnace for refusing to worship Nebuchadnezzar as "god."

The woman during "great tribulation" includes all of those living saints, Jew and Gentile, in Christ at this time. These are the remnant "wise virgins" who have repented in response to the Lord's warning to the end time church (Revelation 2 and 3) and who did not fall away from the faith under persecution and tribulation prior to this time.

These are the metaphorical 144,000 spiritual virgins, who are protected in the supernatural "wilderness" of God for the final three and a half years of "great tribulation," but are not removed from the rest of mankind at that time.

"Wilderness," as used in Revelation 12 is not some remote place in the mountains. It is symbolic of a place of supernatural protection and provision that is not contaminated by the world or by sin, and the "woman" (the 144,000/the wise virgins/the Philadelphian identity) is given the two wings of the great eagle (the Holy Spirit) to "transport" and "keep" (protect) her there.

This specific metaphorical identity of the Holy Spirit is first seen in Exodus 19:4-6a KJV:

> *Ye have seen what I did unto the Egyptians, and how I bare you on eagles' wings, and brought you unto myself. Now therefore, if ye will obey my voice indeed, and keep my covenant, then ye shall be a peculiar* ...(unique)... *treasure unto me above all people: for all the earth is mine: and ye shall be unto me a kingdom of priests, and an holy nation....*(emphasis is the author's)

In this passage "eagle's wings" obviously represent God's presence with them in the form of the Holy Spirit.

Likewise, 1 Peter 2:9 confirms that the kingdom referred to as a "holy nation" of royal "priests" is now a reference to the spiritual body of Christ, the true *ekklesia* or church.

> *But ye*...(born again believers in Christ)...*are a chosen generation, a royal priesthood, an holy nation, a peculiar*

...(unique)...*people.* <u>1 Peter 2:9 KJV</u>...(inserts and emphasis are the author's)

This covenant promise, then, has obviously been fulfilled to spiritual Israel, the Israel of God in Christ, and it is the spiritual body of Christ who are now the unique kingdom of God in Christ, a "holy nation," and a "royal priesthood" in service to our High Priest, Jesus of Nazareth.

Likewise, men have foolishly speculated about Satan's attempt to kill the woman with a literal flood, but we see this event foreshadowed by the supernatural serpent of Moses, representing the living Word of God, eating up and swallowing the supernatural snakes of deception produced by Pharaoh's magicians, Jannes and Jambres (i.e. the truth of God triumphs over the deceptions of Satan).

The "flood" that Satan sends after the woman is a flood of deception, but the flood of deception is swallowed (consumed and made of no effect) by the earth, representing the supernatural protection of the spiritual "wilderness."

The 144,000 (a.k.a. the woman) are not physically separated from the population of the world, but they are a company of fully redeemed "firstfruits" believers, in perfect unity with one another and with Christ, who represent the fullness and glory of the kingdom of God in the earth at the same time Satan and his servants (men and demons) are representing the full manifestation of the beast kingdom in the earth.

The event described in Daniel when the Hebrew children, Shadrach, Meshach, and Abed-Nego (<u>Hebrew</u>: Hananiah, Mishael and Azariah), refused to worship Nebuchadnezzar's golden image as god, illustrates the experience of the 144,000 (a.k.a. the woman clothed with the sun). It was their refusal to worship Nebuchadnezzar's golden image as "god," knowing that the penalty of their refusal was death in a fiery furnace, that caused God to supernaturally protect His covenant children in the furnace. As such, the 144,000 will also experience the presence of the Lord in the furnace of "great tribulation," and at that time they will be perfectly united with the Lord as they minister in the fullness of the Spirit of Christ during the final three and a half years after the 7th seal has been opened.

"That which hath been is now; and that which is to be hath already been; and God requireth that which is past...(to be ultimately fulfilled in the future)...." Ecclesiastes 3:15 KJV (insert is the author's)

Theirs is the most glorious experience that mankind will know prior to the resurrection on the last day. Theirs is the sealing of protection by the Holy Spirit, identifying them as the recipients of the Lord's promise to the Philadelphian church, the "firstfruits" of the entire wheat harvest, as their cup of anointing runs over in the very presence of the enemy, who prior to this sealing will test them severely.

We should also note that the promise of protection revealed in Psalm 91 requires the believer to dwell (continually "abide" and remain) in the secret place of the Most High.

This "secret place" in which we must abide is the revelation of His truth, promises, and commands as we walk in the Spirit by faith. And this "secret" place is known only to those who are abiding (actively living) in Him through their obedient faith responses to Spirit-revealed, Spirit-confirmed truth, promises, and commands.

This was the experience of the Hebrew children in the fiery furnace in the immediate presence of *"one like the son of man."* And it will be the experience of the metaphorical 144,000 who will be in the immediate presence of the Lord during the shocking judgment events of the 7th seal, a.k.a. *"great tribulation."*

Theirs is also the complete fulfillment of Lord's own prayer in John 17.

Neither pray I for these alone, but for them also which shall believe on me through their word; That they all may be one; as thou, Father, art in me, and I in thee, that they also may be one in us: that the world may believe that thou hast sent me. And the glory which thou gavest me I have given them; that they may be one, even as we are one: I in them, and thou in me, that they may be made perfect in one...(why?)...; *and that the world may know that thou hast sent me, and hast loved them, as thou hast loved me.* John 17:20-23 KJV (insert is the author's)

The purpose of bringing the 144,000 to complete, perfected unity with one another and with Christ is to manifest the fullness of the glory of Christ in and through His "bride" as a witness to the world in the face of the presence of Satan's own fully manifested beast kingdom.

...until we all attain oneness in the faith and in the comprehension of the [full and accurate] ...(experiential, relationship)...*knowledge of the Son of God, that [we might arrive] at really mature manhood (the completeness of personality which is <u>nothing</u> <u>less</u> than the standard height of <u>Christ's</u> <u>own</u> <u>perfection</u>), the measure of the stature of the fullness of the Christ and the completeness found in Him.* Ephesians 4:13 Amplified (emphasis and inserts are the author's)

This cannot be a description of the church as it exists today, because Paul is describing regenerated believers having attained the fullness of Christ's own perfection while still in the world. Nor does it relate to a heavenly event.

The metaphorical 144,000, having been sealed for protection and redeemed as "firstfruits unto God and the Lamb," will then be the full representation of Him in the world for the final three and a half years. Thus the woman (spiritual Israel, the Israel of God), who is comprised of the 144,000 (a.k.a. the Philadelphian identity, a.k.a. the "wise virgins") will manifest the fullness of Christ for the final three and a half years as they bring in the final harvest of an uncountable number of tribulation saints in the face of the worst Satan can do through his fully manifested beast kingdom.

286

At the same time, Satan is allowed to wage war against "the rest of her children," meaning the multitude of those who come to Christ after the sealing of the 144,000. "The rest of her children" are that uncountable number from every nation, tribe, and tongue who are included in the final end time harvest of souls.

Many, or perhaps, most of those who come to Christ after the sealing of the 144,000 will be martyred for their faith, and the whore of Babylon empowered by the Jezebel spirit, will be drunk on the blood of these saints.

These martyred saints will be included in Christ on the last day when He appears in the clouds with His angels (where everyone all around the world will see Him at the same time), and He will send forth His angels to the four corners of heaven to gather those who are dead in Christ, and then gather those who are still alive.

The prophetic aspects of Daniel, Matthew 24 and 25 (the Olivet prophecy), and Revelation are completely aligned to reveal the prophetic future of the church, and I will close this chapter with a passage from Daniel 12 that provides us with a brief synopsis:

AND AT that time [of the end] Michael shall arise, the great [angelic] prince who defends and has charge of your [Daniel's]...(covenant)... *people*...(the Israel of God).... *And there shall be a time of trouble, straitness, and distress such as never was since there was a nation till that time*...(the 7th seal of Revelation).... *But at that time your people*... (the Israel of God, a.k.a. the Philadelphian church, a.k.a. the 144,000, a.k.a. the woman clothed with the sun)...*shall be delivered, everyone whose name shall be found written in the Book [of God's plan for His own]*....(the Lamb's book of life)...

And many of those who sleep in the dust of the earth shall awake: some to everlasting life and some to shame and everlasting contempt and abhorrence....(at the completion of this period of time)....

...(a parenthetic going back to the first verse)...*And the teachers and those who are wise*...(the wise "virgins")... *shall shine like the brightness of the firmament, and those who turn many to righteousness (to uprightness and right standing with God) [shall give forth light] like the stars forever and ever*...(the woman clothed with the sun)....

But you, O Daniel, shut up the words and seal the Book until the time of the end....(which time has come)... *[Then]*...(which is NOW)... *many shall run to and fro and search anxiously [through the Book]*,...(that was sealed but is now being progressively opened)... *and <u>knowledge</u> [of God's purposes as revealed by His prophets]*...(i.e. not just Daniel, but ALL the prophets past, present, and future)... *<u>shall be increased</u> and <u>become great.</u>* <u>Daniel 12:1-4 Amplified</u> (inserts and emphasis are the author's)

Many will be purged, purified (made white) and refined,...(the wise virgins)... *but the wicked*...(foolish virgins)...*will behave wickedly. None of the wicked shall understand, but those who are [spiritually] wise will understand.* <u>Daniel 12:10 Amplified</u> (inserts are the author's)

It is not up to any of us to know whether we will be a part of the end time Joshua generation, a.k.a. the Philadelphian identity, a.k.a. the 144,000, a.k.a. the woman clothed with the sun, in the final three and a half years, but the acknowledgment of this prophetic truth concerning the future of the church of Jesus Christ, should stir our spirits to unyielding, uncompromised action as we anticipate the clarion wakeup call of the groomsman, *"Behold! The bridegroom is coming."*

The time of testing will soon be upon us, and those "foolish virgins" who do not respond completely to the Lord's warnings and to His call to repentance will experience the greatest tragedy in the history of mankind.

Conversely, those "wise virgins" who wake up, repent, and endure faithfully under trial will experience an unprecedented time of glorious victory in Christ, a victory and a people, the ultimate

Joshua generation of "wise virgins," who will be heralded throughout eternity as the perfection of spiritual Israel in Christ.

Arise, shine; for your light has come,
And the glory of the LORD has risen upon you.
   For behold, darkness will cover the earth
   And deep darkness the peoples;
   But the LORD will rise upon you
    And His glory will appear upon you.

Isaiah 60:1-2 NASB

So be it, Lord Jesus.

About the author:

Jim Sayles is a prophetically gifted Bible teacher and author focused on teaching Christian believers how to have a Spirit-filled relationship with the Lord as His disciples, "hearing," "seeing," and responding by faith to the Lord's truth, promises, and commands.

A vision given to him shortly after being rescued out of New Age occultism came to him as he was awakened with his name being called.

As he sat upright in his bed he saw John 14:15 written across his mind's eye:

"If you love Me, obey My commands."

Because he had been rescued out of deep Satanic bondage, having experienced the "so-called deeper things of Satan," Jim went through an extended time of intensive spiritual cleansing, and since then he has been used by the Lord to deliver others from various Satanic bondages in order that they, too, might glorify Christ as they walk in freedom manifesting the truth, love, and power of God.

In recent years the Lord has given Jim numerous prophetic dreams and visions about the coming storm, and Jim, along with many other prophetically gifted leaders in the body of Christ, who have been given a true "unsealed" understanding of things to come, is dedicated to the presentation of this truth that brings maturity, unity, and glorious hope to the very generation of the body of Christ who will experience these "things to come" in our immediate future.

If you believe this book should be read by others please write a review on Amazon or on your blog site.

1. In Amazon books search for the title or author;
2. Click: "read reviews";
3. Click: 1 to 5 stars (your rating);
4. Write your review in the text box;
5. Submit

Recommended Reading:

'**The Final Quest**" by Rick Joyner, describing a metaphorical vision of the great end time fight of faith during the 4th, 5th, 6th, and 7th seals of Revelation.

"**The Prophetic Ministry**" by Rick Joyner, describing the current anointing of prophetic ministry, including the purpose of end time apostolic and prophetic ministries.

Recommended Music Album:

The Name Above All Names by Chuck Girard
Intensely inspiring prophetic music and lyrics given to Chuck by the Holy Spirit and confirmed by this author.

The author's companion book, "**UNMASKING the End Time Beast Kingdom**," presenting the recently unsealed revelatory truth concerning the specific entities and events of the end time, identified as the seven seals of Revelation.

The identity of the beast with seven heads ridden by the Harlot coming up from the sea is completely and thoroughly revealed as is the 7th head with ten horns wearing ten crowns.

The identity of the four horsemen/four beasts of Daniel, the "little horn," the "false prophet," and the antichrist "man of sin," are also revealed as demonstrated through their metaphorical representations in scripture.

The exact timing of the entire end time scenario, and the next specific prophetic event on the horizon, are also identified and fully confirmed in scripture just as intended by the Father.

Other books by the author:

Final Instructions – A Bible study guide demonstrating inductive, Spirit-guided, Spirit-confirmed Bible study technique. Based on John 13-17, the Lord's final instructions to His disciples on the day He was betrayed and crucified.

In this He told them how they would "hear" and "see" His truth, promises, and commands by the Spirit of truth after He was resurrected.

These are also our instructions, and therefore the MOST IMPORTANT spiritual skill believers who want to walk by faith in the absolute, immutable truth of God can have in these dangerous days.

All books by the author are available from Amazon, and distributed by Ingram to various bookstores in the U.S., Canada, Great Britain, Australia, and Europe.

Numerous articles related to doctrine, apologetics, overcoming faith, deliverance, freedom, and prophecy by Jim Sayles and others are also available on the website.
www.theendtimeschurch.org

Logos Publishing Company
P.O. Box 2465
Cedar Park, TX 78630-2465

Made in the USA
Coppell, TX
04 March 2021